MAYWOOD PUBLIC LIBRARY
W9-BLF-699

DATE DUE

TRUE
DETECTIVES

Also by William Parkhurst

How to Get Publicity

The Eloquent Executive

TRUE DETECTIVES

THE REAL WORLD OF TODAY'S P.I.

WILLIAM PARKHURST

CROWN PUBLISHERS, INC.
NEW YORK

Publisher's Note: While this work contains actual cases and investigations, some names and other indentifying details have been changed to protect the privacy of the individuals depicted.

Published by Crown Publishers, Inc., 225 Park Avenue South, New York, New York 10003

CROWN is a trademark of Crown Publishers, Inc.

Manufactured in the United States of America

Library of Congress Cataloging-in-Publication Data

Parkhurst, William.
True detectives/by William Parkhurst.
1. Detectives—United States—Case studies. 2. Crime and criminals—United States—Case studies. 3. Criminal investigation—United States—Case studies. I. Title.
HV7914.P33 1989 88-16221
363.2'5—dc19 CIP
ISBN 0-517-56554-4

10 9 8 7 6 5 4 3 2 1

First Edition

To Terry

TRUE
DETECTIVES

1

The only time Vincent Parco ever drew his gun on the job was the day Louis Gloskin called about his unfaithful wife. It was one of those soggy July afternoons when no New Yorker wants to be in town, when sewer gas rises in disease-laden clouds on every street, cabs overheat in strangled traffic, and even the religious zealots, who shout the amplified word of Jesus through bullhorns, are apt to tell you to fuck off.

The thirty-six-year-old private investigator was dieting again, and dieting always turns him into something only fettuccine or an exorcist can fix. But he tried to be nice when Jo-Ann Kunda, his second in command, brought in the open case list and half of last month's accounts receivable were still receivable. He tried to be nice when his handyman, Louie Sedano, left sawdust on the polished parquet floor, then disappeared beyond the reach of a staff who can find most missing persons in less than fifteen minutes.

Parco tried to be *especially* nice when the telephone repairman, who was supposed to be installing a jack in a private garden that connects to his office, offered a play-by-play critique of every episode of every detective show he ever watched on television, including his impressions of Tom Selleck, Bruce Willis, Telly Savalas, and, because he thought he was on a roll, Rodney Dangerfield. Then the guy said he didn't have the part he needed, so he went back to the shop, leaving the two glass doors to the garden open just enough for a huge rat to saunter in and run across the Oriental rug, past Parco's desk, and behind the refrigerator of a little kitchen. That's when Vinny Parco made his decision to kill.

His wife, Carol, had been furious with him last night when he said he'd be home early and wasn't. After fourteen years of marriage, he figured she could be more understanding about his business even if she did sometimes hate it. How could he have known he was going to get a call, just as he was leaving, from a panicked client? There was this slimeball dealing crack on the sidewalk in front of the man's business, and customers weren't coming in. The client was very upset. Clients always get upset at such things, and always at the end of the day when there's no one else in the office to catch the case.

Like all cases, it broke when Vinny found the handle. He had no intention of drawing his gun. You don't draw a weapon unless you plan to fire it and Parco wasn't about to open up on some scumbag unworthy of even a sideward glance. But the gun did its job anyway.

The detective first asked the man nicely to deal elsewhere. Always start with nice. The drug dealer, not surprisingly, was not a fly to be caught with honey. He said he would fillet Vinny Parco with his knife.

After that, Parco had no choice but to let his jacket flap open and show the man his holstered five-shot Walther PPK, James Bond's own weapon, and, because drug dealers aren't always so imaginative, he had to help the guy envision the possibilities of what that weapon can do when shoved up someone's ass and fired. The client was happy, but it took a while and Carol was pissed. Though he ranted back at her, he couldn't honestly say she was unreasonable.

When the rat came in, Parco was seated at his large oak desk, taking calls at his normal clip of three or four at a time. At Vincent Parco & Associates, they don't screen calls so much as hurl them through the intercom. Parco's three secretaries tell most callers that the head of the agency will be with them in a minute and, whether it's a multimillionaire real estate developer or some drooling lunatic who wants to contact Jacqueline Onassis, he will. As Parco handles one call, the next is announced with a tone:

"Vincent, Ray Melucci on one."

"Got him."

"Vincent, Charlie Gordon on two."

"Be right there."

"It's Tony Carter, Vincent."

"Good."

Ray Melucci, a former transit police detective, was reporting in on a debugging job, his specialty. Melucci and one of Parco's investigators had pulled a bug no bigger than a grain of rice out of the client's telephone.

"Bobby found it," Melucci said. "That kid's good. He reminds me of me when I was that age."

"You were never that age," Parco said, then looked toward the door where the rat was making an entrance.

"What the fuck? Jesus Christ, Ray, there's a big rat in my office."

Melucci laughed. "A real one or one of your clients?"

"I'm serious. Wait one," he said, springing to his feet to close the door before anything else got in. "Okay, I'm back. The thing's right behind the refrigerator."

"You might think about an exterminator, my friend," Melucci said. "If it's a female rat, you're going to have problems."

"Oh, shit, you're right. I'm going to blow the fucker away myself."

"Uh, I wouldn't do that, Vinny," Melucci said.

"Of course," Parco said. "It's stupid. I'll get an exterminator." As Melucci talked more about the bug, Parco got up, locked the door to the outer office, then drew his weapon. He aimed it at the spot near the wall where the rat would have to come out eventually. The adult in him demanded that he put the Walther away and get back to running his multimillion dollar business. The kid inside wanted to shoot.

"So, do I sweep the office too, or just the house?" Melucci asked.

"Let me get back to you on that, but I'm pretty sure the guy will want you to do the office too. If they bugged his house, there's sure as shit something in the office, don't you think?"

"Oh yeah, I'd bet on it." As Melucci broke down the cost of sweeping the man's office for room bugs, telephone taps, and checking the windows to see if there was any clear trajectory for a laser bug, the rat ran out from behind the refrigerator and stopped in the middle of the floor long enough for Parco to fire off a shot, had he let his id win, which he did not.

"Shit!" Parco said.

"What now, the rat again?"

"Yeah, he's pushing his goddam luck. He just came right out and stopped by the fireplace."

"But you wouldn't shoot him."

"Guess not. Not with the PPK anyway. There'd be rat all over the place."

Parco made arrangements to meet Ray for a drink the next night, and took a few more calls. Once, while he was talking to a caller whose teenage son was missing, the rat came out again and faced him. It seemed to be giving him the finger. After that, Parco never took his eyes off the refrigerator or his mind off the rodent. Like the gremlin on the wing of the airliner in the old "Twilight Zone" episode, it came out when he was alone and stayed away when anyone else came into the office. During a lull, he unlocked a drawer where he kept a .22 automatic which, if he was going to kill a rat, would be the more manageable weapon.

He finally put the gun and the idea away, and reopened his office to the flow of the late afternoon, which is always busy at the agency.

Vincent Parco is considered a rising star in his booming industry. When he was an investigator of fraudulent medical practices for the state of New York, he drew media attention ranging from small weekly papers upstate all the way to "Sixty Minutes," becoming known in the late 1970s as the man whom alcoholic, negligent, or incompetent doctors feared most. He especially hated butcher surgeons and collected their hides obsessively.

As a P.I., Parco continues to attract the press, though he prides himself on never cultivating reporters or using a PR firm as his critics sometimes claim. The *Wall Street Journal* covered his hidden assets investigations, the *New York Times* has quoted him many times, the *Post* ran his picture next to Bruce Willis, and he is constantly interviewed on local and national television where one reporter dubbed him "The Sherlock of Homes" because his agency investigates more than ten thousand tenants a year for violation of New York's tricky rent control laws.

Among fellow investigators, Parco is known for flamboyance, guile, showmanship, and, in a field not especially known for sportsmanlike assessments of competitors, ego. At 5′7″ and 175 pounds, he struggles with weight control and dieting, a problem exacerbated by a passion for rich foods. He and Melucci constantly accuse each other of impending baldness.

Parco is always expensively dressed. His casual office look is jeans and a pullover shirt, but the ensemble is the meticulous casual of a professional athlete on his way to a disco. Even the pedestrian conservatism of a pin-striped suit for court is offset by a fedora cocked at a precise angle that could only be found by someone for whom style is a genetic gift.

He is a demanding boss, too much so for many. Field investigators, even cops with twenty years on the job, have a way of not lasting in an agency where anything that has to be done has to be done now, right now, not tomorrow, and if you're used to flashing your tin or relying exclusively on your buddies in the precinct to get information, it just won't fly in Parco's town house. Not counting the tenant investigations, there are always more than a hundred cases on the books and, if you want to get along with Vinny Parco, you close them the way he does. You close them today.

Parco hit the intercom button on his phone and buzzed Jo-Ann Kunda's extension.

"What do you need, babe?" she asked. Kunda was downstairs in her office dictating financial assets reports from the company's five telephone investigators, called skip tracers.

"Open case list. I want to finish some of these jobs. You got a minute?"

"Sure, I just want to finish dictating Maroney," she said flipping her Sony dictating cassette recorder on rewind and returning to her place in the report.

"On July 18, 1986, investigator Marla Paul made a field visit to the New York Board of Elections and determined that Randolph I. Maroney, SSN 011-23-8856, lessee of apartment 8-B, 311 East 88th Street, last voted in New York City on November 2, 1975. Current address as listed with the Department of Motor Vehicles is 43 Adler Street, Yonkers, New York 10511. Ms. Paul conducted a field visit to the Yonkers City Clerk's office where it was determined that Mr. Maroney has voted there every year since 1976, last voting November 8, 1985.

"Property on Adler Street is deeded jointly to Randolph and Olivia Maroney. Copies of documents enclosed."

Randolph Maroney was paying $486 a month for a rent-controlled one-bedroom apartment on Manhattan's swank Upper East Side. The unit was now worth about $2,100 a month at current market rates. Under rent control and rent stabilization laws, he was entitled to a lifetime of minimal increases, so long as he occupied the apartment as a primary residence. But Maroney, like 240,000 or so others in New York, had moved out long ago and subleased his apartment at current rates, pocketing a tidy $1,400 a month. That made the landlord mad enough to call Vincent Parco.

Kunda took a shortcut through the garden, climbed a set of cement stairs, and walked through the glass doors into Vinny's office.

"Close the door," Parco said without looking in her direction. He was focused straight ahead past his fireplace and bar at the refrigerator. "The guy from the phone company left the door open and this big mother of a rat came in."

"He's in *here?*" she asked.

"Yeah, right behind the refrigerator. If Sedano ever gets back, tell him I want some Velveeta cheese."

"Uh-huh," she said, looking warily toward the kitchen. Kunda is a twenty-eight-year-old blonde with long curly hair cut fashionably in layers and pinned behind her ears. Her deep blue eyes radiate a secret amusement, as if someone in the White House just told her a chemical had turned most of the world psychotic, but she was spared. Her voice has the smoky, seen-it-all, heard-it-all quality of the young Lauren Bacall.

"So, I hate to ask, Vinny, but what happens when he comes out from behind the refrigerator?"

Parco smiled.

Kunda nodded. "I see. Well, shall we go over the list, or do you want to shoot cans off the back fence to warm up?"

Parco considers himself a lucky man, not because he expects to bill 10 million dollars a year in the next half decade, not because the newspapers and networks run stories on him, but because he chose a business he loves at a fortunate moment in history. The nation's fifty thousand licensed private investigators are the tip of a million strong, private cop industry that is suddenly hot. A 1987 study by Frost and Sullivan, a market research firm, places guard and investigative services at 42 percent of an overall security market expected to reach 18 billion dollars a year by 1990.

The investigative and security boom provides a full range of services from the uniformed guard walking a post at midnight to the Wall Street team of technocrats, lawyers, and accountants breaking an insider trading ring for a million dollar fee. It is a business that has grown 20 percent per year for the last decade and shows no signs of slowing down. Everyone, it seems, wants to find out something about someone and, for the right price, they can.

The private investigator sells information in an information age. The field is too big to accommodate any single image, and most people in it dismiss television and fiction as nonsense. The *last* thing a P.I. wants is the hassle of shooting a gun at another human being, yet stereotypes die hard.

The detective as former cop turned rent-a-cop in a trench coat, fedora, and shoulder holster is a legend that clients and many P.I.'s cultivate enthusiastically as part of the marketing. Most working P.I.'s paid their investigative dues in law enforcement, be it at the city, county, state, or federal level. Once a cop, always a cop. Former police, especially those who have worked the streets of a big city, carry their weapons as naturally as ballpoint pens. To be without a piece, even if the case is a mundane public document shuffle downtown, is unthinkable.

At Vincent Parco & Associates, the television staple of the P.I. with friends in law enforcement is real. The place is always buzzing with cops, from the uniformed traffic officer on a break from directing cars into the Queens Midtown Tunnel to FBI agents for whom Parco has done work that he won't talk about. Officially, information and favors are not passed back and forth, and Parco says information is not the point of having cops around. Having cops around is the point of having cops around. Things get done.

Parco would like to see his company go after more of the big investigative cash cows—mergers and acquisitions investigations, insider trading, computer fraud, embezzlement, insurance fraud, and other white-collar misconduct. Sometimes, there's no misconduct at all. Someone just wants someone else checked out.

Employers will send an executive out of town and have him or her followed. Does he go down to the bar for a couple of drinks? More than a couple? Does he play around? If an operative tries to sell him cocaine will he buy? Often, the P.I. finds the client sleazy and the target a victim, but the job is to get information without the judgment call. It's all business.

Enterprising P.I.'s such as Parco know how to look, talk, and speak corporate, or they hire those who do. Clients who shell out six- and sometimes seven-figure retainers to fight their piece of the 40 billion-dollar-a-year battle against white-collar crime don't warm to the rumpled, wisecracking stereotype with a day's growth of beard and a flask of bourbon in the hip pocket. Anyone with an office on the bad side of town gets bad-side-of-town clients.

Parco believes in guile over gadgets, though he is sensitive to the reality that the high rollers expect a full complement of video, surveillance vans, advanced computers, debugging gear, satellite/microwave security know-how, and always a mastery of financial language. The P.I.'s who work this turf often have law degrees, doctorates, MBAs, and the all-important ease with money and wealth. Parco keeps such specialists close by and calls on his Wall Street clients in very expensive three-piece suits.

Like the lawyers they serve, most P.I.'s aren't hired to do criminal cases, and if they are, the client probably is not wrongly accused. In criminal work, the P.I.'s job is to find every niggling piece of tedious evidence that the defense attorney can use to screw up the prosecutor's case.

Some P.I.'s are just bodyguards with a license to shoot. They are, in other words, goons. The goon doesn't make the papers much. CNN doesn't interview him on the subject of being a "real life" private investigator, and reputable P.I.'s are quick to dismiss this Neanderthal on the record as a throwback who is out-of-step, out-of-place, and out-of-it in today's computer age.

But in the bar with other P.I.'s, they'll say it: Sometimes you need a goon. The MBAs, PhDs, and computer specialists get the press, but sometimes all you need is a goon. When you're attacked or threatened, you need hardware, not software.

Today's P.I. also has to function as a shrink in a frothing, postmodern testament to the dark side of human character. Parco and his staff guide terrified clients through seven-figure lawsuits over fender benders, snatched children, death threats on the phone at midnight, sexual harassment in the workplace, rape under laughing gas at the dentist's office, taps and bugs, ideas that took a lifetime to develop ripped off and flaunted. They come to Parco when the police, social service agencies, the government, and all the bureaucrats say, "Sorry, nothing we can do."

The open case list in the middle of the summer of 1986 was typical. There were the usual half dozen or so matrimonials, which amounted to catching someone in bed with the wrong person, then using it. The scenario was pretty traditional, despite the evolution of modern relationships. Cuckolded men were out to prove the bitch was an immoral slut unworthy of custody, alimony, or child support. Betrayed women wanted to nail the prick and his little bimbo by finding, and freezing, his assets. And, even though P.I.'s say the keyhole-peeping image is yet another gross throwback, the matrimonial clients want pictures, videos, dates, times, and, if the P.I. will tell them, how many times a couple did it in an afternoon. Parco and his team don't go that far, but a lot of P.I.'s do.

"Inga Swenson's been looking for you," Jo-Ann said.

"She's always looking for me," Parco said. "I think she likes my body."

"No doubt."

Mrs. Swenson, a woman in her late forties, was going through a very bad time and had formed a kind of psychological dependency on the agency, and especially on Parco. Her husband had run off to Singapore with a twenty-one-year-old dental assistant, and, as far as the skip tracers could tell, the man had cleaned out his stateside accounts and buried his money in the Cayman Islands, Switzerland, or Hong Kong. It wasn't worthwhile for Mrs. Swenson to go further. She had been a model when she met her husband in 1958. Today she was a broke middle-aged woman.

"Nothing we can do for her," Parco said, shaking his head. "Let's close it out. How much does she owe us?"

"I think we're about square. She paid us for ten hours and that's about what we've done. I'll check the sheets again." The agency charges clients a retainer of $750.00 for ten hours of investigative work. To Vinny Parco, most noncorporate cases can be finished in that time, largely because his staff is trained to use data bases, directories, maps, and especially the telephone to get information.

"You got the Glick file?" Parco asked her.

"Right here," Kunda said. "Nothing much in there yet, though."

Buddy Glick, a P.I. in the garment center, had called Parco for help with a trademark infringement case. He wanted a woman operative, a "girl," he said, to go undercover as a buyer to prove that a blouse manufacturer was selling a design that had clearly been ripped off from his client.

"She's got to look and act Jewish," Parco said to Jo-Ann. "You or Marla?"

Jo-Ann thought a minute. Marla Paul, a twenty-two-year-old freshman field investigator would be a good choice because she is Jewish, but Kunda, who had worked in the garment center, and had far more undercover experience, said, "I think I'll take it. I need to get out."

Parco shrugged. He knew he had to accommodate Jo-Ann's need to be in the field even though he preferred to have her inside where she was more valuable to the agency as an administrator. "You're also going under as a hooker, don't forget."

"I know, Vincent, but two won't kill me." The client on that job wanted to prove that a store owner was a fence receiving stolen merchandise. The man was also supposed to be dealing cocaine. Parco made a note to call his police contacts at Manhattan South. A P.I. can't buy drugs undercover without police backup.

"By the way, Mrs. Janos was not happy with you and Davey. She said the two of you were raving alcoholics."

"What?"

"I'm just repeating what was passed on," he said throwing his hands up in exaggerated wonder. "Who am I to judge?"

"Now come on, you *know* that's bullshit," she said. "We were out in the rain until one o'clock in the goddamn morning. There was like an eighth of the bottle left when she broke it out. An eighth is generous, Vinny."

Parco waved off a story he'd already heard too many times. Kunda and Davey Pagano, a friend working free-lance on this case, had gone to Jersey on a cohabitation job where the client wanted to catch her estranged husband living at the apartment of a new girlfriend. The client's friend, Mrs. Janos, had an apartment that was supposedly right across the street from the love nest. She agreed to let Pagano and Kunda watch the door all night from her living room.

The job called for them to take a picture of the target going in for the night and coming out the next morning. They were to watch the door all night in shifts and be ready to testify that the man went nowhere else until morning.

A couple of things hadn't worked out. Mrs. Janos's apartment was not right across the street, but so far up the block that the only view of the targeted door was an unsheltered balcony. It started to rain about thirty seconds after they got out there, rain that got so heavy that Armageddon itself would have been a relief. The two P.I.'s stood their watch bravely under a single umbrella and a blanket, dodging hailstones, lightning, and gale-force winds that shook the building like an earthquake.

They weren't out there long before they realized they were spying on an ordinary date, more adult than a grade school hayride, but probably a lot tamer than most high school dates in New Jersey that night. The man called for the woman, took her out for a few hours, came back, stayed until one in the morning, and left.

The disputed consumption of alcohol came when Mrs. Janos, a divorcée, got home from a date of her own and offered the investigators tea. They thanked her graciously but wondered aloud if she had anything just a little stronger. Mrs. Janos did have a bottle of Stolichnaya vodka in her freezer which, after seven hours in the rain, went down pretty good and pretty fast.

"Not even a shot apiece," Kunda and Pagano maintained.

"Raving alcoholics," Mrs. Janos said.

Parco sent her a replacement bottle of vodka and his regrets if his investigators caused any inconvenience.

"Marla's out on the Stankowicz case?" Parco asked Jo-Ann.

"Right, chasing the porn queen." One of the landlord clients had called Parco. He was very upset. The woman he planned to marry was, he insisted, the star of an X-rated movie called *Weekend Heat.* He'd seen her at his own bachelor party, he said, and sent *Weekend Heat* over by messenger, along with a snapshot of Lois Messer, his fiancée who supposedly led a double life as Penny Long, porn queen. Parco didn't see the resemblance, but Stankowicz was a good client, so he sent Marla Paul out to follow the woman.

"I. M. Hardd," Parco said, as he ran his finger down the computerized list.

"Closed, but not paid," said Kunda.

That one had gone well. I. M.'s scam was to advertise sexual services in a gay magazine. He would arrange to meet his marks in a hotel room, then beat them up, take their money, and leave them terrified. The magazine wanted him stopped. Two days ago, Parco had posed as an out-of-town businessman looking for a little company. In the next room was Louie Sedano with a video camera, one of I. M.'s former victims, and two people from the magazine. The predator signed a confession of his misdeeds and swore he wouldn't advertise in the magazine again. In return, the magazine agreed not to prosecute.

"Doctor Lynette Simons," Jo-Ann said, getting to the next item on the list.

"We'll send Marla," said Vinny. "I can't have you out on all of them."

"Doctor" Simons, sixty-seven, was accused by her landlord of turning a large prewar apartment into a whorehouse that specialized in bondage and discipline. Tenants complained that strange men and women were seen in the halls carrying bags with chains and whips sticking out, and wearing weird things like spiked dog collars.

The client had taken Simons to court in the past and lost. She showed up with an aluminum walker, and claimed that her health was not good. The noise, she said, was a necessary byproduct of the primal scream therapy she practiced. She said she was sorry if she had disturbed any tenants and would try to keep the noise down. The judge let her off.

Though she was not certified to practice as a medical doctor, psychologist, social worker, or any of the other health care professions, New York has a quirky law that enables anyone to call herself a *psychotherapist.* The term is unprotected by law and requires no formal education or training. If they were going to nail her, they would have to work the prostitution angle.

Everyone with a spare minute in the agency had to look through *Screw, Night Scene, The Wild West Side,* and other publications where prostitutes and madams took ads. If Dr. Simons ran a specialty act whorehouse, Parco figured, there would have to be an ad somewhere.

There were, as usual, several missing-persons cases on the list. They amounted to finding someone who stiffed someone else and left town with the money. Parco figured his skip tracers would track their paper in a day or two, and pinpoint the debt skippers without his having to assign any fieldwork.

Other cases in the missing-persons category included a man wanting to find an old girlfriend, a mother from California whose missing daughter turned up as a homeless interviewee on "Sixty Minutes," and a television weatherman from North Dakota who sent a retainer and a request that the agency find the identity of an actress he'd seen on a commercial so he could ask her for a date. Parco put a red flag on that one. Obsessive romantic pursuits can be as dangerous as radium.

"Call the guy and tell him we'll contact her through her agent and forward any mail. We'll probably speak to her ourselves. If she gets back to him, she gets back to him, but we won't give him her phone number without her authorization."

The man who wanted to find his old girlfriend was one Parco would have been happy to miss, but the man was a friend of a high-rolling landlord client, and his story was sad. He had been scarred in an accident and, though he was not seriously disfigured, the incident had cost him his confidence with women. The ex-girlfriend was easy to find, and single to boot, but the client said he wanted the investigators to arrange an "accidental" meeting. She loved sailing, so they arranged for him to bump into her at her marina. He backed out. He backed out of chance meetings in restaurants, at the opera, outside the company where she worked as a special events manager, and at the health club where she worked out. Every time they set something up, he backed out. In a few days, the investigators would almost literally push him into his meeting, and the case would end on a dismal note. The man would say hello, his old girlfriend would be glad to see him, but he would excuse himself and run off.

Parco preferred not to approach CBS for help in finding the homeless woman. That would take forever. He knew the piece was shot in New York, so one of the staff would watch the tape, pinpoint the neighborhood, then go there. The next day, they found a coffee shop where a short-order cook and two of the waitresses knew the woman and left scraps of food outside for her. The day after, they found her and put her on the phone with her mother.

Parco made a note to tell his front office not to accept any more panty-analysis jobs. A few days ago, he and two other detectives had appeared on a radio call-in show during which a young associate mentioned that Vincent Parco & Associates could confirm a woman's infidelity by running tests on her panties and matching any semen stains with samples of her main man's sperm. Since then, there had been a steady procession of men coming through the front door carrying plastic bags. The secretaries did not want to handle soiled panties and vials of freshly drawn semen. Though each test did bring a quick 150 dollars into the agency, it was not the kind of work Parco had spent seven years cultivating.

Parco had no missing-children cases on the books. That was fine with him because they represent the one kind of case where he is unable to keep his emotions in check. Most of them involve the stealing of a child from a custodial parent by a noncustodial parent, then resnatching the kid. In Parco's view, parents don't snatch children because they love them, but because they have an inhuman, pathological need to torture a former spouse or lover.

There was one murder on the open case list. A bar owner's brother had been shot on a Miami street. It took Parco about three phone calls to learn that the victim had been a gambler, and possibly a drug dealer, with a penchant for not paying his debts. It was a mob hit for sure, but the client wouldn't buy it. He had his own list of suspects that he wanted checked out, and the list changed every few weeks.

AIDS calls were up. Few agencies escape the hysteria. A man found out his wife was having an affair with a bisexual and wanted to know if the lover had any link to an AIDS victim. A woman called to ask if the detectives could check out a man she was seeing. She was starting to worry. For the most part, Parco avoids running sexual résumés, although it's not hard for him to find out if someone took an AIDS test and how it came out.

"Let's not take these on," Parco said. "Once in a while, fine, but no one's going to be happy with us on these. You really can't know everyone someone slept with unless you spend a fortune."

"Fine with me," Kunda said.

Insurance cases, often reported to be the single largest source of income for P.I.'s, are not one of Parco's priorities, but he does them. There were a couple of checks on personal injury claims, a few ongoing lawsuits involving property damage, and an ugly one where two men slugged one of Parco's clients over a rent dispute, then sued him for assault.

Marla Paul came in from an afternoon of fieldwork. All of Parco's employees check in before they go home.

"God, I'm exhausted," Paul said as she flopped on the silken couch.

"How's our porn queen?" Jo-Ann Kunda asked.

"Don't ask," Paul said. "Vinny, you know what we did today? Would you like to hear this woman's exciting afternoon?"

"I'd love to, Marla."

"Well, believe me, you're going to. She went to Altman's, then she went to Lord & Taylor, then she went into a card shop where I didn't think I could follow her without getting caught, so I stood around the sidewalk with men looking at me funny while she picked out a card, and it only took her an hour to pick out that card, then she went into Odd Lot Trading. You ever hear of a porn queen who shops at Odd Lot Trading, Vincent?"

Marla Paul speaks in streams of words that flow out breathlessly and unpunctuated. Her long red hair ranges from a conservative auburn to MTV generation orange and her expensive clothes do little to hide a pinup perfect figure. Her smile guarantees that men will stomp each other to death to give her information that they would not give to a male operative if he tied them up and burned them with a lit cigarette.

"Odd Lot Trading, Vincent. Think about it."

"Well, what did she do after that?"

"I don't know because Odd Lot Trading has an exit I didn't know about. Or maybe she's still in there."

Paul seems a beat off and is teased about her spaciness. When Parco heard that some of the office staff referred to her as the Ozone Queen, he paraphrased Lincoln and said he'd like to bottle the spaciness and send it to all his investigators, for Paul has a viselike mind for detail and can close a case that will stop far more experienced operatives.

Paul can remember names, faces, pictures on walls, dreary lines from public documents, dates of birth, and social security numbers months, and possibly years, after a single glimpse. The most guarded targets, men or women, give her information because, while they may not know what a P.I. looks like, they certainly know what one doesn't look like, and this *girl,* this blend of fawnlike vulnerability and sexiness who probably isn't even old enough to be served a legal drink, can't be anything more than the manicurist, waitress, or bored secretary she claims to be. Marla is a threat because people think she isn't one.

"So you'll pick her up tomorrow?" Parco asked.

"If you insist, Vinny, but I can tell you this lady doesn't make X-rated movies. She's a fat secretary with buck teeth who likes to shop."

"Thank you very much for sharing that with us. Pick her up tomorrow, same time."

Parco went on to tell Marla that she would be contacting Dr. Lynette Simons to set up an appointment. She was to say that she was frigid.

"Thanks a lot," she said. "I have to talk about my sex life to some phony shrink."

"You and me both. I'm going to be your boyfriend."

"Wonderful," she said.

The investigators went back to their desks to write reports. Louie Sedano returned from a hardware store where he had gone to get some wood for shelving. Parco, still determined to be nice, politely asked him to avoid dropping sawdust on the floor, then sent him out for some Velveeta Cheese. It didn't work. The rat stayed behind the refrigerator.

"Vincent, Louis Gloskin on one. He says he's a client of Les Margolis."

Parco thought a minute before remembering that he had gotten a call earlier that day from Margolis, a divorce lawyer with strong ties to the city's various religious Jewish communities.

"Les Margolis, Louis Gloskin, right. Orthodox Matrimonial. Tell him I'll be right there."

He made a notation in the Dr. Simons file and jabbed the line button with his thumb.

"Sorry to keep you waiting, this is Vincent Parco."

"Mr. Parco, my name is Louis Gloskin and . . ."

"And Les Margolis told you to call me because you have a marital problem."

The man paused and stumbled as he tried to speak.

"What's the problem?" Parco asked quietly. It seemed to take an hour before he spoke, but Parco waited him out.

"Is it safe to discuss it on the phone? I don't want to seem suspicious, Mr. Parco, but . . ."

"Be suspicious, Mr. uh, Gloskin, but I'd say my phone isn't tapped. How may I help you?"

The story, though obviously excruciating to Gloskin, was a routine one to Parco. Adultery, as Louis Gloskin found out, one Wednesday afternoon, invades even the most deeply religious households. Gloskin's fervent conviction that a lifelong commitment to daily prayer and the strictures of Orthodox Judaism somehow bought immunity from domestic evil was destroyed in the spring of 1986 when the classic signs of infidelity paraded past him for the first time.

His wife, Sarah, also from a very religious family, had become distant and was suddenly going out on shopping trips alone. She said she just needed to be out, and he accepted it, but she never brought much home, and the remoteness was way out of character. Not that Gloskin required a lot of spousal interest in his wholesale plumbing business, but Sarah had always enjoyed the conversation when Louis told her about the crazy crew in the shipping room, the new girl out front who chewed gum all the time and drove him crazy when she answered the phone that way, or the *gonif* who wanted two thousand bathtubs without putting up a deposit.

"Okay," Parco said, "but she could be going through anything from what I'm hearing so far. You think she's cheating. Why?"

"She is cheating with my best friend and business partner," Gloskin said quietly.

"Oh," Parco said and decided to let the man tell his story.

Gloskin and his partner, Joel Stein, had inherited a business their fathers started in Queens right after World War II. The two boys had been together from the playpen through college. Each had been best man at the other's wedding. It was probably his lifelong friendship with Joel and the sixth sense longtime friends have for each other's patterns that tipped Gloskin off to the affair.

Lately, he'd noticed that Joel, the outside man in the company, had stopped coming in to do his paperwork on Wednesday afternoons, when Sarah went shopping. He'd been acting funny too. Gloskin, who had inherited a damp, some would say whiny, outlook from his late father, Meyer, was used to expecting the worst, but his pessimism expressed itself in medical terms. He thought Sarah was concealing a fatal disease from him, as she would do, and that maybe Joel knew about it.

He went through her dresser looking for prescription drugs.

"And you found what?" Parco asked.

There was an intake of air on the other end of the line.

"I found red silk underwear," he said. "Garments she would never wear."

"Until now," Parco said quietly. "Hey, I sympathize. What you describe, sir, is very common."

"But Sarah is a religious Jew. It's not so common in our community."

Parco didn't tell him that he was wrong. He sees adultery everywhere, and so often that it never surprises him. Instead of punching holes in the faith of an already deeply troubled man, he just asked, "Anything else?"

"Her diaphragm. It is missing on Wednesday afternoons and back in place on Wednesday nights."

"Not a good sign, Mr. Gloskin. And you want proof?"

"Yes, I do."

"No problem on this end, but are you sure you shouldn't just have a talk with the two of them? Not to make light of your problem, but it might be just one of those crazy things people do and maybe it can be worked out without us."

"I don't think so."

"See, Mr. Gloskin, once you bring us in, and the lawyers get involved, and you're fighting in the open, it gets pretty ugly. You have kids?"

"Two children, yes. The little one, my son, is four, and I have a six-year-old daughter."

"Oh, ooh. That's what I'm saying. That's where it gets so ugly, the kids. Hey, I'm a businessman just like you. I'm not here to turn away money, but I'm just saying that these things get ugly. You want evidence for what, custody?"

"Among other things. I also have the business to think about. There are a lot of things. I have to know everything."

"Okay. You say you think they're cheating on Wednesday afternoons."

"That's right. Sometimes she is out on Thursday nights as well, but it's usually Wednesday. Between one and five, I think."

"Well, that's a good start. You have no idea how much time and money gets wasted because we go on a wild goose chase. Do you think he picks her up somewhere or do they just meet at a motel? Mr. Gloskin, this is a hard thing to talk about, especially when we haven't met face-to-face. Do you think you can come in?"

"I will do that, but can you give me an estimate on the phone?"

"I can tell you how we work. Surveillances are billed out at seventy-five dollars an hour per person, and you really need two investigators out on one of these. A team saves you money in the long run. We usually use a male and a female. That way we can get a lot closer to the target than we would if we had, say, one person in a car. You know what I'm saying?"

"Yes, I think so."

"Anyway, we take a retainer of seven-fifty for ten hours of investigation, and I don't think you'll spend much more than that if you have a pretty good idea of when they're getting together. With two people on the job, you won't spend any less, I don't think, but if you do, we'll refund the overflow."

"Do you guarantee your results?"

Oh, Christ, Vinny thought. One of those.

"We're not allowed to work that way, Mr. Gloskin. We sometimes charge a little more by the hour than other agencies, but we're cheaper because I only use top people. You spend a lot more in the long run if you have anything less than a professional on the job. Let me tell you something—may I call you Lou?"

"Louis."

"Good, now we're friends already. Call me Vinny. Louis, how about you come in here and meet us? If you don't want to go ahead, that's fine. No charge. I think you're going to find we deliver what we say we'll deliver."

As he set up his appointment with Gloskin, the rat came out again. It snatched the slice of Velveeta that they had left against the side of the refrigerator and ate it while Parco watched.

That's it, he thought. So what if I have to file a firearm discharge report with the cops? I'll take the hassle, I'll do the paperwork. This thing could be diseased, it could be carrying rabies. It could be carrying other rats. What's an exterminator going to do once the thing gnaws its way into the walls? Lay traps? Poison? Great, then it dies inside the wall. How nice.

"Okay, Louis, we'll look forward to meeting you tomorrow," he said and hung up.

He locked all his doors, told the front office he was not to be disturbed, and pulled out the .22. He steadied his hands, fired, and hit the rat. The smell of cordite and gunpowder permeated the office. The rat stopped, turned, and headed toward the desk.

The bastard's coming for me, Parco thought. He knew better, but part of him thought the thing was coming for its revenge.

He shot again and hit the rat again.

It kept coming. I am not going to fire a third time, he thought.

No way. However, the rat wasn't giving him much choice. It was dragging a thin stream of blood across the smooth, richly varnished floor and in another few seconds it would roll right across the rug and Vinny Parco would either have to live with too much conversation about the stain or give up a carpet.

The third shot was a direct hit and the rat died. Parco felt silly, then a little bad for the brave bastard, then he felt silly again for feeling bad for a rat. Outside, he could hear Jo-Ann shouting to him urgently, asking if he was all right. He sheepishly unlocked the door and let his staff in. They gave him hefty applause and Louie Sedano used a dustpan to carry the rat to its final resting place in a Dumpster outside. Time to go home, Vinny Parco thought. Enough for today.

2

Sam Spade would have whistled and called the lady a classy dame. She wore a full-length lynx coat and Fabergé sunglasses beneath painstakingly casual short platinum hair. She was probably impressed by the proper East Side Manhattan address of the Carney Detective Agency, and probably not too pleased to find an everyday apartment building with a row of doorbells and a strip of blue Dymo-Tape that read only Carney.

She rang once and was buzzed through the building's unattended front door where she found a sign that directed her up a flight of stairs past a company that sells artificial limbs, up another flight, and through an open door with a sign that said, Carney Agency, Walk In.

Dave Cohen, former detective with the NYPD, sat at his desk near the door, writing and talking into the phone that he balanced between his head and shoulder. He beckoned the lady inside by a combination tilt and shrug.

"Wait one, Pablo" he said. "Hi, may I help you?"

"I'm Mrs. Kevelin. I have an appointment with Mr. Howard," she said as she looked the place over without a lot of approval. Her words were tense, measured, and she came through the door like she was about to step in something.

The Carney Agency is a cop shop, a smooth mesh of former law enforcement detectives of various specialties who look and act like the career police officers they once were. They smoke without apology and, in fact, seem to enjoy their disquieting effect on nonsmokers as they light their cigarettes with Zippos at blowtorch force and snap the lids shut in a loud military report.

A cop shop is not set up for the admiration of walk-in clientele, though the scratched gray metal desks, manual typewriters, rotating electric fans, and men on the phone in shirtsleeves and shoulder holsters offer a reassuring streetwise grit. Vinny Parco's American Cancer Society sign thanking a visitor for not smoking would fit into this room as well as a collection of Wedgwood plates or as well as Mrs. Kevelin.

Besides Cohen, there were five men in the converted living room of an apartment. Though they appeared to take scant notice of Mrs. Kevelin's arrival, the room buzzed with coughs, grunts, throat clearing, and other elements of police body language. That Mrs. Kevelin got in at all was surprising to the men because the Carney Agency, a corporate security firm, is not in the business of taking on individual clients. The men waited for the show that would surely start when the blonde met Joe Howard, the fifty-three-year-old president of Carney, who was, at the moment, on the phone long distance.

"Joe, Mrs. Kevelin is here," Cohen said into the intercom.

"Be right out, be right out," he said. Mrs. Kevelin had called from a phone booth insisting on an appointment right away. To Howard, her problem had better be as life or death as she made it sound. The detective was talking to his old friend, former FBI agent Joe Chapman, who specializes in art fraud and museum security.

"So, how can I screw up your life, Joseph?" he asked, as he reached to snuff out a cigarette butt that had been smoldering in an ashtray.

"Ever hear of the Calgary Archive?" he asked.

"No."

"Ever been to Philadelphia?"

"Not so you'd notice. Why, what've you got?"

"Well, there's this small private library and museum up there. It's been hit a number of times, and again last night."

"And, let me guess. They don't have a great accounting of what's missing."

"I knew I called the right man."

Howard groaned. Art theft, according to those who work near it, is an enterprise that may net up to a billion dollars a year, taking a backseat in numbers only to narcotics. Despite a genteel, Cary Grant image, it attracts vicious crooks across the board from the street skel out to trade a vase for a vial of crack to big-time smugglers, drug dealers, and the Mafia who use art to bleach illegal money.

Art theft is largely invisible to the general public because museums, libraries, and private collectors don't like to go public with their losses, especially if the art was acquired under shady circumstances in the first place. Even at the most legitimate levels, recordkeeping gets fuzzy, especially since a wise art thief knows how to destroy documents.

"The cops know?"

"They do, yes."

"That's a breath of fresh air," Howard said. "Inside job, I assume."

"I assume too."

"How soon do you need me up there?"

"As soon as you can go."

"Tomorrow, I think. I'd like to take Marty Meehan up if I can get him away from his golf clubs."

"Whatever you need," Chapman said. "They're grateful for anything we can do."

"I'll bet."

Joe Howard needed a road trip like he needed another bullet in his spleen, but he made a note to call Marty Meehan and get this art thing moving. He walked through a small pantry that serves as the agency's bookkeeping office to the living room where Cohen was looking desperate as he tried to engage Mrs. Kevelin in small talk.

"Sorry to keep you waiting, Mrs. Kevelin," he said, offering her his hand. He motioned her to follow him into his office. "We ever going to see the sun again or what? I have coffee and not very good tea, if you want anything."

She declined the offer of a beverage, but let him hang up her coat. As a very decorated detective with the New York City Police Department's prestigious Safe, Loft, and Truck Squad, Howard recovered many a truckload of hot fur. He couldn't resist a brief scan of the label and lining to see if the lady paid full price. She did and then some, he decided.

Howard took a minute to settle into his chair while Mrs. Kevelin checked out a wall of citations from the New York City Police Department, including the rare Medal of Honor for heroism in a shoot-out. They give out one of those a year and you usually have to die or come back from the dead to get it.

If Mrs. Kevelin didn't approve of the ambience of a cop shop, she certainly could appreciate the tailoring of the man who ran this one.

Howard is always dressed to meet an upscale clientele. He favors Bill Blass, Brooks Brothers, and custom tailoring on the conservative side of tweedy. He is as youthful as a man in his early fifties ever gets, with his black hair nearly as dark as it was in 1957 when he joined the force.

His eyes, which are even darker than his hair, telegraph the seen-it-all assurance that makes many high-rolling clients insist on cop shops when they buy detective services.

Joe Howard is so 1940s in swagger and style that his presence turns a room into the set of a black-and-white movie. He snarls at the absurd storybook image of the private dick, but does so as he evokes its most poetic fragrances. He speaks in a staccato, Bogart-style delivery from the side of his mouth, where a nonfiltered Camel bobs up and down with the words.

He spent his first eleven years in Ireland, and between the Bogart muffle and the B-movie pace, his voice reveals a trace of brogue, a little Cagney in the equation. He drinks lots of coffee, black, no sugar, and his handshake is an iron claw-hold. It's not hard to imagine him kicking down a door just because it's in his way, claiming, as the splinters fly, that real P.I.'s don't do such things.

"Well, Mrs. Kevelin, how may I help you? I should tell you up front that I do not do divorce work."

She smiled. "It's not a divorce problem, actually." She reached into her purse and handed him a file card with the typed name and address of a couple.

"How much do you charge for your services?"

"It kind of depends what those services are, but I bill at sixty-five an hour, if that helps you any."

She nodded. He read the card and said, "Who are they?"

"They're elderly people who live in an apartment my husband and I are thinking of buying. I need to know if either of them has a terminal illness, like cancer or a heart condition."

Howard removed his glasses and looked to the ceiling, as though he could get the words he needed from some tile up there.

In the frenzied, frothing, real estate market of contemporary Manhattan, many landlords sell their rent-controlled apartments at bargain prices to buyers who must wait, without interfering, for the tenants to leave.

"How old are they again?" he asked.

"Eighties. He's probably close to ninety."

"Then they have a terminal condition, don't they, Mrs. Kevelin? Their lives are over."

"How long would it take you to get me this information?"

"I don't know because I have to turn down the opportunity."

For the first time since she'd arrived, Mrs. Kevelin removed her sunglasses. She looked at Howard as though he had just urinated on the carpet in front of her. "I don't understand," she said.

"I'm saying I don't want the case, Mrs. Kevelin. Won't take it. Period."

She hissed like an angry cat, grabbed her coat, and ran through the office so fast that even Howard couldn't keep up. Dave Cohen flinched at the breeze created when she slammed the front door, which Howard saluted and said, "Have a *nice* day, Mrs. Kevelin."

The investigators, fulfilled in their expectations of a good show, broke into applause and cheers.

"I guess she didn't like our rates, Joe," Cohen said.

Howard told them the part of the story they missed with the poise and timing of a stand-up comic. Like most Irishmen, he loves an audience and makes the retelling of an event more sparkling than the moment itself.

Five years ago, Howard might have gladly taken Mrs. Kevelin's case, and a few that offended him more. He was not billing a million and a half a year for his work with the top museums, banks, book publishers, multinational corporations, and government agencies then. He was learning one very big difference between being a cop and being a P.I.; cops don't have to hustle business, pay staggering rents, and meet a payroll. He was nearly bankrupt after stretching his limited assets to set up shop. Thanks to a twenty-thousand dollar loan from a Greek businessman whose hijacked furs he had once recovered, Howard survived the crisis, and his timing could not have been better.

The field set up in 1849 by Allan Pinkerton with the logo of an open eye and the motto We Never Sleep has, according to

Forbes magazine, evolved into "one of the fastest growing services in today's service economy." By 1990 private police will outnumber sworn officers by a ratio of four to one. Howard's piece of the market is white-collar crime which, according to the U.S. government, costs the American economy $44 billion a year.

Half of all employees in any business steal. In some businesses, such as retailing, the figure can rise to 75 percent. A quarter of those who steal go for the big-ticket items such as VCRs, copying machines, cameras, cash, computers, and cars. Any corporation can assume that eight out of every hundred employees steal repeatedly.

Payments of casualty and loss insurance awards increase at the rate of 500 percent a year, accounting for the industry's pretax operating loss of $3.8 billion in 1985. In 1985 Americans spent $744 million on information security, mainly to keep intruders away from computers. That figure will increase 171 percent to $2.1 billion by 1993.

Illegal wiretaps, product counterfeiting, and industrial espionage are so rampant that corporate security directors spend more than $3 billion a year on state-of-the-art hardware, a figure likely to triple in the next decade.

Small-ticket shoplifting of the stuff-it-in-the-purse variety costs retailers $58 million a year, not including the cost of security personnel and hardware. The elderly are bilked of $10 million annually by pharmaceutical charlatans who peddle modern day snake oil largely in the form of bogus cancer remedies.

Ten thousand phony doctors and any number of marginally trained quacks with medical degrees worth scarcely more than the parchment they are printed on lick their chops at the financial potential of phony medical claims which, according to fraud investigators at Aetna Life and Casualty, amount to a million dollars a *day*.

"It's not like TV," Howard says. "In some ways it's worse. On TV, crooks get caught and sent to jail. In real life, we catch them, but the client doesn't want to prosecute a lot of the time. We're not in the jailing business anymore, and that's a tough thing to live with when you're used to locking the bastards up."

But even if Joe Howard could lock them up, the crooks wouldn't stay long or do very hard time. One FBI study estimates that bank fraud with a computer nets a criminal an average of nearly half a million dollars, while robbing the same bank with a gun will yield less than twenty-five thousand. The gunman, tagged with videotape and probably marked money, may well get caught and do fifteen years in a maximum security institution. The computer crook will probably walk. If he is caught, the perception of respectability attached to his clean hands and education is on his side. Even in the harshest cases, sentences of more than five years are rare. The white-collar criminal, a first-time offender most of the time, is probably going to do his time in a minimum security institution.

Howard shares his office with his son, twenty-four-year-old Jeremiah Howard, Jr., who joined the company after college and a short stint with a brokerage house. It will be up to him to keep the Carney Agency technologically au courant.

Both men trust the leathery worth of street hunch as the premier gift in private security. The senior Howard calls it "common sense for Chrissake, no big deal"; others call it seasoning. Howard goes out a lot and reads faces, watching for twitches, eye shifting, the subsonic wavering of a voice, or any subliminal quirk that brings an investigator to say, "Hey, something isn't right."

He likes it boring. He's been involved in eight shooting incidents, and has one old wound that remains life threatening twenty-five years after it almost killed him. In 1984 he developed peritonitis from the wound and fell into a coma that nearly wiped him out for the fourth time. Excitement, at this point, he can live without.

"Being punched *hurts*," he emphasizes. "On TV, you don't see the guy spit out his teeth and miss a week of work. These clowns on the detective shows fight like Muhammad Ali with a referee in the ring. That is bullshit. In life, three guys will kick you in the balls and work your head over with a crowbar. They could give a shit if you die there or if your family has to wheel you around in a chair for the rest of your life.

"Don't get me going on guns," he adds. "I hate the goddamn things. I haven't carried one on a job for two years."

Carney's hundred and twenty-five part-time security people are all off-duty police officers, correction guards from the country's toughest jails, federal marshals, or fire investigators. "These people at least have some training," he says. "I look for the guy who hates guns as much as I do. That's the one who makes me feel secure. A lot of these morons out there shouldn't be armed with a squirt gun."

"Boring, boring, boring. The real world of the private detective is boring," he says. Blondes don't usually walk through the door. Instead, detectives receive calls from attorneys, do the investigation as quickly as possible, and send a bill.

Howard does most of the agency's investigations himself. In the winter of 1986, he had half a dozen cases to think about. A young man had been arrested for stealing video equipment and his attorney wanted some background information on the merchant making the charge.

"A normal, boring case," he says. "If there's dirt, fine, if not, I'll say so and that will be that."

A construction company wanted him to check out a would-be client to "find out what kind of an outfit he was dealing with." The client wanted some very expensive work done, and the contractor had to evaluate the financial risk involved before bringing in expensive equipment, added help, and costly materials. Howard had gone to Brooklyn to talk to the company's neighbors and employees.

The manufacturer of a patented tool felt that several former executives were now illegally manufacturing and selling the product. It would turn out that the tool had been produced with sufficient design differences to warrant its own patent.

An industrialist wanted his daughter's fiancé checked out. He didn't like him. That's all he knew. The young man, who claimed to be an attorney, would turn out to be a con artist with a long string of aliases, phony credentials, and ripped-off fiancées.

He delayed returning a call from Clara Trow, but supposed he'd have to face her sooner or later. She was a "bedbug" case who believed she was being hunted by aliens and wanted an armed escort on a two-day trip to Washington so she could tell the politicians about it.

He returned a call to his friend Gus Chakas, who owned a coffee shop and several buildings on the very trendy Upper West Side. Gus's problem was not a case Hollywood would race to option. Four peddlers had set up their carts on the sidewalk near the chic boutique and shops that paid Chakas premium rent.

"Well, as you know," Joe told Chakas, "the police up there have been trying to keep them away."

He heard a frustrated sigh on the line.

"Joe, Joe, you're a businessman," Gus said. "You think summonses are going to scare these people? My tenants pay ten, twelve, fourteen thousand a month rent for their shops. I'm losing thousands myself. I can't tell them, 'Well, we're working on it.' I got to do something, you know? Maybe my father's right. Do it the old way. Bring my brothers in and beat the shit out of them."

"Great idea, Gus. Let them sue the ass off you and they'll be able to move into your stores because they'll own them. We'll figure something out."

"Please, Joe. Those assholes are making kissing sounds when the women walk by. They smoke dope right out in the open."

"The trouble is, Gus, they're not selling it. If they were, we'd have them out already."

"And they're always drinking goddam wine or something out of bottles in those paper bags. Hell, this is supposed to be the best area of the city now, but no one told these pricks that."

"We'll tell them, Gus."

"Please," he said.

Howard dispatched Joe Junior and Bob Katchen to check things out in the neighborhood that afternoon. Somewhere between goon tactics and ineffective summonses, there was an answer, and he'd find it if Gus could hold out.

Howard got up and walked into the pantry to pour himself some fresh coffee. Yesterday, he'd thrown out a doctor who wanted two armed guards to keep his own mother from coming to his wedding. Twenty minutes ago, Mrs. Kevelin had burst in off the street breathlessly needing to know how long two people close to ninety were expected to live. He had just sent a pair of intelligent grown-ups to the Upper West Side to handle peddlers making kissing noises at passing women.

As he dialed Marty Meehan's number to talk about the Philadelphia art theft, he noticed the note to call Clara Trow about her aliens. She was beginning to make a lot more sense to him.

3

Les Dinkins and Buster Mallory were supposed to be cleaning up the huge Arco station off Interstate 81 near Roanoke, Virginia, where they had shared the graveyard shift for about a year. Since management didn't check, they did what unsupervised overnight workers do at twenty past four in the morning; they dozed over their magazines, Les behind the register nodding gently over airbrushed breasts in *Penthouse* while Buster snored on a chair by the door with *Car And Driver*'s centerfold of a red Corvette working its way, inch by inch, from his lap to the floor.

Their hypnagogic bliss was assaulted with the rudeness of thrown ice water when a massive 1980 Buick Century came from nowhere and stopped with a screech right outside the door. A medium-sized man in his midthirties got out of the driver's side and leaped to the passenger door so fast that the car was still rocking on its axles. Les and Buster were now fully awake and near panic, for the man had one hand behind his back.

Oh, shit, Buster thought. A gun for sure. Young night workers who handle cash have heard stories about the old days when all you had to do was give a robber the money he wanted and you wouldn't get hurt. Now, you'd give up the money and maybe get killed anyway. Everyone knows that. Dinkins and Mallory stayed frozen in place as the man, dressed in jeans, a windbreaker, and a mesh New York Mets cap, opened the passenger door.

A second man got out awkwardly, for he was chained up like a wild animal. His hands were cuffed in front of him and the chains seemed to run from his sleeves into his crotch and down his pants to his ankles where his legs were bound. The one with the Mets cap was waving a big black T-shaped stick with his left hand, while his right hand stayed behind his back.

"Okay, Wayne, nice and easy now," he said, gently guiding the prisoner out of the car and pointing him toward the office.

"Excuse me," he shouted through the open door. "May I trouble you for the men's room key?"

Dinkins, a red-haired man of twenty-five with a beer gut way beyond his years, stared with awe for a second or two before he could answer. "Ain't no key. Just walk right on over there, sir."

The man in the baseball cap was Peter Castillo, an Arlington-based P.I. who occupies a rare and dangerous corner of his field, one where car chases, high-caliber weapons, and criminals for whom violence is a shrug are part of the landscape. Castillo is a bounty hunter.

When criminals post bond and fail to show up for trial, the bondsman calls a professional bounty hunter to bring in the fugitive for a piece of the forfeited amount, usually 10 or 15 percent. Castillo packs a formidable arsenal of weapons, yet takes pride that he has never had to fire a gun. He is quick to separate himself from the buffs who read post office posters and charge off with their pistols drawn. All of his work comes from bondsmen he knows in the Washington area or from referrals.

Castillo works all fifty states and always travels with letters of authorization from the bondsmen who hire him. Legal precedents dating back to British Common Law, and especially the Supreme Court case of *Taylor v. Taintor*, have established the jurisdiction and right to arrest of the person holding a bond or his representative. According to the high court, "They may imprison him. . . . They may pursue him to another state; may arrest him on the Sabbath, and if necessary may break and enter his house for that purpose. The seizure is not made by virtue of new process. None is needed. It is likened to the rearrest by the sheriff of an escaping prisoner."

In some cases, a bounty hunter's authority transcends that of local police who must seek extradition when a criminal crosses into another jurisdiction. Bounty hunters are paid either quickly or not at all. There are no retainers, no calculation of hours spent even if the case didn't work out, and no misunderstandings. Find the crook, get the bucks. Lose him and weep. Castillo, the only full-time employee of his firm, would collect five thousand dollars for turning in his prisoner this morning.

He was racing back to Washington to meet a matrimonial client. Aside from the unusual sideline of capturing armed criminals, Castillo's caseload is the routine fare of the working private investigator. He is not much of a joiner or a collaborative personality. He prefers to keep his own counsel, follow his hunches, and close his case without partners.

The prisoner, Wayne Johnson, was a small-time drug smuggler wanted on a murder charge in Washington. From what Castillo had heard, eye contact was probably reason enough for Johnson to draw his .357 and blow someone away. He liked the mess. Castillo had tracked him to Florida where the Miami PD was very helpful in aiming him toward the bars and hangouts of the "cocaine cowboys."

Johnson had made two classic mistakes. He assumed no one would be looking for him a thousand miles from home, and he couldn't stay away from his girlfriend.

"They never give up on their girlfriends, even when the women have given up on them," Castillo says. "I usually find the girlfriend by her girlfriends or by watching relatives."

Genealogy is a big part of Castillo's investigative repertoire. He spends hours tracking relatives and charting family trees, interviewing friends, local merchants, and others who would have reason to know a family's pattern. The names of out-of-state aunts, uncles, or cousins, the closeness of a family, all form a loosely structured, but often accurate map. Through such interviews, Castillo traced Johnson's girlfriend to Fort Lauderdale, Florida.

Wayne Johnson accommodated Peter Castillo's educated hunch quickly. He came out to empty the trash and Castillo met him by the Dumpster with a sheaf of legal documents and an Intratec nine-millimeter semiautomatic, a cannon of a weapon fierce enough to make Dirty Harry mellow.

"How's it going, Wayne?" Castillo asked. "You know, they want you back in DC and we're going right now."

The nine millimeter looks like a machine gun. Johnson, no stranger to the weapon himself, just stared at it and said, "Sheeeeit."

Castillo had notified the Miami Police that he had his quarry and was now moving north on 95. He also notified the Florida Highway Patrol of his route. He prefers not to fly with fugitives because airlines don't like the attention and their captains have a way of ordering that a prisoner fly unchained.

If he drives all day, he usually deposits the prisoner in a local jail and spends the night in a motel. This time, he didn't do it that way and he was beginning to regret it. He shook a little sleep from his eyes as he followed Johnson into the men's room of the gas station.

To his relief, it was one of the more modern facilities with a dozen urinals and stalls. Peter stood about a foot behind Johnson as the drug dealer relieved himself.

"Okay, Wayne, now I want you to put your hands right up against that wall over there," he said, gesturing toward a large tiled area next to the hand-drying machine. "Just look at the wall, don't let me hear the chain rattle. I hear even one link, you go down."

Castillo relieved himself without incident.

As he zipped up, however, he noticed Johnson doing something extremely dangerous. He had turned his head around and his eyes were scanning the room.

"Don't even think about it, Wayne," he said sharply, but without raising his voice. He walked slowly toward Johnson with his stick in striking position.

"I wasn't thinking about nothing, man."

"That's good, Wayne. Real good. Now just walk back to the car slowly and don't let your mind get tempted. You know I'll drop you, Wayne. You know that."

Johnson made a hostile gutteral sound that was the equivalent of spitting. Then he walked slowly back to the Buick. Les Dinkins and Buster Mallory watched from the gas pumps as Johnson walked, one small step at a time toward the car, with Castillo a few feet behind him.

"Thanks, guys," Peter said to them. Buster nodded, Les stared until the taillights of the Century disappeared on the interstate.

"Thirty thousand," Johnson said. "You stop up ahead, I make one call and you've got thirty thousand tonight. I stay with you till my man brings it. They catch me on something else, it never happened, man. Thirty thousand, like that."

Castillo kept his eyes on the road and drove silently. He'd been waiting for the offer. It's always there.

"Fifty thou, man I swear, I won't even miss it. It's chicken shit. I'll make the call. You name the place. How much you gonna get for bringing me in?"

"Five thousand honest dollars, Wayne. Five thousand dollars

for four day's work. To you, that's a joke. To me, it's decent money."

Johnson again said, "Sheeeeit." It was the last remark that passed between them.

Castillo did not collect his money that morning, but picked it up the following day. He went home to his garden apartment in suburban Washington, showered, slept for two hours, and was in his Alexandria office by ten o'clock, wearing a dark blue suit, white shirt, and red tie. Tonight would be bliss. Tonight he would go to bed early and sleep all night.

Castillo, who does not smoke, drink, or even scowl, comes close to the lone wolf legend of the private investigator. He shares a receptionist and office space with a political action committee that lobbies conservative causes, but has his own entrance, and functions as the proverbial one-man operation.

Castillo usually wears cutoff jeans and a T-shirt while working. When he meets clients or goes to court, he wears neat, but not power-grabbing, dark suits. He favors white shirts, red, yellow, or dark blue ties. He could be a realtor, an insurance executive in middle management, or any of a million government functionaries who keep the machinery moving regardless of who's in the White House.

Perhaps because he grew up in Pennsylvania and moves with the unrushed poise of a midwesterner, he is mistaken for every nationality but his own. "People think I'm Iranian, Israeli, Indian, whatever, but they never take me for a Hispanic."

Castillo was born in San Juan, where his father was a police officer. When he was five, they moved to Scranton, Pennsylvania, where he grew up in the late fifties and early sixties, with the unapologetic patriotism of an astronaut.

He learned much of his trade in Army intelligence in Southeast Asia, specifically in Thailand near the Vietnam border. He won't say what he did, even now. After the Army, he served as a police officer in Fairfax County, Virginia, before leaving to slug it out as a P.I. in 1980. He'd transported prisoners as a cop. Bounty hunting made sense.

"Ninety percent of the people out there claiming to be bounty hunters should not be there," he says. "It's a job where you have to be very professional. You can't just kick down a door and go in there like John Wayne."

Five years ago, Castillo caught ten escapees a month. His

service as a bounty hunter remains in great demand in the Washington area, but he's slowed down the flow in favor of more conventional cases.

In the summer of 1986, he had several debugging cases. Washington P.I.'s get them all the time. Castillo is a high tech enthusiast and tries to keep abreast of new developments in electronic countermeasures.

He continues to find missing children, sometimes for only expenses if a family is unable to pay. He is a fierce believer in giving something back to society. He was tracking several missing teenagers.

He received a call from Ron Grace, the bondsman responsible for Wayne Johnson's appearance in court.

"Just wanted to say thanks," he said. "Are you too tired for another one?"

"Too tired today," Castillo said. "What's doing?"

"Got a real nasty one this time," Grace said.

Thomas Everett Lang, twenty-three, had never been convicted of rape, but the rape squad of Washington's Metro Police believed he was linked to as many as twenty brutal attacks in the past eighteen months. Though his usual victims were young adult women, they suspected he had also raped a ten-year-old girl and an eighty-three-year-old woman.

"They finally got him," Grace said. "Brought him into court this morning. We posted twenty-five thou on the guy."

"And he's gone already?" Castillo asked.

"Yeah, right. Guy gets out of court at eleven. Three o'clock, St. Mark's Hospital, when the shift changes. This nurse comes into the parking lot and he's there waiting between the parked cars. Her jaw's broken, she's missing teeth, and one eye's closed, but she made an ID. So, the cops go up to the house and guess what?"

"They haven't seen him since court."

"Right again, my man. I think he's probably out of state already."

"Okay," Castillo said. "You know my routine."

"Take your time, take your time. Let him settle in," Grace said.

Castillo put a few bills aside for his bookkeeper to pay when she came in at the end of the month. As he waited for his matrimonial client, he opened the file on a case that had occupied his time for several weeks.

Stapled to the manila file folder was a business card. High Is Heaven was the motto in black lettering against a pink background. In the corners were drawings of capsules representing barbituates, amphetamines, hallucinogenics, and other drugs. This was the handiwork of Walter Williams, the Sugar Daddy, who had flooded northern Virginia with both the cards and the pills.

The Sugar Daddy was not a drug dealer. The pills were fake. They were made by a mail-order pharmaceutical house in Pennsylvania and sold as cold medicine or caffein tablets, but looked so much like the real items that police could only be cynical about the stated purpose of their manufacture. Williams even had an exaggerated view of himself as a savior. The way he saw it, the four dollars per pill he took from junior high and high school kids was money they wouldn't spend on real drugs or with real drug dealers.

The police did not agree. The fake drugs gave the Sugar Daddy's young clientele (he favored seventh- and eighth-graders) a false sense of security. They took the pills by the handful, unaware that they were ingesting only caffein and nasal decongestant. But when the Sugar Daddy had fled to another school, he left behind plenty of customers for school yard traffickers in the authentic substances. The students then gobbled down the real thing and overdosed.

The police had done their job and the Sugar Daddy was caught. That he'd served sixteen years for murdering a cop in 1970 did not seem to affect the judge who released him on a bond of two thousand dollars. The Sugar Daddy found that a reasonable price to pay for his freedom. He never showed up for trial.

No one expected a serious bounty hunter, or even an amateur, to take the case. At the usual 10 to 15 percent rate, it would mean practically working free. The police detectives were now on to other pursuits. But Castillo had been a second generation cop and cops do not care for people who kill their law enforcement brothers. He wasn't too crazy about the bogus drugs either. He'd get to it. He'd find and bring back the Sugar Daddy.

4

In his office across Jericho Turnpike from a Burger King and a Friendly's in the Long Island suburb of Westbury, Barry Silvers waited for clients he didn't want to meet, about a case he didn't want to take. Yesterday, the fifty-five-year-old former federal rackets investigator had received a call from a woman named Karen Girard who wanted him to find the biological mother of her husband, Jeff. Her husband hated the idea. He told Mrs. Girard he'd meet with her, but his gut said to pass on this one.

Natural parent cases are emotional land mines even when the outcome is successful, which it isn't at least half the time. They can also be very gratifying, filling a void that looms in the subconscious as a constant yoke to an adopted child.

A successful investigation can be a reprieve to the parent who, more often than not, conceived the child out of wedlock as a very young adult and has lived a lifetime with a decision too heavy to make at any age. A month ago, Silvers had a happy ending when he united a thirty-nine-year-old woman with the man who had fathered her during World War II. That's the high end of such a case.

The low end is that clients have a way of expecting incandescence when there is none to be found. Kids romanticize their biological parents. When the mother they pictured as a beautiful, confused young girl who went on to marry a millionaire turns out to be a hooker still turning tricks in her sixties, or the father they fantasized dying over France in an aerial dogfight with the Luftwaffe is a belching wino who keeps warm by hiding in the toilet of a Greyhound terminal, the dream is over for good.

Silvers was also uneasy about taking money for results he probably wouldn't get. Jeff Girard had been born in Providence,

Rhode Island, two hundred miles away. Silvers had never been there and knew no one who had. If he took the case, there would be a lot of costly, puddle-jumping travel and at some point, he'd probably have to hire a local P.I., someone with the all-important contacts in the area. Such a person would know how to work the city and state bureaucracies for public documents.

Silvers could easily spend five thousand dollars on this one and he could not even remotely suggest any reason for optimism. When states seal adoption records, the courts are on their side. The task is to make an end run around the bureaucracy, piecing together information from legal sources and interviews, then corroborating the evidence to the satisfaction of investigator and client.

Finding biological parents has become a big item for any P.I. who wants to take on the work. Adults with money to spend are suddenly discovering that, long shot or not, there is a chance to fill the hole in their lives. As with anything that draws money, there are also black marketeers and con artists who promise results and either don't deliver or falsify their findings. Such practices are a cousin of illicit baby sales and make Silvers shudder.

But the part of the story he liked least was that Karen wanted to find her husband's biological mother and Jeff did not. She had asked if Silvers could make the inquiry without her husband's involvement in the case because she was worried that her newborn daughter, Laura, might have a hereditary disease such as Tay-Sachs, MS, or a hundred other medical problems where a knowledge of family history is pivotal for a doctor's diagnosis. The baby had been crying repeatedly at night and the physicians could not find anything wrong.

Silvers said he wanted, if possible, to talk to Jeff as well. The young man had agreed to a meeting, but was furious about the whole thing; a fury, Karen said, derived from another piece of the script that investigators who do these cases know only too well. Jeff's adoptive mother would become hysterical if she found out. That, Silvers thought with a sigh, can turn out to be the biggest problem of all. The young man would feel cornered, torn between what his wife wanted, the suffering he believed he would cause the woman he knew as his mother, and, somewhere in there, he would have his own emotions to plumb.

The Girards had called to say that they would be late because a tractor-trailer on the Long Island Expressway had jackknifed, causing the traffic to back up for miles. Silvers was philosophical. The LIE is known to anyone who drives it as the world's longest parking lot.

Silvers was grateful for the breather. Two days ago, he had returned from London, and in a day or so would leave for Rio on a well-paying, but time-consuming, embezzlement case. He had stayed in his office until 2:00 A.M. the night before, "seeing wood," or excavating the paperwork of his customary seventy-five or eighty project caseload, from his desk.

Introspect Investigations is a small agency, employing only Silvers, a secretary, two full-time investigators, and an assortment of free-lancers for periods when the surveillances and fieldwork become too heavy. There are also offices in Toronto, Montreal, and London, where Silvers conducts business through his alliances with local agencies. He, in turn, serves as their New York office.

He is an unlikely prospect for international intrigue. His vice is donuts. On a hot July Monday in 1986, with the air conditioner not in top form, he worked in a crisp, short-sleeved, white shirt with a tie neatly knotted against the top button, and not so much as a degree off center. He looks more like a pharmacist filling a prescription than a former G-man with three decades of experience in criminal investigations.

Jeanine Simmons crossed an empty reception area to his office and leaned in.

"Barry, your desk looks so neat, I'm scared," she said. Jeanine is twenty-five and has been with Barry for less than a year, first as a secretary, now as an investigator trainee.

"I know," he said, "I'm scared too. Now I won't be able to find anything, like your paycheck."

"That's because it's so small, I have a hard time finding it myself. When's Diane coming back?"

"We should be done with that job by next week. God, I can't wait to get her back."

Diane Kowalski, the agency's secretary, was working in an office Silvers had set up to receive stolen merchandise from a group of thieves who specialized in hot auto parts. The ring usually got the parts from chop shops, or garages where cars stolen from the nearby New York airports were stripped. He needed a person in the office full-time and chose to use Diane instead of an investigative operative. Now, he was thinking twice about that decision.

"Is there any more coffee?" he asked Jeanine.

"I just put a pot on. It's not Diane's coffee, but it's fresh. Let me get it for you."

"No, I can use the exercise," he said, getting up and walking to the coffee maker for his third cup of the day. When he returned to the office, he continued to go through the papers in his office as he reviewed his caseload.

A P.I. gets used to working the middle of a case with no sense of how it began or where it will end. A client calls, an attorney calls, the P.I. gets the information and bills it out. He might just pound on doors until he finds someone who saw a three-car accident. He couldn't care less what the attorney or insurance company does with the report. He might get a call from Italy where a member of the World Association of Detectives is looking for an heir to settle an estate, as happened last week. Silvers would never know or care to know if the fortunate client made fifty cents or fifty thousand dollars.

During his twenty years as an investigator for the Federal Organized Crime Task Force, he got used to working the middle, but it never dampened his enthusiasm for his work. To Silvers, every piece of paper on his desk represents a story, a human drama that is more fascinating to him than any movie. If the end isn't so clean, and the beginning is so vague no one can even remember how the client got there, the middle is more than enough.

Silvers doesn't like files. Once he sees wood, he starts covering the desk with credit reports, airline tickets, four or five color snapshots of people he will soon follow or find, notes he writes to himself, retainer checks, legal documents, and always, a Dunkin Donut box.

The joke around Introspect is that Barry's real office is his shirt pocket. The amount of material he can jam into a small breast pocket of a white shirt should, they feel, make the *Guinness Book of World Records* or "Sixty Minutes."

No one seems to have told Silvers that detectives become jaded after thirty years of checking out human sleaze. He is cheerful enough to overwhelm a true cynic and sets a tone of unabashed corniness. Yuppies suddenly remember urgent business elsewhere when they look at the handmade signs above Diane Kowalski's desk:

INTROSPECT INVESTIGATIONS, INC.
INSPECTOR BARRY CLU-SO
DIANE KNO-NO
ANSWERING ALL YOUR CRIME NEEDS AT A MOMENT'S NOTICE
GIVE OR TAKE A DAY OR SO

There's another sign under that:

DEBUGGING
MURDER
ATTEMPTED MURDER
SUICIDE
FUNERAL ARRANGEMENTS
YOU CHOOSE IT, WE RUSE IT

And finally:

COLD COFFEE AND DONUTS OUR SPECIALTY

"He's a doll," Kowalski says. "It's more like working for a friend than working for a boss. He just never stops being nice, no matter how tense the work gets."

People have a habit of giving him their life stories, whether he asks for them or not. As he drank coffee and munched on a donut, he tried to figure which cases he could close today.

For two weeks, a pair of free-lance operatives had been tracking a department store theft ring. They posed as part-time employees, worked different shifts, and never contacted each other when their schedules overlapped. They had learned that televisions, microwaves, power tools, and other expensive items were being carried out the front door with coded orange "sold" stickers, and the front door guard was being watched carefully.

Silvers knew that his operatives would find these thieves and he'd soon be called back to look for more. The loss prevention business never dries up.

He'd returned a call that morning from a wholesaler. Could he come to Brooklyn immediately? A truck had been hijacked. Silvers sent another investigator out to meet the client, and would go himself in the afternoon. Hijackings are one of his specialties. The work is quick and urgent, but this time there would be no helicopter or out-of-state police cooperation needed. The eighteen-wheel Peterbuilt had been stolen from a truck stop in Connecticut more than twelve hours ago. By now, it was unloaded and ditched somewhere.

There were also a couple of matrimonials that would wait until next week, a forgery, and the undercover operation that was keeping Diane out of the office.

He had to go to Rio on a case that he knew was taking up far too much time and energy lately, but he couldn't stop thinking about it. Barry Silvers will not say precisely how he first became involved with Richard Peter Hammond, a man known to Interpol, the FBI, about a dozen other law enforcement agencies, and countless marks as the Duke of Audley. He acknowledges only that one of his millionaire clients lost a lot of money to Hammond, and that the young man caught on to a truism known to cons since the beginning of time: If you know what you're doing, it is far easier to con the rich than the middle class or poor. More than any con artist Silvers had seen, the Duke knew what he was doing.

The key to Hammond's success was his intimate knowledge of social networks, and the vulnerability of his marks to them. He would latch on to an extremely prominent host or hostess, then get that person to introduce him to someone just a smidgeon down on the social ladder. The Duke would then become instantly close to his mark. They might go sailing together, play tennis, or ride horses, and Hammond would invoke the name of the person with higher status as though the two of them had taken a blood oath of eternal friendship. The sting victim would later find out that the Duke was only a casual, and very recent, acquaintance of the person who made the introduction.

He also traded on the tendency of nouveau wealth to revere British nobility. Rich Americans crave its proximity and will buy a royalty scam with astonishingly naive fervor when it comes through the tight, clubby channels of their social circles. Most of the Duke's marks believed not only that he was a real duke, but a polo-playing buddy of Prince Charles who could deliver an invitation to Buckingham Palace.

Hammond also understood American royalty, celebrity, and its draw. He constantly got himself photographed with top rock musicians, athletes, politicians, and movie stars. Though the poses were nothing more than the usual vacant embraces that stars accept as inevitable when they go to a fund-raiser or wait in a VIP lounge, Hammond parlayed the illusion of association into a string of swindles.

In the early stages of a sting, Hammond treated money as a vulgar, and irrelevant, necessity to his life-style. He gossiped, dropped names relentlessly, and was a generous check grabber. He was a big gift-giver, insisting that his new friends accept an engraved Rolex watch, a rare bottle of wine, or a cherished antique. He was even known to give away Porsches and Jaguars as a token of his good faith when he got to the nitty-gritty of deals.

The deals themselves varied, but usually amounted to the Duke confiding that he, and a very few important people above the mark's status, had the inside track on something that couldn't miss. The mark would tentatively ask if there was any chance he could buy in. The Duke would solemnly claim he'd do his best, but he had to be honest. His partners wouldn't care for the idea. How high could he go? If the mark was serious, maybe the partners could be persuaded.

The Duke's favorite currency was bogus certified checks. Police said he could produce the ink and paper to fake a check so real that it could fool even the most discriminating banker. He knew the proper numerical codes, where to punch the holes, and how to blend the rare inks. There were bounced checks running into six and, in at least one case, seven figures anywhere Hammond went.

Though he stung a lot of people stateside, the Duke kept a relatively low profile here. He was at his most flamboyant in the Caribbean and South America where he could make the wealthy almost beg him for an audience. They met him at the airport in their stretch limos as he flew in on a private jet borrowed from a high roller or celebrity. He traveled with an entourage of well-heeled, Dom Perignon–guzzling young people from the wealthiest families. Being in his presence was a social must for a while. A week or two later, his marks would wish they had never heard of the Duke of Audley.

The rich are proud, too proud to admit to being victimized by the kind of raw swindle the Duke pulled off. He not only took their money, or their jewels, but seemed to want to make his marks feel stupid, the trademark of a psychopath. That degradation was probably as rewarding to him as the money itself, not to mention the protection it provided from disclosure.

Silvers didn't know what he'd find on his trip to Palm Beach, St. Maarten, and Rio, but he was sure it would be an eye-opener. If the arrest warrants, complaints, and police files on his desk were correct, the Duke stung more than a dozen people and ripped off close to a million dollars. Some estimates went as high as three million. It took him three weeks to do this.

5

Louis Gloskin left his Toyota Camry in a parking garage underneath an apartment building near Vincent Parco's office. He scanned the posted rates and bristled at the fifteen dollars he'd have to spend if he was gone even two hours, and that didn't include a tip for the surly attendant who was now leaving a trail of rubber as he dive-bombed the sedan toward a far wall of the garage, stomping the brake a millisecond before impact.

It was sunny and clear outside, but Gloskin hardly noticed. He'd been feeling bad since he gave in to his impulse to look in Sarah's dresser and found that awful red garment that a harlot would wear in a whorehouse. The world went into the slow motion of a very bad dream after that. Sometimes, when he was playing with little Melissa and Adam, his hands would shake and he could hardly stop the trembling.

He wondered if Sarah could tell that he knew. He tried to act normal, but the harder he tried, the more conspicuous he felt. It seemed to him that everyone around him would have to know that he was hiding his feelings. Time had taken on a frightening cast. He could sit in his living room from seven until bedtime with only the dimmest awareness of hours going by. He could even hear himself talking to Sarah, but sounds were hollow and images unreal, as if the world were at the other end of a pipe and he couldn't get through to it.

Sometimes his mood floated from paralysis to resignation to the giddiness of a child. He would drive to work and even talk to Joel and everything would be routine. Then, at odd times and usually when he was alone, he would see Sarah's face moving slowly toward Joel's for a kiss. He would shut his eyes tight to make the image go away. The thought of a slow, longing kiss between his wife and his best friend bothered him more than the sex he knew they had.

He hoped this detective, this man Vincent Parco, would help him get back the control he'd always had over his life. Gloskin placed predictability and order above all other personal virtues. At New York University, he had pitied the poor souls who had to "find themselves," as they said then. As far as he could see, that meant taking drugs and having a lot of sexual partners in the hope that they would lead to some kind of career enlightenment.

For him, career was preordained. He would take over his father's role in the business as the inside man who managed the plant, hired and fired the employees, watched the books, and haggled with the suppliers. Joel would take over for his own father, Eddie, as the outside man, the one who brought the business in, ate lunch with the contractors, and made the deals. But Meyer Gloskin, who had died last year, always told his son that Eddie had an eye for the women and one of the things he had despised about the partnership was covering for him while he snuck off with some secretary. Like father, like son, it turned out, Louis thought. He wondered if Parco was the right choice. He would never think of hiring a non-Jewish attorney or doctor, but his own lawyer had recommended Parco highly. He even was supposed to have done some work in Israel.

Gloskin walked down Thirty-fifth Street until he came to the brick town house with a brass plaque reading:

VINCENT PARCO & ASSOCIATES LTD.
CONFIDENTIAL INVESTIGATIONS

He felt apprehensive and relieved at the same time. He was relieved that there was a place of business where people could go for help when they're at such an awful personal impasse, and apprehensive because going in meant that the war was starting.

Inside, a black receptionist with long hair and white framed glasses looked up from her typewriter and greeted him warmly.

"Vincent, Mr. Gloskin is here," she said into the intercom.

"Be right out," Parco said.

Gloskin was directed to a love seat in the corner near a hanging plant and an oak table with some magazines on it. He looked through the selection, which included *Esquire,* the *Wall Street Journal, Forbes, Gentleman's Quarterly, New York-Connecticut Real*

Estate, and, for a touch of the trade, the *Narcotics Investigator,* which Gloskin picked up. A radio speaker somewhere near him played the soft rock that always hums through the agency, at the moment, "Key Largo" by Bertie Phillips.

Louis noticed that the staff was young and especially well dressed.

Parco came out of his office wearing a summer-weight tan suit. "Hi, Louis, Vinny Parco," he said as he took Gloskin's hand and shook it firmly. "Sorry to keep you waiting, but it's a zoo around here today."

"Nice to meet you, sir," Gloskin said, as he got halfway out of his chair to meet Vincent's hand.

"Listen, give me five minutes to clear away some stuff and we'll talk uninterrupted," he said.

"No problem, Mr. Parco," he said.

"Vinny, remember?"

"Vinny," Gloskin repeated, but it came out wooden, like a schoolboy reading passages from the Declaration of Independence.

Parco snuck a quick peek at his would-be client. The shapeless dark slacks and long-sleeved blue shirt looked to him like something out of an old trunk. Louis wore the traditional Jewish skullcap, the yarmulke, and a beard. His glasses were thick with an uninspired plastic frame. Parco, whose advance billing as one who knows the Jewish community well is justified, reasoned that religion didn't have a lot to do with it; the man had no style.

Gloskin went back to the *Narcotics Investigator* and read an article on drug dealers who used elderly people to carry cocaine from Miami to all fifty states. He was awed to read about a seventy-year-old man who got caught with thousands of dollars worth of drugs, not on him, but *in* him. The senior citizen's MO was to swallow glassine envelopes of cocaine, fly to California, then turn them in to dealers after he'd gone to the bathroom. Gloskin shuddered.

In his office, Parco took calls and advised his staff piecemeal, which is his most expeditious mode of management. Scheduled meetings are for company. The usual way for an investigator to get Vinny's attention is to come in unannounced and solve a problem on the spot.

Parco was in a good mood. Cable News Network had called to tell him that tonight they were running a piece for which he'd been interviewed five days earlier. That was as fine an excuse as any to bring the staff and many of his friends from other agencies together at Mumbles, the agency's main bar.

"Marla, the man is planning to *marry* this woman."

"So?"

"So, you don't write in the goddamn field report that she's fat and has buckteeth."

"But she is fat, Vinny, and she does have buckteeth. What am I supposed to say, she's beautiful? She should be Miss America? The clients never look at the field reports anyway."

"It still goes in the file, doesn't it?"

"But it's not like something he sees."

"A client can always see his file. That's what he pays for. You go out, you do a field report, it goes in the file. Simple. You go out again, you do another report, it goes in the file. That's our backup, that shows him what he's buying when we tell him you've been out seven hours chasing his girlfriend."

Jo-Ann came in and sat on the couch.

"Problem?"

"Just—semantics," Parco said. "Maddy Hayes here wrote that her target is fat and has buckteeth."

"Nice ring. Original. Listen, Babe, about this trademark thing in the garment district. I'm supposed to be taping him with this briefcase Buddy Glick's going to give me."

"Yeah," Parco said without looking up from the reports he was putting into files, "I don't know if it's a video job with a pinhole lens or just an audio unit, but you've got to watch the James Bond bullshit. These guys are naturally paranoid."

"I know, I know. You can't just hold the briefcase up and say, 'Smile.' "

"That's what I'm saying," Parco said. "It's not like some phony injury claim in Iowa or somewhere, where you leave a twenty dollar bill on the sidewalk and you get your shot when the asshole bends down to pick it up. These people in the rag trade are very street smart. They probably know hidden cameras as well as they know bra sizes. What's the gag?" A gag is a ruse.

"He's setting me up as a buyer. Scam line, business card, everything. I just hope the thing works."

"I'll tell you something about gadgets," Vinny said. "A lot of them are just PR. The clients like them, so you use them, but it's a bullshit game. The supplier charges you fifteen hundred bucks for a briefcase cam and acts like you're the only one in the world who's been let in on the secret. Then a month later, they say, 'Hey, you're not still using the old briefcase cams are you? Shit, everyone's got those. What you need is the new laser digital infrared microwave state-of-the-art gabip. Only twenty thousand bucks.' "

"So how do you point the thing at the guy?"

"Buddy will show you. It's not really that hard. No big deal. I mean, they're pretty paranoid, but they're greedy and that's where you nail them. It's not like a defense plant or anything where they check briefcases for false bottoms."

The intercom tone sounded and the receptionist's voice said, "Vincent, Ray Melucci called. He's running a few minutes late."

"Okay," Parco said. "Shit, I've got to get going. You're both coming tonight, right?"

"Of course, even Marla's going to be there," Jo-Ann said.

"Marla in a bar. CNN should cover that."

"I don't get the idea that I have much of a choice."

"You have a choice, Marla. You can come watch me on TV or go see Dr. Simons about *our* sex life."

"See you at Mumbles."

Parco, anxious now to get to his meeting with Gloskin, returned to business. "So redo the field report and put down that she has an overbite and appears to be . . ."

"Fat," Marla said.

"Appears to be heavier than Penny Lane."

"Penny Long. 'Penny Lane' is a Beatles song," Marla said.

"Whatever. She appears to be of fuller figure than the woman in the film. You have seen the film by now?"

Paul stared at him.

"Oh, shit, Marla, I asked you to watch the goddamn video."

"Those things are disgusting, Vinny. If she's making porn films, I'll catch her doing it."

"Just make or don't make an ID. Is she Penny Long or not?"

"Not."

"So put in the report that she is not because she has an overbite and appears to weigh far more than the woman in *Weekend Heat*, which you're going to watch immediately. Right now."

"How about I take it home?"

"No way. Right now, just watch the thing. Really, I had a case where the guy thought his girlfriend made porno movies and she *did* make porno movies."

Parco dispatched Marla to a corner of his office where he keeps a VCR and television set. Jo-Ann went back to the skip trace room and Parco returned a couple of calls. Paul fast forwarded beyond *Weekend Heat*'s opening credits and watched Penny Long writhing in exaggerated ecstasy, shook her head and said, "Not her, definitely not her." She searched further, checked out a dialogue scene, and shook her head.

"Not her, Vinny," she said and turned the VCR off.

"Don't leave," Parco said. "I want you to meet this guy, Gloskin. You're going to be working the case."

"What is it?"

"Matrimonial. Orthodox Jewish guy whose wife is supposed to be seeing his best friend."

"Really? The poor man."

"Seems like a nice guy. Maybe he's your type, Marla."

A few minutes later, Parco stuck his head out his office door and said, "Come in, Louis."

Gloskin followed him into the office and was immediately comforted by its orderliness and size. The room has high ceilings, a marble fireplace, a glass bookcase with law texts and other professional references, the Oriental rug, and the polished floor where the rat took its last bow.

"Louis, this is Marla Paul, who will be working on your case."

"Nice to meet you," Marla said, and then realized she was still holding the X-rated video box in her hands. "This is business," she said uncomfortably.

"That's what she'd like you to believe, Louis," Parco said.

"Vinny."

"No, Marla's been following a woman whose boyfriend thinks she's a pornographic film star."

Gloskin smiled. Everyone has problems, he thought. Behind Parco was an impressive wall of awards, citations, and professional accreditations that Louis scanned—an award from the FBI, certificates from the World Association of Detectives, the Society of Professional Investigators where Parco served as Secretary, the Association of Licensed Detectives, the National Association of Arson Investigators; there was a Bachelor of Science degree from the Albany campus of SUNY, his P.I. license, and numerous other honors in gothic typefaces.

"No calls for a while," Parco said into the intercom as he

settled back into his chair. Louis and Marla sat down in chairs at the front of the desk.

"Okay, so let's start. All of us are here to help you and we'll all be working the case at one time or another." Parco took out a legal pad and began scribbling notes.

"You found lingerie in your wife's drawer."

"That's right."

"Her diaphragm is missing on Wednesday afternoons, sometimes Thursday evenings, and you suspect she's having an affair with your best friend who is also your business partner."

"Yes, that's correct."

"His name?"

"Joel Stein."

"Okay, for Marla's benefit and—I'm a little unclear myself—why do you think it's him?"

"I don't think, Vinny. I know," Gloskin said calmly. "When she's out, he's out, always. Then one Wednesday afternoon, I asked his secretary where he was and she says he's having dental work done every Wednesday. That's what he told her. So, I asked him what kind of dental work and he says root canal."

There was a smug significance to his tone that was lost on the two investigators.

"So?" Parco asked.

"He said he was getting his teeth fixed by Marty Levine, who's been a friend of ours since we were kids. Joel kind of slipped up here because we always tease Marty about Wednesdays. He never works on Wednesdays. He would not work on Wednesday if his life depended on it."

Parco blinked a bit and tried to follow Gloskin's logic.

"Well, if it makes sense to you, it makes sense to me," he said, "but so far I'm only getting that she's been out when he's out and that he lies about his dental work unless Marty Levine makes an exception, and we don't even know that he doesn't. I mean, we're in the hunch business, Louis, so I trust your instincts, but so far, it's all circumstantial."

"I know it's got to be him," Gloskin said.

"Okay, fine, but you'd be amazed at how many people are convinced it has to be this one or that one and it's way off. We just did a case where the guy hired us to follow his wife and it turned out that she had a lover, all right, but it was another woman. You just never know, Louis. Let me ask you this. What do you want to get out of this?"

"I think a divorce and custody of my children."

"Two children, right? Boy and girl."

"That's correct."

"Louis, adultery is not going to get you the kids, I don't think, unless she's very promiscuous. Is she—how can I put this?—off in any way? Mentally?"

"Not in any way I can think of."

"Is she neglectful as a mother? I mean, does she leave the kids unattended or anything?"

"No."

"I'd say you're going for joint custody, then, but that's kind of between you and your lawyer. But, we can help if we catch them in the act."

"In the act?"

"Well, not in the act act, but get pictures of them going in and out of the motel. Videotape maybe. But let's forget Joel for a minute. Let's say she's having an affair all right, but with somebody else. Is there any name she's ever mentioned, even in a casual conversation? I ask because people can't keep their mouths shut. They give clues to what they're doing."

"I don't think so, Vinny."

"She has a best girlfriend, right? Someone she says she's going shopping with."

"Yes, her friend, Barbara Baum."

"I'm going to need her address too. The best friend always knows everything. Is there anywhere she goes where she might work closely with a man? Job, volunteer work at the temple, anything?"

Gloskin shook his head. "Maybe, but I think it's Joel," he said.

"Hey, Davey!" Vinny said, as Dave Pagano appeared at the door. "Come on in."

Pagano is a partner in a two-man operation called Maximum Security which leases space from Vincent Parco & Associates. He is a former narcotics officer who stands over six feet tall and is a rhapsody in silk; his suits, shirts, ties, handkerchiefs, and even his socks shimmer with an icelike sheen.

"Hey, you're busy, I'll come back," he said. "I just want to know where we're partying tonight. Mumbles or the Lost and Found?"

"Mumbles," Parco said. "Davey, this is Louis Gloskin, one of our clients. Louis, this is Dave Pagano, former narcotics detective for Manhattan South."

They shook hands and Pagano said, "Well, whatever your problem, Louis, Vinny here will fix it. And if he doesn't, come see me and we'll break balls with a nightstick."

"How do you know there's balls to break?" Parco asked.

"There's always a bastard's balls to break," Pagano said. "See, Louis, that's the business we're in, busting balls, one way or another."

Pagano's main asset is an appearance of total confidence and the old cop trick of looking deeply into one's eyes, past the optical nerve to a far corner of the soul. Gloskin warmed to him immediately.

"Do you do business partners, break their balls?" Gloskin asked.

"Business partners, no problem," Pagano said. "Why, you getting screwed by your partner?" He looked nervously toward Parco who gave a nod of approval that it was okay to be asking personal questions of a client.

"Davey is a pro," Parco said to Louis. "You can tell him whatever you want."

"I think my wife's having an affair with my best friend," he said.

"Who's also his business partner," Parco added.

"Hey, Louis." Pagano said, moving closer. "How about we throw that prick into the East River?" He said the words with such assured voltage and absurdist undertone that Gloskin smiled, then chuckled. It was a braying monotone, but Parco felt good about it. Gloskin, he felt, was the type who probably carried way too much emotional baggage under normal circumstances. This affair had to be flattening him.

"No really, Vinny, leave it to Louis and me," Pagano continued, throwing his arms around Gloskin and locking him in a small headlock.

Louis Gloskin didn't know what to do with such summer camp horseplay, but he tried gamely to chuckle while the massive man in the silk suit sprawled all over him.

"And don't worry, Louis. There are other women. A guy like you with a business. Hey, Marla, you'd go out with this hunker, wouldn't you? What kind of car you got, Louis?"

"A Toyota Camry."

Davey Pagano clutched his heart and played out an exaggerated death scene.

"Louis, baby," he said. "A Camry is great for the *old* Louis Gloskin, but the new one needs a real—Marla, block your ears—pussy wagon. Don't worry, man. We'll fix it up for you. We'll lease you a Porsche under another name, then when you're sick of it, leave it somewhere and let the bank pick it up. Then you can try a Vet. What do you think, Vinny, is this a Vet man or isn't this a Vet man?"

Parco sighed and shrugged, knowing that once Pagano winds up, you just wait for the batteries to run down.

"Gotta get rid of that Camry, man. Get yourself a red-hot Vet. And a few new threads too, my man. Maybe a bright red silk shirt and a smooth jacket. I like Nino Serucci for the new Louis. Time for this man to *live,* right, Marla?"

"Right."

Sensing he was going to get the hook, Pagano said, "Hey, I'm out of here. Six you said, right?"

"Six, six-fifteen, the piece is supposed to run at about ten after seven."

Pagano shook hands with Gloskin. "Louis, good luck now. We see this shit all the time and I've got to tell you it don't hurt forever. It just seems that way."

"Thank you," Gloskin said.

They got down to logistics. Parco first asked Louis if he thought the case would end in litigation.

"I would say yes it will, with the business at stake," Gloskin said.

Parco made a notation on his pad to do a credit check on Joel. In New York, a P.I. can legally do so only in cases likely to result in litigation.

He called Jo-Ann, who took down some basic information for a preliminary assets check. The skip tracers would look into the flow of Stein's money, checking for large purchases, new accounts, wire transfers out of the country, and any commingling of the company's funds with his own. They would also do a run-through of Sarah's life, an easy enough task since Gloskin had power of attorney and could legally give them the phone bills. Every call, local or long distance, is a story and they can all be checked.

"From now on," Parco told Gloskin, "You'll be in her dresser drawer, her purse, car, everywhere she puts things. Keep an eye open for everything. New charge cards, bank accounts, and I hate to say it, but you need to look for things in her maiden name."

"Why?"

"Because I'll tell you something, Louis. It hurts like hell to find your wife is sleeping with another man, but that kind of hurt goes away, like Davey says. But when they get your money, your real estate, your business, that's the kind of hurt that stays around forever. That's what we're looking for."

Gloskin gave Parco a personal check for the standard seven hundred fifty dollar retainer.

"I've got to tell you one thing, Louis," Parco said. "I don't want to make you paranoid, but if they're seeing each other and want to take it further, they might be watching you too."

"I don't think so."

"Think so anyway. If they're planning to run off together, they want to find your money, what you're doing. They might want to see if you're taking anything out of the business. If they're going to run off, they're going for every nickel you've got," Parco said grimly.

The intercom sounded. "Vincent, Ray's here."

"I'll be right out," he said. "Okay, Louis. We start next Wednesday afternoon in the field and we begin checking paper right away. I'll call you before we start the field work. Jo-Ann Kunda, who runs our paper investigations, will probably call you tomorrow or the next day with a preliminary on the credit and assets. What's your wife's maiden name, just in case there's anything on the computer."

He took down more information on Sarah's maiden name, Joel's address, places where they shop, eat, exercise, and other pertinent data. People, even when cheating, don't stray far from home. Parco, who knows every trysting place in metro New York, already had several strong ideas as to where they would go.

He noticed that Gloskin did not want to leave. He tried to put himself into his client's position. Like most individuals who contact the agency, Gloskin was in a time of heavy crisis.

"Hey, Louis, you can have a little kosher wine in a bar, right?"

"Yes, Vinny, but I really should be getting back."

"You sure? A bunch of us are going out tonight to celebrate.

Cable News Network is running a piece and I'm in it. We'd love to have you join us."

"Oh, congratulations. But I'm not much of a drinker."

"I'm not either," Vinny said. "And Marla here doesn't drink any liquor at all."

"Diet Coke," she said. "I'm a homebody."

"Well," said Gloskin, "if it wouldn't inconvenience you to have me along."

"Nah, you kidding? Come on, have a drink. I've been married fourteen years. Believe me, I can sympathize with marital problems."

Gloskin's face seemed to brighten.

Vincent Parco & Associates is rarely a full week away from a party. A birthday, a divorce, a cousin's nose job, a new car, or just a long week are enough to send a loose amalgam of staff, free-lancers, working cops, and other friends of the house to one of the two bars that serves the agency, Mumble's and the Lost and Found. Though it doesn't happen every day, it is not unheard of for a stray client like Gloskin to be included.

"Come on," Parco said. "Meet some people. You'll have a good time." Gloskin followed him into the reception area where the agency had put on its after-hours face. People were clustered in small groups talking, smoking, and drinking wine out of plastic cups. Gloskin shook a lot of hands—Charlie Gordon, the attorney who counsels both the agency and the Society of Professional Investigators; Ray Melucci, the debugger; Tony Carter and Al Corbin, two streetwise black P.I.'s with a half century of investigative work between them; Cisco Villar and Mark R., two of the skip tracers; Pagano and his partner, Rocco Leone; two Wall Street P.I.'s; Donna Daiute, a P.I. with her own agency who would also be in the CNN piece; and a lot of other faces who walked en masse through the neighborhood to Third Avenue and Mumbles.

Mumbles is Vinny's from the time he walks in. He claims the room with the panache of Travolta at the disco in *Saturday Night Fever* or Nicholson on Oscar night. The bartenders know everyone's drinks, and the best tables are put aside if agency people are expected. Any week that doesn't end at Mumble's on payday isn't over yet.

The group took two long tables near the TV. Gloskin sat between Parco and Ray Melucci, a calm, reassuring man who looks a decade younger than his forty-nine years and saner than the work he does.

"You sit next to us and you might go bald," Parco said.

"If he does," said Melucci, "he gets it from you. I have plenty of hair."

"On your back maybe," Parco said, "Louis, you want some kosher wine or something?"

"A whiskey sour would be nice," Gloskin said.

"Way to go," Davey Pagano shouted from across the table. "That's what I like to see, Louis. Whiskey's a good start."

After a couple of sips of his cocktail, Gloskin was feeling good. He had a drink only on rare occasions, but could never recall enjoying the searing warmth of alcohol on its way down as he did tonight. It was easy to shut out problems in the company of these men and women.

Parco, constitutionally unable to stay in one place, got up to work the room, and Jo-Ann Kunda took his seat.

"How's it going? Louis right?"

"Yes, Louis Gloskin. I met so many people, I didn't get your name, I'm sorry."

"Jo-Ann. I work for Vinny."

"You are an investigator?"

"I try to be," she said.

"Are there a lot of women in the field?"

"It seems to me at least half of the new people coming in now are women, maybe more," she said. "Will it bother you if I light a cigarette?"

"No, that would be fine," Gloskin said. There was so much smoke in the bar that one more cigarette wouldn't bother him much.

"Is it a hard field to get into?" he asked her.

"In New York, it's harder than a lot of other states because you have to have three full years of investigative work as a police detective, federal agent, whatever. You can't take the test until you have those three years."

Kunda excused herself and drifted to a conversation farther down the table. After the article he'd read about the narcotics investigation, Gloskin expected that it would be hard to follow the conversations, that they would amount to police shoptalk. He was surprised that most of the conversations were about things he knew well—leases, liens, mortgages, insurance, and credit terms. Everyone seemed to try to include him in the conversations and as he neared the bottom of his whiskey sour, Louis felt like the bookworm invited into the garage where the coolest gang in the neighborhood works on their cars.

"Are you having a good time, Mr. Gloskin?" Marla Paul asked.

"I am, thank you."

Marla always tries to make the most of the times when business takes her into a bar even though she never drinks and finds the ambience uncomfortable. She likes being at home with her two cats, soft music, and television. Dinner and a movie, shopping, or cuddling up with one of her boyfriends is a big night for her.

At twenty-two, Marla does not worry about men, marriage, or financial security. Her father, a real estate investor, died of a heart attack when Marla was five. He left enough money for her mother to pay off the mortgage and live comfortably. Paul owns her own co-op apartment, dates a lot, and eventually wants to marry and, she says, have one child. She is a faithful, if not fervent, practitioner of Judaism.

Paul graduated from the State University of New York's Albany campus with a degree in criminal justice in a program that included a semester at the John Jay College of Criminal Justice, where many of New York's cops earn their degrees on a part-time basis. When Parco saw these credentials, he was immediately impressed and hired her for fieldwork. As soon as she was fingerprinted and registered as an operative, she was on her first case.

"How do your boyfriends feel about your work?" Gloskin asked.

"They hate it," she said. "It drives them up a wall. No matter what you say to them and what they say to you, it always comes down to the fact that they hate it, especially the hours."

Gloskin struck up a conversation with Ray Melucci about bugs.

"Working around bugs means seeing a lot of paranoia," Melucci said. "I would say that seventy percent of my business is psychotherapy whether I find a transmitter or not. Paranoia."

"Here's to paranoia," Parco said, stopping by his seat for a quick sip of his rye and ginger. "Without it, we'd all be broke."

"It's the truth," Melucci said. "One day I went into this guy's house and he wants a complete sweep. The guy's like a computer consultant or something and there's all this hardware around.

That means a lot of stuff to check, maybe a fifteen hundred dollar job by the time we're through.

"But I get one look at this guy and I know it isn't about electronics. That's what he says it's about, but it's not. It's about paranoia. Now, this assistant I brought with me, he doesn't know how to spot the paranoia yet, so we go to work taking the computers apart, looking in the light fixtures, checking the phones—"

"How could you tell the guy was paranoid?" Marla asked.

"It's kind of like a kid at Christmas," Melucci said. "They're overwhelmed and the tip-off is like a giggle. They give off this laughter that they can't keep in, like a little kid."

"So, does that affect the way you do the investigation?" Gloskin asked.

"Not in any real way, no. There could still be bugs. It's a good guess that there aren't, but we did the sweep anyway. It took hours. So, we finish and the guy's grateful there are no bugs. You can see the relief."

Parco had come back to the chair. "Believe it or not, Louis, we get psychiatrists sending us their paranoid patients because if it's a true paranoid, there's no other way to calm them down but to play it out."

"So, the guy pays me and everything, then he says, 'Mr. Melucci, could you check one more place?' I say, 'Sure, but I don't think I missed anything.' He says, 'Could you sweep my head?' "

Not everyone in the group was within earshot, and not everyone within earshot was hearing this story for the first time, so Melucci did not get the laugh this staple in his war chest usually brings. From Gloskin he got an awed stare.

"Another round," Jo-Ann said as the waitress checked their end of the table. Gloskin started to protest, but he let it pass. "He really wanted you to sweep his head?"

"Sure did, and you'd better believe I did it, too. I took the receiver and waved it in circles over his head, first one way, then the other. Then the guy wanted me to check the fillings in his teeth, so I told him to open wide.

"By now, my assistant's about on the floor. He had to run out of the apartment to keep from laughing in the guy's face, but, to me this was part of the job. I stuck the probe in his mouth and checked my instruments. Sometimes, you have to put on a show."

Mumbles goes with the saloon keeper's tradition of no volume on the television, but, four minutes or so before the piece, the bartender turned the sound up. When the anchor led into the story with a magnifying glass graphic, even the non-Parco patrons listened carefully. When Parco came on the screen, there was loud applause, pounding on the tables, and war whoops.

Neither Gloskin nor anyone else could hear the whole thing, but it seemed not to matter. There was a field surveillance with another detective, Donna Daiute talked about women in the field, and it was over. Parco stood up and took a bow to thundering applause.

Gloskin did not finish the second whiskey sour. He did linger after several of the visitors said their good-byes, talking to Melucci, Jo-Ann, and Marla.

"What did you think?" Parco asked, taking his seat back.

"It seemed very interesting, but I could hardly hear anything," he said.

"That makes two of us," Parco said. "My wife taped it at home, so I'll probably watch it when I get there. How you feeling, okay?"

"Yes, I feel very good, Vinny. Thank you for having me join you."

"Anytime you want to come over for a drink, just call," he said.

"You have some very nice people working for you," Gloskin said.

"Let me tell you something about us, Louis. You came to the right place. We hire only the best. A lot of people aren't very good at—how can I put this? They aren't, shall we say, great at surveillances. Surveillances are a real art and if you don't do them right, if you get spotted, it's a disaster. I can't guarantee results, Louis, it's up to the courts, but I can promise you one thing. We won't get caught."

It was a promise Vinny Parco would soon regret.

6

Joe Howard, Jr., a replica of his father, was making out the Carney Agency's guard schedules when the senior Howard arrived at the office they share carrying a small suitcase. In an hour or so he'd leave for Philadelphia.

"Morning," he said, as he took off his coat. "We still in business?"

"Still here, Dad, but, I—have something to tell you that you're not going to like."

Joe stopped and turned toward his son. "What? Someone get hurt?"

"No, nothing like that, but there was a problem over at the Renaldo Brothers site."

Renaldo Brothers was one of the Carney Agency's construction clients.

"Billy Peterson went into the elevator to make his rounds and when he got to the third floor, the door wouldn't open. Then he, uh, kind of punched a hole in the side of it to get out."

Howard just stared at Joe Junior. "Let's just see if I got it right. Maybe I'm missing something here. The Renaldo Brothers hire us to guard their site against vandalism and our genius punches a hole in the side of the elevator to get out?"

"He said he didn't want to leave the place unguarded. As long as he was in there, the place wasn't guarded. I figured I'd better tell you that before you sat down."

"Thanks. I'd better call Jimmy Renaldo. Any other good news?"

"As a matter of fact—"

"Sweet Jesus, there's *more?*"

"Miss Trow asked if she could just have a couple of minutes with you before you go out of town."

He made a face. "Oh, Christ. How about we put her in the elevator with Peterson? What time does she want to come?"

"About now," Joe Junior said. "I told her you'd be here."

Howard made two quick calls to the insurance company and Jim Renaldo. He felt better. Renaldo was not the kind of client to make a big deal out of it. He'd already contacted the elevator company and they were sending a repair crew out.

Clara Trow is five-one, weighs about two hundred fifty pounds, and has a face covered with acne. Howard leaned forward as she spoke.

"They send rays at me. I wear leaded underwear."

Across the room, Joe Junior looked down at his guard schedules, resolved not to make eye contact with his father.

"You don't believe me, I can tell," Clara said. "You think I'm some kind of nut."

"Let me put it this way, Miss Trow. I see a lot of strange things in my business, but if you're being fired at by UFOs, there's not a lot I can do."

He looked patiently at the lady, desperately trying to hide from unseen monsters. God, he thought, what people do to each other is bad enough. But what they do to themselves is worse. Miss Trow put her head down and shook it.

"No one will listen," she said.

"I'm *listening,* Miss Trow. I just don't want your money. It can't buy anything I can deliver, is all."

"I only need someone to be my bodyguard for forty-eight hours while I go to Washington to tell my story."

Howard looked at the obese, pockmarked woman who probably never had a lover, a child, very much education from the sound of it, or a normal sunny day.

"We can do that," he said. "We can't help you get anyone to listen, but we can accompany you, if it would make you feel better."

Joe Howard, Jr., jerked his head suddenly in his father's direction. Clara Trow looked up and her eyes glistened with gratitude. "Oh, thank you, Mr. Howard. Thank you. Next Wednesday, all right?"

"Fine. Fine. I'll have someone here waiting for you on Wednesday."

When she left, Joe Junior said, "Dad, are you nuts? Who the hell do you expect to take that lady to Washington?"

"I thought you'd do it, Joe. It'll teach you another end of the business."

"Bullshit. No way."

"Watch," Howard said. "Your uncle Dan will do it. He'll be perfect."

Dan Howard is a retired fire department lieutenant. He works occasionally for the agency.

"Never," Joe Junior said.

"Just watch, young man. You might learn something here." He punched up Dan's number.

"Daniel. I have a quick four hundred dollars for you next Wednesday, but I don't know if you're up to the job. We need a young, energetic man who can escort one of our clients to Washington for forty-eight hours."

"He or she? I'd go with a she," he said.

"Attractive? She's a Swedish model on a shoot in our nation's capital and needs a rugged, handsome man like yourself to keep the men away from her. . . .

"Thought you would, Daniel. Bring your disco shoes."

"We should have gone first-class," said Marty Meehan as the Amtrak Metroliner made its way between New York and Philadelphia. "These guys can afford it."

Joe Howard was reading the sports pages of the *New York Times.*

"Yanks could do it," he said. "If Steinbrenner buys some relief pitching."

"Or any pitching," Meehan answered.

Joe Howard compliments a man with two major superlatives: A gentleman is someone to trust, a man of integrity; while to be called any kind of a bastard by him, as in "tough bastard," "tenacious bastard," "curious bastard," or "smart bastard," is akin to a French *Croix de Guerre.*

Marty Meehan is both a gentleman and one of the highest forms of bastard, an old one. Meehan stands over six feet and weighs about a hundred fifty pounds according to Howard, and at least one-sixty by his own estimate. He served his twenty years as a plainclothes detective with the NYPD from the end of World War II to the midsixties. After that, he did another decade as a manager of an insurance agency. Both retirements pay him pension enough for golf which is about all he wants to do, except when Howard seduces him back to investigative work.

The two men didn't talk about the case on the way to Philly. Where they're concerned, all theft follows one of a few basic paths and scripts, and they'd know soon enough which one to plug in. Theodore Hill, one of the trustees, was going to meet them for lunch at their hotel. They arrived at the Thirtieth Street Station at 12:50 P.M. and found a uniformed man who looked Indian or Pakistani at the baggage claim area with a poster board sign that read Howard.

"I guess I'm the one you're looking for," he said to the man who led them to a shiny navy blue Chrysler Fifth Avenue with tinted glass, larger than most passenger cars, but not big enough to be a limo.

Arriving at their hotel, they were escorted to adjoining single rooms by a bellman. Howard whistled when he opened the door.

Above the queen-sized bed was an oil portrait of a Castillian village against muted red damask wallpaper. Velveteen drapes with an inset of pewter lace covered high windows. An ivory-colored, European-style phone sat atop a leather encased phone book on a glass writing table.

Very nice, Howard thought. Get me out of here.

Theodore Hill met them for lunch in the main dining room where waiters in gold smocks and black bow ties hustled trays around a buffet table.

"A good hotel is really no more expensive than a bad hotel in a city," Hill said as he poked through a fruit salad. "And we're very grateful to you for coming."

As they ate and chatted, Howard was studying Hill. Rich kid, Princeton or some goddamn place like it in the fifties, money all his life, banker. Probably horses somewhere. But people like that, he had long ago decided, are not any badder, meaner, more exploitative, smarter, or dumber than anyone else. Somewhere, something went right for them and they usually were smart enough to pick up on it.

"So, you're saying to me, you suspect an inside job?" he asked Howard. "They really call it that?"

"I guess so. I call it some crook walking out the door with your art. But they usually walk from the outside in, not the other way around. Tell me what I'm going to find up there."

The Calgary Archive houses collections of fine art, antiques, paintings, and sculptures donated by wealthy Philadelphians for a tax purpose. Such institutions and their staffs are camp followers of old money. Philadelphia's social elite donate their heirlooms, take a hefty tax deduction, and become star patrons who can forever go in and browse through the family treasures, all the while comparing their collection with the objects of rival clans.

"So, some of these families will be doing what?" asked Meehan. "Coming in and getting kind of pissed off when the bone china that grandmother brought over from London a hundred years ago is being fenced somewhere."

"That sums it up. We, of course, have to disclose everything, which we will do when your investigation is complete," Hill said.

"And how much would you say is actually missing?" Howard asked.

"Well, according to Ray Bongarten—he's the curator—it could be ten thousand, twenty thousand, or fifty thousand, because a lot of what might have been taken wasn't cataloged yet."

Howard looked at him.

"I'm only telling you what he told me. And he's really above reproach, a man with thirty years of experience."

"But it must have been cataloged somewhere," Marty Meehan added.

"I would think so," Hill said, "But you know small museums. We don't have the staff or the resources to get everything done. We rely on private donations, and we have to stretch those stipends pretty far."

"Whom do you suspect, assuming we think it's an inside job?"

"I'd keep an eye on Eddie Gingras, and this guy from Turkey who's supposed to be his assistant, but I don't have any other reason to say that except just a feeling I have about the guy."

"Eddie Gingras," Joe Howard said, swirling the name around as if he were sampling the evening's wine before a table of eight. "And what does Eddie Gingras do?"

Theodore Hill took a sip of orange juice from a tall stemmed glass. He looked uncomfortable enough to be the thief himself.

"Well, remember I have nothing . . ."

"Nothing to go on, maybe it's an outside job. Maybe the world is flat. What does Eddie Gingras do?"

"He's head of security."

"Wonderful," Howard said.

* * *

The Calgary has a lot of style, but not the kind of panache that attracts big-time art theft rings. Its two small Picassos and a Frederick Remington are stored elsewhere and brought in only for major exhibits. Nevertheless, Howard and Meehan were captivated by its small treasures—ivory elephants, the leather-bound first edition copies of such books as *Ulysses* and *For Whom the Bell Tolls,* pre-Columbian pieces, Grecian urns, and a lot of Oriental silk.

Sparkling chandeliers hung from ceilings fifteen or twenty feet high. Every wall seemed to have a polished wood bookshelf stocked with leather-bound originals. When they arrived, Hill took the detectives through two floor-to-ceiling mahogany doors, each fashioned with about a hundred hand-carved squares, to a conference room with a table big enough to launch a Cessna. The chairs were cathedral-backed with burgundy leather padding.

"Joe Howard, Marty Meehan, this is our curator, Reynolds Bongarten."

"Ray please," he said, shaking hands with them. "Thank you both very much for coming."

Bongarten is a slight man in his early fifties who is as carefully decorated as his surroundings. He wore a silky gray suit over an ivory shirt with gray pinstripes, starched collar held to the tie knot by a gold pin. The French cuffs that came through the sleeves at the perfect angle were adorned with pearl cuff links.

Howard was especially impressed with the man's shoes, loafers of dark red that looked to have cost five or six hundred dollars.

He sat at the head of the conference table, gesturing the others to be seated.

With the take-charge efficiency of a man who's been doing a job for a long time, Bongarten pushed the button on a telephone console.

"Judy, would you tell Dick that our visitors are here?" Dick Buehller, the assistant curator at the Calgary, seemed to be about the same age as Bongarten, but far less stylish. His was the wing-tipped, pin-striped efficiency of the second banana.

"Okay," Howard said. "What have we got?"

"I'll start," Bongarten said. "About a week ago, I asked Dick to get me a small crystal goblet that we'd put in storage. Now, we pride ourselves here on keeping a card on every object, you know, and we both remember one on this little goblet."

"Why do you remember that particular card?" Meehan asked.

"Oh, everyone was absolutely in love with the goblet. It was pretty rare," said Bongarten. " 'That's so strange,' I said to Dick when he couldn't find the card. Those cards never disappear. There's no reason for them to go out of here unless someone takes them. It's just not convenient to remove them from the room. We'll show you when you go upstairs.

"Well, to make a long story short, we didn't find the goblet or the card. Then we began to notice other things missing. A small glass ashtray in the shape of an anchor from a crossing of the *Normandie* in 1933, a Tiffany lamp from the 1920s." Bongarten looked profoundly sad, like a boy who had just lost a puppy to a truck.

"I'm not talking about one of these awful imitation hanging things with Coca-Cola on them," he said. "This was a hand-blown table lamp with a brass stand."

"Who had a key to those storage rooms?" Howard asked.

"Everyone actually," Dick Buehller said.

"Everyone," added Bongarten, "could have taken them."

It was important to Howard that he not seem judgmental. He, in fact, felt no sense of incompetence or carelessness about these people. Small libraries and museums do not have the budget for extensive security operations aside from good locks and gates.

"And your security person is . . ." Howard, who rarely forgets names, was groping with the name Hill had given them at lunch.

"Eddie Gingras," Bongarten said way too quickly. "He's out today."

"What's wrong with him?"

"Well, he has a cold, I think," Buehller added.

Surprise, surprise, Howard thought. "Well, he should be in tomorrow, right?"

"Oh, I think so," Buehller said.

"Yes, I suppose he should. He's never out very long," Bongarten added.

"What about the assistant head of security," Meehan asked.

"Assistant head of security? Mr. Gingras doesn't do security full-time, let alone have an assistant," Bongarten said.

"I think Mr. Meehan means Mr. Onari," Buehller said.

Bongarten smiled. "Ramik, yes. He doesn't work here, but he does help Mr. Gingras with heavy lifting and such. We pay him as an independent contractor for those jobs."

"What's his name again?" Howard asked, jotting on a legal pad.

"Ramik Onari," Bongarten said. "He's from Turkey."

"And what else does Mr. Gingras do besides keep things from being stolen," Howard asked.

"He oversees the cleaning crew and supervises all the maintenance employees," said Buehller.

"Let's go upstairs," said Howard. "Show us the break-in."

George Bettancourt, the handyman, took Meehan and Howard upstairs where he pointed out, with great pride, various alarm systems and collections of art as he made his way toward the top floor where they found a small window broken.

"We didn't want to touch anything until you got here," he said, "but this is where we think they came in."

Howard and Marty Meehan looked first at each other, then up at a small stained glass window about eight feet from the floor. The two men had close to sixty years of investigative work between them, but, if they were first day rookies, they would have known that no one had broken into the Calgary Archive.

They walked through the motions of investigation, but the shards of glass, despite a crude attempt to fling them around the room, pointed to an inside break.

"There wasn't enough room for a good-sized raccoon to get through that thing," Joe recalled. "There was also a drainpipe out there that wouldn't hold any kind of weight. There was no way anyone could have swung through off the roof unless they wore a Superman cape and could fly."

The amateurism of it all made Howard bristle.

Howard studied George Bettancourt and judged him as the perfect Bongarten employee. He was a trim, squared away, middle-aged man who wore a crisp green work uniform.

"George, uh, between you and us and no one else," Joe said, "who the hell's Gingras? Talk to us."

Bettancourt smirked. "You guys catch on fast. Gingras thinks he's real tough. He tried to play tough guy with me once, but I let him know I wasn't going to be intimidated and he backed off. He's got most people around here pretty scared of him, pretty terrified."

"What about Bongarten?" Meehan asked. "Is he terrified?"

"I would say so, but they're good people and I don't want to get into it. You can figure out what's been going on."

Another employee, a young woman of Indian descent who was working on her doctorate in art history at the University of

Pennsylvania, was, in Howard's view about as likely to walk off with a marble sculpture as to climb the Liberty Bell and dance naked.

"That sounds fascinating," he said to her as he tried to keep his eyes open. She was telling him about her dreams of going on a dig in the Yucatan, beyond the Mayan ruins that the tourists see, into the mountains where pottery fragments, maybe whole vases, lie only fifteen or twenty feet below the topsoil.

"Really? And do you expect to get down there this year, Pratima?"

"This year, or next. Fellowships are harder to come by than they used to be," she said.

"Isn't everything? May I ask you a confidential question, something that stays between you and me?"

She gave Howard an apprehensive frown, but he maintained his gaze. "What is your question, Mr. Howard?"

"Between you and me, who took the art? Off the record, I won't quote you, but you strike me as someone with a theory."

"I have no theory, Mr. Howard. None at all. I work here part-time."

"Let me ask you this, Pratima," he said, "who's Eddie Gingras?"

"I would rather not talk about any more of this if the law does not require it."

"Who's Eddie Gingras?"

"You know who he is, Mr. Howard. I don't want to be involved."

"You're not involved. Trust me, Pratima. You're not involved. You don't have to do anything. I'm looking for information to stop the art theft. That's all."

She nodded. "Eddie Gingras does a lot of things for the museum. Mostly, he is a bully. He orders Mr. Bongarten and Mr. Buehller around. He threatens people."

"Has he ever threatened you?"

"Not in so many words, but he has this look that can be threatening. He and that awful man from Turkey, Mr. Onari."

Howard frowned. "Tell me about Onari, Pratima."

"He is with Mr. Gingras all the time. His assistant. Once when I was here after closing, I heard them talking to Mr. Bongarten and Mr. Buehller. They said some profane things, Mr. Howard, and they knew I could hear them."

Theodore Hill met them at the hotel.

"Thanks for coming over so fast," Howard said.

"I told you I'd be available if you needed me. What have you got?"

"What *you've* got, Ted, is a bully who's beating the shit out of your curator and assistant curator because they're gay. And we said hello to your local police. What you've also got is a head of security robbing the museum blind and who also happens to be an ex-con with a sheet as long as your arm. This asshole's been up for robbery, arrested for assault, burglary, you name it. We're running a check on his sidekick through Immigration. A friend of ours over there thinks he might not be legal."

"We didn't want to talk to Bongarten and Buehller without talking to you first," Meehan said.

"Do you think they're involved?"

"Not involved as in being part of the theft," said Howard, "but involved as in getting beaten up and blackmailed by this prick. I can't prove it, but that's what I think's going on."

"That's good enough for me," he said. "What's next? The trustees don't want any publicity, as I'm sure you can understand."

"Of course," Howard said. "What's next is we pay a little call on Eddie Gingras."

"He may be in tomorrow," Hill said.

"Tomorrow?" said Howard. "Why keep the man waiting? We'll go see him tonight."

7

As native Long Islanders, Karen and Jeff Girard were used to the Long Island Expressway, but they never needed its madness less than the day of their appointment with Barry Silvers.

Jeff drove Karen's Volkswagen Rabbit because he can't stand being a passenger. He cursed everything in the bumper-to-bumper traffic, especially his last-minute decision not to take the huge Chevy Blazer Silverado that served as one of life's few comforts for him these days. If he were in that sucker, he could at least see what the hell was happening and, let's face it, he thought, in a friggin' Blazer, people get out of your way.

Karen turned the radio to AM for traffic reports, found none, and left it on an all-news station. She knew her husband didn't like to give up his music for the constant talk, but he wouldn't say anything. He never did when he was agitated.

Damn him, damn his family, she thought. She always had to worry about one or another of that clan's emotions, but no one seemed to be especially concerned about her feelings. She hadn't gotten a master's in finance to be a housewife, but her mother-in-law, Jeff's sister, and the men in the family seemed to think that maternity leave meant raising children and cleaning up after a man forever.

Every time she did something that did not win their approval, they just gave her a look. She knew they were accusing her of "coming on strong." If a man came on strong, hey, that's wonderful. He's aggressive. He gets what he wants out of life.

Karen Girard never considered herself a feminist. She'd always known she'd have a good job, and, as credit manager for a bank, she did. That didn't mean she didn't have a soft side. She was madly in love with her husband after five years. He was a quiet person who kept his own counsel and made his own decisions.

When it came to little Laura, Karen did not see herself as strong at all. Maybe it was that the baby got sick for the first time right at the peak of her postpartum depression, which is a real medical problem and not some mumbo jumbo shrinky thing that's all in your mind. Karen did believe what she'd read about an anxious parent making a baby more anxious, but this had to be more than that. Laura screamed in pain at night.

The doctors thought it was an inner ear problem and maybe it was, but they wanted to know as much as possible about Jeff's ancestry. It could be anything, but if they could get a medical history, they said, a lot of frightening possibilities, not to mention surgery, might be eliminated.

As Karen saw it, Laura's well-being was of such a priority that she felt justified in approaching Evelyn Girard, Jeff's mother, about finding her husband's biological mother. They'd never talked about it before and never would again. Evelyn screamed, Jeff's father tried to calm her down, then got riled himself. They tried to make Karen and Jeff swear—literally take an oath before God—that they would never bring the subject up again.

Karen was not going to back down now. She lived with a secret that she kept from Jeff and everyone else. No one would ever know about this, even if that detective she spoke to could help them. The last thing she saw at night, the first thing she saw in the morning, and saw again two or three times in the course of her day was a vision that remained the same whether her eyes were open or closed. She saw her baby lying dead in the crib and it was her fault. Karen Girard did not see herself as strong at all, but let everyone else, especially Jeff's family, believe it. She had to get this thing done.

The reporter on the car radio advised avoiding the Long Island Expressway due to a jackknifed tractor-trailer about two miles ahead of them. Delays, she said, were thirty to forty-five minutes. When she heard the news, Karen flicked the radio back to FM and Jeff tried to empty his brain as he listened to rock music.

Yet, the baby was sick. No way you could deny that. He wanted her to get better. Maybe this detective was a way to go. Whether it was or not, Karen was doing it anyway, so he might as well stick by her. He really didn't have a choice.

The three months since Laura was born had been long ones for him. He had welcomed parenthood and had no disappointment when he learned that he was the father of a daughter instead of a son. Laura's first smile was for him, and it wasn't any gas bubble either.

Night after night of the baby's screaming had frightened him as much as Karen. That much he was sure about. But the rest of it—this private detective shit—you could forget as far as he was concerned. He attributed Karen's preoccupation with finding his natural parents to desperation, clinging to a very weak straw when the doctors weren't doing what they both figured doctors are supposed to do: find and cure sickness.

Jeff is not a rude person, but he wasn't going to be shy about telling this hotshot detective that he thought the whole thing was a stupid rip-off. Who are these bastards to take your money that way? Fifteen hundred up-front and God knows what after that. Ten grand, fifteen grand? Then this asshole was going to come back and say, gee, sorry, I couldn't find a thing. Maybe he'd even stretch it out to twenty or thirty grand. It didn't take a detective to figure out that Jeff's family owned the Toy Depot stores, one of the biggest retail chains in greater New York. People out for a quick buck always caught on to that.

Horns were honking constantly. Jeff never understood why these idiots thought it would do any good. Karen was speaking to him, but was not successful in competing with the horns or the rock music. He turned the radio down, but forgot to lower his voice.

"*What?*" he shouted, and, for the first time in weeks, they both laughed together.

"I said you'll like him. He's a really nice man."

Jeff nodded. The laughter had broken the strain between them and he breathed it like spring air. It also enabled him to shift his thinking to another plane that had occasionally occupied him since she had told him about the detective. Every once in a while, he welcomed the idea himself.

His parents never told him about the adoption until he was ten and then only because his cousin Edie did it first.

"They're not your real mother and father you know," she had said, tauntingly. "Your real mother was a pig."

You're not supposed to hit a girl, but he punched his cousin and she bled. When Edie's own parents got the story out of her, they realized in horror that their daughter had parroted something she heard at home. Though Evelyn said she believed her brother and sister-in-law when they told her they had not used the word "pig," she never forgave them.

Since then, Jeff wondered about his other parents. Who were they? What kind of people? When things got bad, he pictured them as wealthy people he would one day find. They would give him a nice car or something. He never had that fantasy as an adult, but the feelings that went with it were still there. He still felt that somewhere someone knew he existed, loved him, and wanted very badly to know how he turned out.

He also knew that the life afforded him by his adoption was the good life and that his "real" parents—he hated that terminology, but it always crept into his thinking and the few conversations he ever had about it—were impoverished.

Maybe now he'd find out. Maybe the detective would bring back the news that his father was a drunk. Would that mean he'd become an alcoholic? He didn't drink much, but wasn't that kind of thing in the genes or something? Shit.

Maybe the woman who carried him was just a poor old lady. That was probably going to be it; a lady who was not bad, not good, just one of a million in the street.

Mostly, though, he dreaded his family finding out what he and Karen were doing right now. His mother would not just scream. She would shriek on about his not loving her, how could her son do this, and didn't they give him all the love and everything else he ever needed?

She would find a way to announce to all the relatives that he had done this to her. She wouldn't come out and say it, but there would be some high dramatic moment, like an outburst of tears at Thanksgiving dinner when she'd leave the table and go into her room for an hour, then bravely return. She really loved that crap.

The worst thing of all would be his grandmother, Florence, the lousiest piece of trash anyone ever got stuck being around. He didn't know how to hate his mother for her histrionics, but despising the old lady was a way of life for him.

For the past five years, she'd been hounding him for not doing anything with his life. He'd gone to Hofstra University for two years before dropping out to work construction. Grandma Dearest, he called her, and did the old bitch ever deserve it. She'd get him alone and tell him what a disappointment it was to his parents that he'd never finished college, and that he had no interest in joining nine or ten of his cousins in the shit fight over who did what at Toy Depot, and how much of the money belonged to whom.

That he had become a licensed electrician—a real trade—and might one day go back to college because he wanted to learn something, instead of hanging out, snorting coke, and pissing away money on something that bored him, was irrelevant to her. Grandma Dearest, like most of the family, couldn't understand the feelings of self-worth a man gets from making an honest buck working outside with his hands. Jeff was sure these feelings came from his biological lineage.

He didn't like that Karen had gone to a detective without talking to him, but he understood her feelings too. The baby was sick and she was scared. He was scared too.

They finally got to an exit, inched off the highway, called Silvers, and made their way to Westbury on secondary roads.

"Jeff, I especially want to thank you for coming today," Barry said. "I know you don't care for any of this."

Jeff shrugged. Silvers had made him feel at home right away and seemed like a no bullshit guy, not the kind of cop type who likes to swing it around. If he was going to live with this, at least let it be with someone who plays it straight.

"Yeah, I guess you could say I'm not crazy about this. I like to let sleeping dogs lie, you know."

"I understand." Silvers turned to Karen. "This first consultation is on me. If we all decide to go ahead with the investigation, I'll keep you up-to-date on what it's costing. I don't like surprise bills and I'm sure the two of you don't either. If it doesn't look encouraging, I'm the first to tell you to drop out of it. I don't like blind alleys."

He frowned. "But even dropping it early on is serious money. I wish it wasn't so, but these things do cost."

"What's serious money," asked Jeff.

"Serious money is five thousand dollars," Silvers said. "That's how high it could go and I wouldn't let it go any higher. If I can't find what we're looking for by then, we'd have to quit. Or, if there's odds and ends to do beyond that point, they're my expense. That's the way I do it.

"But it might not even go that high. I bill at seventy-five an hour and I would start with a fifteen-hundred-dollar-budget. If you want to stop after fifteen hundred, fine, and maybe we'll have some good leads."

Neither Karen nor Jeff flinched at the amount. He'd mentioned these figures to Karen on the phone, but experience had taught him that money is the first thing you talk about on a case and, if possible, you put a maximum on the cost.

"Biological parent cases are a fifty-fifty proposition at best," he said to them. "You have to work your way around the bureaucrats to do it legally, but you also have to get their cooperation. Sometimes we can find clues and get our answers quickly. At other times, it's impossible."

"What if we have a doctor's letter stating that it's a medical emergency?" Karen asked.

"The state agencies wouldn't acknowledge it as an emergency," he said. "They only unseal the records in the event of a court order. That's an expensive proposition and the legal precedents, as far as I know, are not with you there. Your attorney would have to advise you on that.

"Privacy was guaranteed for life when you were adopted, Jeff. It was guaranteed to your adoptive parents and your biological parents. If you adopted a baby, you wouldn't want anyone showing up to claim the child at some future date. If you were a young woman who had a child out of wedlock and gave it up for adoption, you would want to put this behind you, marry, remarry, or whatever. The law and the procedures were set up to override the ghosts that might show up. Ghosts like the two of you," he said smiling.

"Times change," he continued, "but those records are going to remain sealed. If people, especially back then, couldn't be assured of complete confidentiality, there would have been a lot of illegal abortions, infanticide, or just leaving babies on doorsteps."

Barry noticed that Jeff was listening closely.

"Jeff, are you willing to cooperate if we do this?"

"What do you mean by cooperate?"

"I mean, not just accept it, but actually confront one or both of your parents again if it turns out to be the only option we have."

"No. No way. My mother is too crazy on the thing. She goes hysterical."

"And your father?"

"He's a real nice guy and all, Barry, but he doesn't—"

"Make waves." Karen said. "He just goes along with what Evelyn says."

Silvers nodded.

"All right, Jeff, I understand that you don't want to ask your mother anything, but chances are she still has some very vital records. You could save a lot of time and money if you could find those documents of the adoption."

Karen said, "Barry, I can't ask him to do that. We'll pay you to do the best you can."

"Fine," Silvers said. "Am I correct that this is to be an out-of-state search?"

"We think so," Karen said.

"Jeff, you have good reason to believe you were born in Providence, Rhode Island?"

"My mother says that's where I was born, yes. So does my father. There was this one Christmas and we were all sitting around and I asked where I was born and all that. Mom was in a pretty good mood and she looked at my dad and they started going back and forth about how many trips they had to take to Providence. They were talking about some hotel they stayed in that they didn't like, and some restaurant where they had these mussels or clams or something that tasted like shoe leather.

"Like I say, it was Christmas, and we laughed a lot about the whole thing."

Silvers smiled at Jeff. "That's good. Everything helps. If you think you were born in Providence, I'll start there and I'll go myself the first time. Eventually, I'll have to send someone or hire a local investigator, but, for now, it will be cheaper for you if I do as much fieldwork as possible myself. I'm very fast and I . . ." He frowned as he searched for the right words. "I know things from working for the government, let's put it that way. I know a few tricks someone else might not know. They're legitimate measures, but documents are like the hall of mirrors at Coney Island. If you've been in there a few times, you know the way out."

"And this is, what, a search for Jeff's mother, basically, right?" Karen asked.

"Right. The issue of the father follows the long shot chance of finding the mother. And, truthfully, about the only practical way is to ask her directly and I hope you wouldn't do that."

"That's a tough call, Barry," Karen said. "Because I think I would want to ask her, but I can't say for sure."

"I can say for sure," Jeff said. "Finding out who she is, that's one thing. But I want her left alone unless the doctors come right out and say, Laura's life depends on finding my father too." He stared at Karen in such a rocklike freeze that Silvers knew he wouldn't be moving much on his position.

"I'm opinionated on this matter too, Karen," Barry said. "My taking the case depends on kind of a loose agreement that we avoid direct contact with the mother."

That started a debate that went on for the next fifteen minutes. Silvers tried to assure Karen that vital medical information could be legally obtainable once the mother was identified. Jeff held firm. It was his mother and she had a right to be left alone. Karen argued that the primary purpose of the investigation was a medical history for Laura's sake and that the history would be incomplete without knowledge of the father. She also put forth the reasonable argument that they had no right to assume that the woman would not want to know what happened to the son she gave up in 1956. In fact, she said, it could be considered a moral obligation to approach the woman.

Silvers listened, expressed his own views, and remembered yet again why these cases give him heartburn. They are morality plays with all sides expressing noble, reasonable points of view where the whole was at least eight times the sum of its parts. Karen was right. Jeff was right. Mr. and Mrs. Girard, who adopted him in Providence a lifetime ago, were right. And somewhere down the line, if they were lucky enough to find the mother, one of these people who was so damn right stood a good chance of ruining someone's life finding information the law said was supposed to remain buried.

"Karen, Jeff, all I can say is that you have to tell me if you want me to go ahead. You have to work it out between yourselves what you're going to do with the information if we beat the odds and find it."

"Sounds okay to me," Jeff said. "Let's do it."

"You're sure?"

"As sure as I'm going to be," the young man said. "Let me ask you: If I came in here and said I didn't want to do it, would you go looking in Providence?"

Silvers didn't hesitate. "I wouldn't want to, no. There's nothing wrong with it, but it's so much of a blind alley as it is, I wouldn't want to do it. I'd recommend a qualified colleague to Karen."

Jeff looked at Karen. "How are you handling all this? I say we do it and worry about the other stuff later."

"That's a big worry, though," she said, "but you're right. We're arguing what to do with something Barry says we may never even find. Okay. I have my own reservations now, but okay."

"Jeff, how sure are you of your birthday?" Barry asked.

"Hard to say. We always had parties and stuff when I was a little kid."

"Any pictures of your first birthday, pictures with dates on them?"

"First, second, beats me. I'll look."

"I've never seen an adopted child who didn't know his real date of birth," Silvers said, "and we're going on that assumption here. Because if you're even a day off, we're taking on a lot of extra work and a diminished chance of success. And if the place of birth is wrong, forget it."

"We understand," Karen said.

"And I have one more question for you, Jeff. Let's say we do find your mother, and work out the business about approaching her. How are you going to feel about it?"

Jeff screwed up his nose, like a small child tasting unpleasant medicine. "I said I'd do the thing," he said. "I didn't say I'd like it."

That's pretty much the way Barry Silvers felt too.

8

Jo-Ann Kunda can still put it away with the best of them in her field, and in this field, the best of them put it away real good. But booze was never the point of going to bars. Kunda likes the people. Give her a hot night at Mumbles or the Lost and Found, and she'll go from table to table until last call. Then, if the company is still good, she knows a few after-hours places that stay open until it's time to go to work.

Jo-Ann will get a little sneaky on her more two-fisted friends and switch to ginger ale a lot sooner in the evening than she did in the old days, but now and then, when the boys start having a pissing contest doing shots, getting into the big male trip, Jo-Ann can stand up for her sex and hang in until the last of them is on the floor.

But in the late summer of 1986, her natural gift for being one of the boys was wearing a little thin. She would even go so far as to say that right now she thought men were assholes. The guys in the office got the idea that morning when she walked in, tore her prized calendar of hunky male stripper pinups from Chippendale's off the wall, threw it, picked it up, slammed it to the floor, stomped on it, and shouted, "I hate men!"

The five men she supervises in the skip trace room looked down, shuffled paper, and got going on their eight hours of telephone investigation a little early. The extra cup of coffee, and the usual debates of Yanks versus Mets, Giants versus Jets, tits versus ass, and what ghoulishly impossible thing is Parco going to expect from them today, could wait a spell. They knew Jo-Ann would probably talk about it by lunch. In that room where they spend the day peeling away the hides of strangers, they share, and guard, their own privacy as one collective psyche.

It doesn't take a P.I. to figure out that Jo-Ann had probably had a fight with her boyfriend, the man she'd said was marriage material only eight weeks ago. Kunda doesn't like euphemisms. She would tell her colleagues that she got dumped again, an assessment they would find destructively harsh, but they'd leave it alone. They would also know, from their own painful experiences, that the work is threatening. Spouses and lovers hate it.

And men, goddamn them, can't get by some asshole notion about the work as an aphrodisiac. Through some combination of media hype and their own performance anxiety, they think a woman alone with a man on surveillance will start panting and beg to be taken.

Yeah, right, Kunda thought. Seeing some poor lady sneaking into a hot sheet motel off the Cross Island Parkway surrounded by bus fumes and betrayal really gives you the old hots. And your partner on the case is probably just a nice guy with Winstons and salami on his breath doing a little night work to supplement the police pension. Where Kunda wants to be taken after a surveillance is home to a nice guy who knows that this blue-eyed party animal, boogie-till-dawn blonde is ready to spend her after-hours time with cats, her flute, books, and, down the road, kids.

Hell, guys, Jo-Ann figured, you want to know who's going to have an affair? Try the little homemaker who never gets out. Try the chickie who's spent so much time building her life around a man's wants that she doesn't know who she is anymore. Or look to the wife of the guy who takes a side order of nookie as his due. You think women don't know something's going on? Men. What jerks they could be sometimes.

Kunda is a Brooklyn girl, raised in a close-knit Polish family. Her mother, Anne, is also a night person who loves partying with her daughter, hitting the slots at Atlantic City, and heading down to Chippendales with Jo-Ann to howl approval when the guys start taking off their bikini underpants.

Kunda went through the New York City public schools in their full blackboard jungle splendor, graduating as the sole Caucasian in the class of 1980 from Manhattan's Central Commercial High School. She's still paying off college loans from her four years at the Brockport campus of the State University of New York where she majored in radio and television.

Most of the people who succeed in New York radio and

television do so after a healthy apprenticeship in the heartland. Kunda didn't want to leave New York, nor did she want to compete with a thousand would-be's to get a low-paid gofer job in the bowels of a station or network.

She took a job as a trainee with Equifax, one of the major information-gathering corporations, and spent three years as an insurance investigator. She advanced fast and well, learning the full spectrum of credit reporting, public document searches, data base access, medical information retrieval, and how to get in all the other nooks and crannies where personal information lies like the *Titanic* waiting for the halogen lights of explorers.

Like thousands before her, Kunda was dazzled by the biographical color of the paper that documents the existence and chronology of every human being. Like an archaeologist piecing together the wonders of a civilization from its artifacts, the paper investigator sees, feels, smells, and almost touches a target, following a story richer than a novel from flat computer printouts.

Paper intersects with other paper to reveal the loves, fights, competitions, medical complications, comedies, tragedies, and travesties of relationships. Kunda learned to merge computers with the telephone to make a crystal ball, to get a look at the kind of car a person drives, the clothes she wears, where she's lived in the past ten years, and even where she's going next year.

Most intriguing is the rogue paper, the red light reports on quacks, embezzlers, con artists, and other arguments for Lucifer's existence. It's the bad guys that keep the adrenaline flowing. The good guys are boring. Kunda learned to track the paths of these scuzzballs, chart patterns, and make educated guesses as to where they would next go to rip people off.

She was on a good course at Equifax until her boss asked her to become an investigator of other investigators, sort of a corporate internal affairs agent. Kunda, who has dozens of friends and relatives in law enforcement, found the idea appalling. And, having turned down a career advancement opportunity, she felt she would have stagnated at Equifax.

A friend told her about an opening for a skip tracer at Vincent Parco & Associates. She met Parco and found they shared a sense of perfectionism and a basic investigative philosophy: Do it right, do it fast, close the case. She also found a place that welcomed her dramatic flair, her ability to become anyone she wants and pull it off.

She moved up fast, becoming head skip tracer, then a junior partner.

The intercom on her desk rang.

"Hi, Jo-Ann, Vinny."

"Morning."

"You sound depressed."

"Nothing that a little castration wouldn't solve."

"Don't say that too loud, my wife might hear you."

"You're out on that fence thing this afternoon, right?"

"Right. I should be back late in the day sometime."

"How's it going on the Gloskin case?"

"I talked to Louis this morning as a matter of fact. Joel's got the house in his wife, Deborah's name, not his own. He bought this place out on the island in 1981 for something like a hundred eighty thou. You want the exact figures? Mark's got them."

"I'll look at them later. What else?"

"There's eighty or ninety thou in money markets and he's got both an IRA and a Keough. There's also an IRA in Deborah's name. Those account for another sixty, seventy thousand. Louis's putting in a request for all local calls from the business so we're going to find out if he talks to a stockbroker or whatever on his office line. We'll go further after we get that stuff."

"Sounds pretty normal for a guy with a going business," Parco said. "And if the house is in his wife's name, I'd say he's in no hurry to break up his marriage just yet."

"Right. It doesn't look like he's up to anything so far, except for the fact that he's getting it on with his best friend's lady."

"If he's even doing that," Parco said. "Louis struck me as a naturally suspicious guy. Someone's banging his wife all right, but I'm still with the theory that it's an unknown. By the way, if you get arrested in that hooker outfit, don't call me."

"Thanks."

The relationship between working cops and private investigators is cozy on television. To Vinny Parco, there's nothing funnier than watching a prime-time P.I. walk right into the captain's office to open a file. Or, when the lieutenant snarls grudging respect at that what-will-he-think-of-next dick who pissed off the whole police hierarchy, got so much media attention that the mayor himself demanded action, but drat, solved a crime that mere cops couldn't figure out, and they go for coffee.

In life, any P.I. who infests the police sanctuary with politicians, even inadvertently, is going to pay. You'd sooner piss off the Shiite Moslems. If you want touchy information, you don't put a good cop at risk by asking him for it at headquarters. You have a beer, the guy says he'll see, and you wait for his call. The P.I.'s workload, and usually his economic base, comes from civil, rather than criminal cases, where the police wouldn't be of much help anyway. But no agency can afford to be without friends on the job, more to open the bureaucracy than the files. Such was the case when Jo-Ann Kunda went undercover as a hooker.

Manhattan South is Kojak's old precinct, one of the busiest processing plants for hardened criminals in New York. The cops there trot a genre of remorseless street criminals through the criminal justice system in numbers that rival Christmas crowds at Macy's. These criminals, called skels, mutts, perps, maggots, or just plain slime, play their part of the game, and the police play theirs. Time is spooned out on a triage basis, like a combat field hospital where medics treat those who have the best chance of living, and let the dying die. Aside from ACLU lawyers, about the last thing they want to see at Manhattan South is a private detective.

Vinny Parco needed police help to break the lease of a drug-dealing fence that Jo-Ann had been visiting in her hooker role. A P.I. can be charged with compounding a felony if he buys drugs without police backup. Parco likes cops. He does not ask, and does not expect, information from them, but there are times when a friend at Manhattan South can move the legal process along.

Jo-Ann checked herself out in the bathroom mirror. She knew her white minidress was going to be snug—it was bought to fit that way when she was in college—but it was too damn tight. God, she thought, just what my self-image needs right now, a dress that doesn't fit.

She checked her jewelry—oversized crystal earrings, a heart necklace, and a slave bracelet—for overkill, but was satisfied. She walked across the hall to Vinny's office.

"You've got the ring?" Vinny asked.

"Right here," she said, holding out a diamond ring worth about fifteen hundred dollars.

"How much you gonna ask for?"

"Seven hundred."

"Good. You're a junkie, let him get you all the way down to seventy-five or a hundred. He won't get suspicious. Remember—"

"Yes, Dad, don't buy any drugs from the guy without backup from Manhattan South. It's compounding a felony. How do I look?"

"Too good. Watch out." They both knew that dressing as a prostitute is no trick-or-treat gag in New York. Hookers trigger the most base hostilities and weirdnesses, the darkest things men think they can do to women. They are meat for every slice-and-dice pervert on the street. As a whore, Jo-Ann was also in danger of attack by pimps and prostitutes who might see her as taking a stand on their turf. It wasn't likely, but possible.

Jo-Ann does not carry a gun. She shoots regularly with Vinny at the range, and would love her own Walther PPK, but she also would like to buy a clarinet. Dressed as a hooker headed for a fence, the gun won easily, but at home, as she practiced on the flute she's played since the seventh grade, a new clarinet was much more of a turn-on. She could buy a cheap pistol and a less expensive clarinet, but she knew she'd have to go first class with one or the other. Right now, it didn't matter because she still had about three hundred to save.

If Vinny Parco thought Jo-Ann would be in real danger, he'd follow her, but he wasn't overly concerned, so long as she took a taxi each way. He never had to worry about her in the field, but the agency needed her more inside than out right now. He hoped the cases she'd work in the next couple of weeks would get her over this field thing soon, but, as he knew only too well, a P.I. needs to be out in the fresh air sometimes. They especially need it when the personal life is a little unsettled. Parco understood that too.

"Okay, you're coming back later?" he said.

"I'll be back."

As Kunda hailed a cab, she felt invigorated, and very glad she'd pushed for the fieldwork. To make it as a P.I., you have to know more than good investigative technique. You have to get to the business stuff and master the financial paper flow. Bookkeeping, sales, marketing, advertising, and enough law to keep the shop legal, are as big a part of your on-the-job-training as gags and guile. A lot of P.I.'s go down because they think being a good investigator is enough.

Jo-Ann knows she's good. She's good at about everything she

tries. She was good at Equifax, good at retailing when she did that, she's good with both the clarinet and the gun. That was the thing. Finding something you're good at is a problem for some, but for Jo-Ann, it was finding the right thing you're good at. You think a lot about that when you get close to thirty. What do I really want to be when I grow up? And for a minute, though she swore off thinking about men for the day, she wondered who she was going to be grown-up with.

Jo-Ann had other offers in her business, but she is grateful to Vinny Parco for going beyond his more chauvinist impulses not only to show her the business, but to make her a partner. She'd stick with both Parco and the P.I. business, no question there, but wondered what part of it interested her most. What kind of client does she want to be around, and, God, would it interest her when she got close to forty? She shook it off.

"It's a piece of shit," the fence said. The store typified the kind of retail outlet that seems to grow, like fungus, out of nowhere once a city gets to about a million in population. A frayed sign with very tentative lettering said Lost Our Lease, Everything Must Go. Kunda figured it had been up for about three years.

The windows displayed calculators, cameras, computers, video games, the Sony Walkman and Watchman, onyx chess sets, tapestries of Christ and the apostles at the Last Supper, and a full line of handcuffs, badges, police nightsticks, and huge knives sheathed in camouflage cases. While many such stores are the legitimate legacy to the pushcart and represent the American Dream to a new generation of immigrant merchants, they are also frequently dumping grounds for bogus brand-name merchandise, fenced jewelry, credit card fraud, and many other modern scams.

The fence's name was Lenny. He was a large, but not slovenly, man with deceptively kind eyes and a beard.

"Lenny, you telling me this ain't a diamond ring?" Jo-Ann asked.

"It's a diamond, but a piece of shit. Look at this cut," he said, holding a magnifying glass over the diamond. "See how uneven that is? I can't give you more than seventy-five bucks and that's a gift."

Jo-Ann decided to push it a little further.

"I think we're talking at least a hundred, hundred fifty, man," she said.

"I think we're talking seventy-five," he said quietly, and the kindly eyes told her that she could take her business elsewhere, but they both knew she would not. "Take it or leave it."

"Mean streets, babe," she said. "You've got it." It was the third time she'd been in, and she knew he was buying her as a hooker.

"Uh, Lenny," she said. "Do you sell just radios or do you handle the stuff I like to spend my money on, you know?"

"Like what?"

"Like coke," she said with a sly smile.

He looked at her carefully. "Seventy-five bucks don't buy a lot of coke."

"I know, but I make very good money, Lenny."

He shrugged and said, "Very good money is always nice. Show me some and maybe I can help you out."

That was as far as she wanted to take it right now.

When she got outside, it had started to rain. Oh, no, she thought. Jesus Christ, I'm stuck out here on the street in this getup. Kunda can probably find any missing person in the country, and most every dollar he or she ever earned, but she cannot find a taxi in Manhattan when it rains. No one can.

For all its mass, New York is parceled into a thousand tiny occupational and residential hamlets where the same people pass at the same time every day. It was getting to be rush hour and Kunda knew that several of her mother's friends, along with a hundred people she knew from Brooklyn, worked nearby, and were due to pass. She walked through the rain to the subway, and she'll never know if some nice guy she always wanted to date, a friend of her mother's, or an old college buddy, spotted her dressed for turning tricks.

Kunda got a call from the client the following day.

"Nice work, Jo-Ann," he said, "you people really know your stuff."

"Thanks," she said, "uh, we try." She had no idea what the man was talking about.

"Yeah, they took old Lenny right out of there in cuffs. That was beautiful," he said. "I thought you were going to bust him next week."

Kunda was stunned. The detectives at Manhattan South, busy with their own workload, had promised her that they'd bust the fence this week or next, they couldn't say when, but they'd call her. They sure as hell wouldn't do it without her. This fence just wasn't enough of a big deal to merit a full sting from the narcs.

"Well, I knew it was going down, John," she told the client, "but I was sworn to secrecy on that."

"Well, very good work," the client said. "Just send me the bill."

"I will," she said and hung up. She then called her contact at Manhattan South and asked, in polite, but shocked terms, what the fuck was going on. How come they arrested him?

"We didn't, the Feds must have done it," her contact said.

The Feds had no record of the guy either.

It took more detective work to find out when and why the target was arrested than it would have to arrest him themselves. Investigators from another detective agency representing a watch company had used their own contacts at Manhattan South to throw the guy in jail for product counterfeiting. He had been selling fake brand-name watches as the real thing.

It is not unusual for one detective squad in a busy precinct not to know what another is doing until well after an arrest is logged. Parco's contacts in narcotics didn't know that their colleagues in anticrime were also taking time away from the muggers, murderers, and rapists, to help a P.I. close a case. Either way, it just wasn't Lenny's week. It might have been the first time in history that an electronics store with a Lost Our Lease sign lost its lease.

9

South Philadelphia is Joe Howard's kind of place, a working-class scoop of urban America so traditional that Roosevelt's Fireside Chats seem fresh in the living rooms of aluminum-sided, two- and three-family houses. Stallone played Rocky Balboa in South Philly, and the real Rambos—the guys who went to Vietnam because that's what you *did*—live out their lives peacefully in a neighborhood that didn't need two decades to welcome them home.

Kind of like Queens, Joe Howard thought. Kind of like home. And, like home, there are scuzzballs among the good people, shitheads like Eddie Gingras who was now probably in a bar as Howard and Meehan waited outside his rooming house in a cramped Nissan Sentra they'd rented that afternoon.

"The poor man must be seriously injured," Marty Meehan said. "He's probably in an emergency room getting treatment for his head wound."

"What head wound?" Howard asked. "He has a cold, remember?"

"Yes, but before that, Mr. Buehller told me he got into a fight in a bar and hurt his head."

Howard lit a cigareette. "Yeah, well, let's hope we can help make him more comfortable, just like he's making us."

The detectives, at 11:00 P.M., were in the third hour of their stakeout. Once in a while, two or three locals would shag by and eyeball the car with proprietary arrogance, but stopped short when Howard, Camel butt drooping from his stubbled jaw, eyeballed back.

Stakeouts, even when done properly by a team, are hallucinogenic. Time slows to a dirgelike pace. The little sounds of a summer night—the settling of the car engine, the murmur of conversation from a stoop down the block, or bugs hitting the windshield—press against the nerves to those not used to it. And, for those who haven't done it for a long time.

"I'm way too old for this shit," Howard said. "This is for kids."

"You are a kid."

"Compared to an old bastard like you, I suppose I am." Hour after hour, the investigator has to keep his gaze on a single spot, often a doorway. A blink, a scratch, or just changing stations on the radio can blow the watch. It's not unusual to lose a target, for he can come out the door and disappear in a matter of seconds.

There were no outstanding warrants on Eddie Gingras, but Ramik Onari, his alleged assistant, was a delectable treat to the Department of Immigration and Naturalization. He was also wanted by the FBI in a forgery case. The Philadelphia police had picked him up an hour ago. Howard and Meehan would have to go through his lawyer to question him, but that would have to come later, if at all. Right now, they just wanted Eddie.

"Just like old times, Joseph," Marty said. "Just like the job."

"Right, Marty. Just like it."

The job. Once you've been a New York cop, you can throw your plastic Patrolman's Benevolent Association card on the dash and park where you like in a city where tow trucks operate with the moral authority of hit men. You can still go to the cop bars and be welcome even if no one in the old joint knows you anymore. You can get your muffler fixed at cost, your hair cut, or pick up a bike wholesale for your grandchild, you can still eat free, and your money just might not be good at Yankee or Shea Stadiums where, even in a hot series, there's always a good seat or two for a cop. Cops always know someone who can get it done and cops are cops forever.

With one exception.

The only thing that can stop it all happened to Joe Howard. It was a nightmare that almost destroyed him in a way that would have made death from his eight gun battles seem like a night of trick or treating. Joe Howard was officially accused of not being a good cop. To a good cop, there's nothing worse.

Howard was born in County Mayo, Ireland, a rocky patch of the west that almost lost its whole population to the potato famine. He calls Mayo "the West Virginia of Ireland." His parents were determined to move the family to New York, and accomplished the feat by working hard in the depression and sending for their children one by one.

Howard, the youngest of four, was left with the husband of his mother's sister, a retired farm laborer named Anthony Carney, a man whom Howard describes with his highest accolade, "a gentleman, a real gentleman." More than forty years later, he would honor Carney by naming his detective agency after him.

School did not interest him enough to attend with any regularity either in Ireland or New York, when he finally arrived in 1945 at age eleven. He got as far as the seventh grade and later passed a high school equivalency exam.

In 1952, he enlisted in the Navy where he spent three years in the engine room of the aircraft carrier *Intrepid*, now a museum in New York. He served his time "as far down as you can go in the goddamn thing," he remembers. Way down there, he started to think about how Joe Howard wanted to spend his life. He knew he wasn't going to be a sailor and anything that took a lot of school was out for him. One day it hit him. He wanted to be a cop.

If he'd lived in a small town somewhere, the dream might have been easier, but in the New York of 1955, there were about eighty thousand other guys with the same idea. If you knew the mayor or something, you could get to the top of the list, and if you were an Irish kid with three generations of pull on the job, okay, you had it. But if you were Joe Howard, you had a couple of years to wait.

Howard worked as a bank messenger and did other odd jobs, and almost lost his chances of ever seeing the police academy up close because of a childhood prank that seemed like a thousand years ago to him. As he recalls it, he and three brothers—Pat, Martin, and John Beasty—were caught by the Garda, the Irish police, for borrowing a mule from Johnny Kelly's farm. They were scolded and warned to stay out of trouble, and maybe to go to school once in a while.

That incident resurfaced when the NYPD did its check on Howard and, if not for some fast talking and a little intervention by a cop who liked the kid, Howard would have had to find another career.

After he graduated from the police academy in November 1957, Howard was assigned to foot patrol in the twentieth precinct, the Upper West Side. Today rock stars live nearby on Central Park West and yuppies get together for brunch at the restaurants on Columbus Avenue. In Howard's rookie year, the region was a cesspool with all the slum trappings—prostitution, drugs, street gangs, congestion, filth, and weapons. *West Side Story* was set in the Two-Oh.

Howard and his partner, Mike Hickey, watched their streets from rooftops. When they saw drug deals or a little gang warfare, maybe a pimp beating up on his woman, they swooped down like hawks and had the perps in cuffs before they could even wince.

In those freewheeling years when the economy boomed and the Warren Court was something not even a Greenwich Village beatnik could imagine, a street slug learned fast that "sir" was the way to address an officer of the law, and your rights were guaranteed by the Constitution of the United States of America as long as you made it easy for the arresting officer to grant them. The word was out. Mess with a cop and you could die of old age waiting for due process.

The rookie learned the street and its code fast. There were always drunks, crazies, or kids mean enough to draw weapons. Throughout his police career, Howard was cited for disarming men with dangerous weapons.

He also learned to play the game, keep his nose where it belonged, work through the system, and to confine any wave making to the street. He got to know the difference between the official rules and the unofficial ones, which sergeants favored which kind of arrests, what to bring back to the station house and what to leave on the street.

Howard was, according to Mike Hickey, a star in the making, discovering what he was born to do, and doing it beautifully. He was popular with his superiors as he knew how to be a good Irish son as well as a good cop, a team player who worked hard without complaint, and earned the respect of other cops. He kept his streets under control, which was all he was supposed to do.

He was also aggressive. The Two-Oh had no shortage of "good" arrests, those that result in conviction, during his three years there. But an ambitious cop has to move on and Howard's chance came in October 1960. He'd spent the day in court in lower Manhattan, after which he left some seized heroin in a lab.

He passed 400 Broome Street, home of the Safe, Loft, and Truck Squad.

Safe and Loft is cop heaven, an elite cadre of detectives with the authority and budget to override other police fiefdoms in their pursuit of bank robbers, fences, hijackers, Mafia front operations, and a thousand other big-time, high-profile crooks. Safe and Loft was under the command of Inspector Raymond Maguire in 1960. According to Howard, Maguire was a tough, by the book, old-timer who was such a disciplinarian that a single personal call in the office got a cop warned and into a kind of unofficial probation. The next call got him bounced from the knighthood.

The way Howard tells it, he was young and arrogant enough to think he could get a job with Safe and Loft by swaggering in and asking for it. On the books, a uniformed cop is supposed to be able to do that, but the workings of the NYPD call for a more diplomatic approach in the form of fraternal sponsorship within a division. Howard knew no one in Safe and Loft, but Maguire apparently saw something he liked. Howard was a detective a month later.

His reputation and record appear to have soared so quickly as to be embarrassing to him. He is uncomfortable talking about the early sixties, but microfilms and old clippings scream hero.

Safe and Loft in those days was a TV cop show without the grit scrubbed away. They were real cops chasing real crooks with real guns. Howard remembers a blur of undercover jobs where he'd do surveillances with his buddies in taxicabs, panel trucks and, for a while, a Dodge Charger V-8 that would blow serious smoke at today's Trans Ams or Iroc-Z Camaros. He says his Savile Row tastes in the 1980s probably stem from so much work in khaki pants and sweatshirts.

"Joseph, you and I have seen far better surveillances," Meehan said.

"If I followed a cat up a tree, I'd have seen a far better surveillance," he said, letting out his breath in disgust.

Howard is grateful for boring work, but that doesn't mean he can't gripe about surveillances that lead to nothing more interesting than some punk like Eddie Gingras with one very swelled idea of his own toughness. He wouldn't trade such "make-believe" work for the kind of stakeout he did on the job, the kind that nearly got him killed a few times. One such "real surveillance" started in February of 1962 when the head of security for Railway Express Agency, a forerunner of UPS, noticed that one of the company's trucks was being followed.

Howard and his four partners caught the case and soon learned that they were following Patrick Huston, Albie Taylor, and Kenny Cavanaugh, members of a family with a long history of high-yield robbery. The Railway Express truck proved to be only a window shopping expedition.

"These guys were pros," Howard recalls with the grudging respect that an experienced cop yields to a gifted enemy. "They only did about one score a year and they picked it carefully."

The surveillance took seven months. The detectives stuck with the gang as they scouted banks, armored car transfers, payroll deposit runs, and other big money opportunities for its annual harvest. They finally seemed to settle on an armored car company which, in the course of its rounds, took a lot of cash out of the Franklin-Simon department store at 360 Washington Street in lower Manhattan. For weeks, they watched as the car made its pickups from the store. As Paddy Huston and company patiently absorbed the armored car's schedule, Joe Howard and his colleagues took notes of their own.

Utilizing police intelligence sources in the criminal underground, the group was ready for a robbery when one occurred on the afternoon of November 16, 1962. Howard and three detectives waited in a cleaning truck they had rented from Hertz. Six backup cops took their places in doorways, behind parked cars, and in other concealed spots.

Newspaper reports indicate that the officers waited while the thieves completed their task in a transaction that is a textbook case of good guy–bad guy etiquette in the old days. The crooks didn't kill the guards and the police shouted out a warning of their presence, actually saying, "Halt, police!" Today's cops are often criticized for skipping this little professional courtesy, and they, in turn, accuse the criminals of blood lust and all the fair play of Gila monsters. Urban crooks today, many police officers feel, will amuse themselves by beheading some poor cashier with a .44 Magnum or some other Pentagon-sized weapon. Yelling "Halt police!" might have to be forfeited. But the papers say someone in Howard's party did give Paddy Huston his warning before the scene turned into a classic B-movie. The robbers drew weapons and began firing. Twenty-nine shots later, two of the three were dead and Joe Howard was on his way to the emergency room of St. Vincent's Hospital with a bullet in the spleen, courtesy of thirty-three-year-old Kenneth Cavanaugh who died instantly. Howard still carries Cavanaugh's lead.

The scrapbooks, with page after page of front page headlines, tell the rest of the story:

BRAVE IRISHMAN
2 THUGS SLAIN IN GUN BATTLE; HERO COP SHOT
HE EARNED TOP HONORS FOR HEROISM

The stories went on as front page headlines for months throughout Joe's recovery. The stories tell of the twenty-six-year-old cop joking with nurses as he was wheeled into the operating room. There are pictures of his wife, Anne, and their daughter, Jo-Ann, and one-year-old Jeremiah Junior. Anne was pregnant that Christmas season with their third child.

THEIR JOINT FATE IN HANDS OF GOD
CHIN UP COP'S WIFE CARRIES ON
HE'LL LIVE!
SALUTE TO A HERO

Even before the shooting, Howard had received eight citations for bravery, five of which were for disarming persons with dangerous weapons. Newspaper photographs show a smiling, defiant man being visited by professional athletes, politicians, and various representatives of police organizations. Police Commissioner Michael J. Murphy said, "I have never met a man with more courage. His fight for life is as great as his bravery under fire."

Joe Howard won the Medal of Honor, making him the officially designated bravest cop in New York.

The heroics went on for as long as Howard was a cop. The headlines in his scrapbook point to more than a decade of supercop voltage:

CRACK COPS SMASH HIJACK RING, SEIZE $6 M LOOT
SEIZE 2 BOMBS, 2 MEN IN MIDTOWN
EX-CON WITH DOPE HABIT & WIG HELD AS BANDIT

The clippings in the late 1960s and early 1970s show Joe Howard in his midthirties, still in the game. There's Joe in 1970 handcuffed to a woman in a paisley miniskirt, one of three radicals who attempted to finance revolution by robbing a branch of First National City Bank. His expression, caught by a *New York Post* photographer as he headed for Central Booking, was the wary eye of a cop who had seen about a year too much of the Age of Aquarius.

There's Howard involved in one of the first NYPD helicopter chases, a shootout at Kennedy Airport, a big-time rare coin heist that he solved, and the smashing of an art theft ring where the veteran cop recovered a Goya worth $200,000 in 1969.

Joe Howard is the first to support the need for the Knapp Commission, the panel convened by Major John V. Lindsay to investigate allegations of corruption in New York's police department in the early 1970s. That the commission found cops on the take is beyond dispute. That it created a department of cops expecting to be yanked off the street by internal affairs for a free cup of coffee is also beyond dispute.

Cops who survived the "Serpico Era" comment about it carefully, usually with a raised eyebrow and a grunt. If they're on the street, they might even spit, and if inside, extend a middle finger with a kiss for the politicians.

"The paranoia that came out of those times," Howard says, "produced the most honest and least effective police department in the history of New York. Do I think it was necessary? Absolutely. Was it also a witch-hunt that brought down a lot of innocent men? Yes, I'm afraid it was."

Joe Howard did not have problems with the Knapp Commission *per se*. He did choke on its residue, beginning one day in 1971 when his first wife, Anne, was asked by the children's dentist for a favor.

"The dentist was very upset because the fellow upstairs was selling narcotics," he recalls. "He asked my wife if I could do anything about it. He knew I was a detective."

"You know we never work narcotics," he told his wife. He reported the activity to the narcotics unit of the Queens District Attorney's office and let it go at that. But whenever the kids went to the dentist, the dealer continued to operate on the stairway.

His usual four-man team at Safe and Loft was between major cases and working burglaries in the nineteenth precinct on Manhattan's Upper East Side. Anne continued to ask her husband if anything could be done.

"I got a little teed off because it was my wife and kids involved. I called the Queens DA's office again, nothing happened. Another month went by. So I went to my boss, Tom Cassain, and said, 'Jerry, Tony, and I aren't doing anything right now. Why don't you give us a whack at this guy?' Bottom line is we set a surveillance up and within two months I think we had made twenty arrests. And each time we made an arrest we told the users they could do themselves a favor if they testified against this dealer, which they did.

"And during this investigation, we came up with a man we suspected of being this guy's supplier, a guy named Frank Augiar, known as Jamaica Avenue Frank. We got a search warrant and hit his place in Kew Gardens. Empty. Case closed."

The investigation did shut down the dealer above the dentist's office and the three men, along with Bob Deeter, the fourth member of their ad hoc narcotics unit, went back to work in the more familiar terrain of Safe and Loft. They were working on the mob hit case of Joey Gallo when they read in the paper that Jamaica Avenue Frank had been arrested for selling drugs.

"This was two years later," Howard says. "We didn't pay any attention. But he came up with a list of who supposedly shook him down. Jerry Hernandez, Tony Bonham, Bob Deeter, and me he picked out. We allegedly shook him down for fifteen thousand dollars and two nickel bags of heroin."

It's not unusual for a drug dealer to make such accusations, and the police department's Internal Affairs Division, the despised police force set up to investigate cops, always conducts its probe. When they can't find any further evidence than the accusation of a street criminal, they lock up the files and call the whole thing off.

Joe Howard claims there was no evidence to back up Jamaica Avenue Frank's allegation, but "the paranoia that came out of that Knapp Commission was enough for them to suspend us for fifteen months and bring us to trial. And when the case was finished in the trial room, when the prosecution had finished their case, the case was dismissed."

When he remembers the incident, Howard's voice slows down,

each syllable is deliberate, and his eyes take on the look of a bear hit three times with a shotgun, but not directly enough to keep him from shredding his hunter.

"We never even presented our case. That's how *lousy* their fucking case was. But by that time, Jerry Hernandez was dead already, and Tony Bonham was cracked up. He lives in a room somewhere out in New Jersey. I go see him once a year, but he's not quite in it. That's the kind of paranoia that came out of the Knapp Commission."

His partner, Jerry Hernandez, died of a bleeding ulcer, probably, Howard says, brought on by the amount of drinking he did during the fifteen-month suspension. The four men had visibly suffered the ravages of the accusation as one avenue of appeal after another was turned down. Most devastating to them was the refusal of their offer to testify before the grand jury without immunity. Tony Bonham suffered a stroke that brought on severe memory lapse. All were cleared, but only Bob Deeter and Joe Howard had survived well enough to return to duty at full pay.

Theirs was not much of a Knapp Commission story. The commission's investigators, in fact, were not interested in even speaking with them. There were no blaring headlines about the disgraced hero, no television cameras with the defendants hiding their faces, no elected officials on the political bandwagon of finger pointing.

The *New York Times* gave the story a paragraph on the bottom of page 18 on Monday, April 3, 1973, and never mentioned the incident again. The big story of that day was red meat and a nationwide boycott of it. The Nixon administration was loudly shouting down Watergate as a third-rate burglary and trying to deport John Lennon on an old marijuana charge. The *New York Post*, a more subdued tabloid in that era, said nothing at all.

The fifteen-month suspension was not the end of Howard's ordeal. He was returned to modified duty—office work—without his gun and gold shield until 1975, when all charges were finally dropped. His accusation had drawn five lines. His innocence was never reported. And in July of 1976, when Howard and his colleagues were cleared, there was no coverage.

But, by then, Howard's drinking had accelerated to a full-scale problem, his marriage ended in divorce, and he was, by his own account, a very difficult man to live with.

"Let's not bullshit, I was a drunk," he says with a bitter smile. "No point in calling it anything else. Anne and the kids went through the worst of it."

Maybe. But Joe Howard had been betrayed by a job that he had been willing to trade his own life for, again and again.

The experience gave Joe Howard a bitterly different perspective on the scrapbooks and the Medal of Honor that made him the number one cop of 1962. One day during his suspension, he heaved all of it—the citations, clippings, plaques, and the lifetime of honors that sang his heroism as loud as a jukebox—into a roaring blaze in his fireplace.

Joe Howard, Jr., then fifteen, came into the room and stood up to his father by diving into the fireplace and rescuing the flaming material. Young Joe wasn't going to let it happen. No commission, bunch of politicians, or whatever those people were, was going to shake the young man's faith in his dad, or take from him the special pride in being the son of a hero. And no fury on his father's part, regardless of how well justified, was going to take the physical evidence of those honors out of Joe Junior's life.

They weren't the old man's to throw away. They also belonged to the family. Even though he was only fifteen, young Joe knew he'd one day show them to his own children, they to their children, and descendants all the way down the Howard line would know that a hotheaded, brash, hero cop from County Mayo set the tone and tradition of this family.

Once he was cleared, the senior Howard started to look for other priorities. He didn't want to be a cop anymore, not after "that bullshit." He couldn't. That was the problem. The fire was gone. For a while, he owned a taxi but, as he recalls, "It's hard to make a living as a cab owner if you throw as many people out of the taxi as you allow in."

And there was the alcoholism to deal with. He had to put away the scotch. He didn't do it alone and he didn't do it overnight. That's all he'll say about the recovery program. Today he lunches with attorneys, museum directors, and book publishers in Mon Paris, a very fashionable French restaurant where, like Vinny Parco at Mumbles, he owns the joint when he shows up. He orders authoritatively from the menu and, between sips of Perrier, makes his recommendations from the "fancy schmancy" menu.

His second wife, Susan, and grandson, Jeremiah Howard III, have also provided him with a grounding and perspective the young gunslinger never knew. Some might even say Joe Howard has mellowed a bit, but usually not if he's within earshot. He works hard as ever but, by all accounts, he can relax more, leaving the agency in the hands of Joe Junior.

Kenny Cavanaugh's bullet nearly killed him again in 1984 when it shifted slightly. Peritonitis set in and Howard went into a coma. There were no newspaper headlines or reporters bugging the nurses for medical bulletins this time, but there were a lot of veteran cops, and family wondering desperately if the tough son of a bitch would come back again. He did, but his left side was paralyzed. They said he might never walk again and maybe he would lose some of his mental acuity.

"Screw that," he says. It took almost a year, but he walks, has all his mental powers, and still sends an occasional curse with Kenny Cavanaugh's name on it. His convalescence gave a brash kid from another generation a shot at the game.

Joe Junior had just taken a job with the Carney Agency after getting bored on Wall Street. The idea was to see if he liked it. During the senior Howard's convalescence, the young man had no choice but to run the place. His business degree, administrative flair, skills with the polygraph and other technology are natural additives to bring the agency into the next century. Guards and security will continue to be its direction. The younger Howard is an active member of the American Society of Industrial Security, a trade group with high standards that keeps its members abreast of sophisticated approaches to corporate security problems.

Two years after his peritonitis, Howard returned from the dead again when he underwent heart surgery. He thinks he's still around because "The Big Guy" wants him to do a little more work. The work isn't catching the Eddie Gingrases of the world or chasing away the bedbugs. That's his living. The work that counts to him now is helping cops fight the sauce, and if a few nonpolice happen to stumble into alcoholism, he'll be there for them too.

The Medal of Honor plaque presides over the office shared by father and son for all the Mrs. Kevelins, lawyers, bedbugs, CEOs, and retired cops to see when they come to the Carney Agency.

But if they turned it over, or thumbed through the scrapbooks, they would find the charcoal traces of a man's worst hour.

"Hey, Marty," Howard said. "How about we get some sleep and see this genius when he comes out in the morning?"

"Fine with me, Joseph. It's been a long night."

"Too long," Joe Howard said.

10

Walter Williams, the Sugar Daddy, had a habit of visiting his former girlfriend who was, according to Peter Castillo, terrified of him. Williams had put his bogus drug business on temporary hold and was back to armed robbery, a consistent staple in his life since age twelve. The woman agreed to a meeting with Castillo in her attorney's office, where she passed along the information that Williams was planning to rob a small store on the edge of an industrial park, basically a self-service gas station with a few convenience items. Tonight was supposed to be the night.

Castillo's friend, Sergeant Ed Kinsella of the Fairfax County Sheriff's Department, joined him in a stakeout of the store. It was getting toward 8:00 P.M. and the moon, at least, was cooperating. It shone full and bright through the clear skies.

Castillo views the hazards of his work the way a bacteriologist looks at a killer virus in a petri dish. Don't drop the dish, and you have nothing to worry about. Screw up, and your day has come.

The ex-girlfriend's tip was good information a few days ago, but criminals aren't the most focused people in the world. The Sugar Daddy could have changed his mind. Hunch did its job and Williams showed up on foot.

"That's him," Castillo said.

Kinsella squinted. "You sure?"

Castillo was. His symphonic system of jangled nerve endings, all going off in harmony, confirmed it. Something was starting.

The Sugar Daddy was alone, walking up the street wearing jeans, leather boots, a flannel shirt, and a dark blue jacket.

Castillo looked at a snapshot, looked toward the man now

getting near the car, and decided that it was time to work. He put on his high beams and said, "It's him, Ed. Let's go."

They got out of the car carefully, Castillo standing behind the door as the man approached.

"How's it going, Walt?" he said quietly. "How you doing?"

The man stopped walking and sized up his two-man posse.

"You guys got the wrong man," he said. His eyes started to shift left and right.

"You know, Walt, I have a capius for your arrest," Castillo said quietly.

"Well, you got the wrong guy," he said, then suddenly ran away across the street, down an embankment, and into some heavy woods.

Castillo and Kinsella took off after him. Before he reached the top of the hill, Castillo grabbed him by the jacket. Williams wiggled out of the sleeves and kept running. The movies do not depict foot chases very well, according to those who have tried them.

"Pine trees hitting you in the face make it very hard to catch someone. It really hurts," Castillo remembers.

Fortunately, he was as appropriately dressed for the chase as the Sugar Daddy, wearing a windbreaker and jeans himself. Occasionally, he stopped and listened for branches cracking, then turned in their direction. The moon helped, but the woods were very dark and Castillo knew that the Sugar Daddy could be behind any tree waiting for him with a loaded gun. Or a knife. He could swing from above, grab Castillo and rip a hole in his jugular in less than five seconds.

Castillo got lucky. He came to a clearing and saw Williams's shadow as the Sugar Daddy made his way across a rutted field. He caught his breath, drew his nine millimeter, walked down the hill slowly, and called out, "Walt. Don't do anything foolish, Walt, because, if you do, I'm going to shoot you."

The Sugar Daddy, as Castillo remembers, danced around a tree and said, "Kill me, kill me, go ahead, kill me." Castillo leveled his gun directly at the Sugar Daddy's head, and cocked the hammer.

The Sugar Daddy took off.

The firing of a gun at a human being is probably the least well-represented aspect of the business on television. The responsible user of guns disciplines himself to go to the farthest edges of the brain, where the left and right hemispheres meet, and hang there frozen as time stops. Once the gun is drawn, he must assume that firing it is an inevitability. At the same time, he must withhold the impulse to fire unless he sees a clear threat. If he hesitates on either end—if he perceives a threat which the courts later decide wasn't there, or if there is danger and he sees it too late—someone gets killed.

Shooting at someone brings a truckload of paperwork. There are teams of ballistics people combing a field for every shell casing, interrogations all over the police department, bureaucratic jurisdictional hassles with city, state, or federal investigations, complications from licensing agencies, and professional associations. Since the Sugar Daddy did not draw a weapon or charge at Castillo, he decided not to fire.

On stakeouts, Castillo always carries a small jet black aerosol can of Smith & Wesson, Mark IV CS gas. Mace. Spray it in someone's face and the burning fumes reach to rip out the eyes, trachea, and stomach for a spell. He caught up to Williams who put up a furious struggle. Castillo finally overcame him long enough to spray the Mace. After that, the cuffs went on pretty smoothly. They heard a rustling through the trees and Ed Kinsella showed up with the Sugar Daddy's jacket.

"May I have my jacket please?" Williams asked, shaking his head to clear away the gas, and reaching for it. Kinsella stepped back. Castillo took the jacket, went throught the pockets, and came out with a .38 and a full clip of ammunition. Williams was also carrying a knife.

The Sugar Daddy had served his time for murder. There was no evidence to prosecute him on anything stronger than bail jumping and selling bogus drugs to kids. But the hunch work that has saved his life many times told Peter Castillo that, given half the chance, the Sugar Daddy would have killed him that night.

11

Barry Silvers was working late again, "seeing wood" and studying a stack of criminal indictments on the Duke of Audley.

THE UNITED STATES OF AMERICA

V.

RICHARD PETER HAMMOND

1. Beginning on or about May 11, 1983, and continuing to on or about March 1984, in the State of New York and elsewhere, the defendant, Richard Peter Hammond did, together with other persons known and unknown to the grand jury, combine, conspire, confederate, and agree to transport in interstate commerce, with fraudulent intent, falsely made, counterfeit, and forged securities, namely checks, knowing the same to have been falsely made, counterfeit, and forged in violation of 18 U.S.C. 2314.

2. It was part of such conspiracy that defendant and coconspirators would and did obtain counterfeit and forged checks drawn on cash reserve management accounts at the Mariner's National Bank of New York (now known as the Greater New York National Bank) of New York, New York, specifically a check in the amount of $1,500,000 drawn on the account of Sidney Rowlands and a check in the amount of $500,000 drawn on the account of Namco Textiles, Inc.

> 3. It was further a part of the conspiracy that defendant and coconspirators would and did cause such checks to be made payable to Robert Browning, an alias selected for defendant Richard Peter Hammond.

Silvers shook his head and tried to imagine someone with the nerve to rob Sidney Rowlands, a television evangelist famous for vindictive litigation. Any reporter assigned to his story could expect a suit for even a hair's breadth misstatement. Other TV ministers, even the most dedicated fundamentalists, gave him a wide berth at conventions. There were no theme parks or sex scandals in his ministry, no big cars, no tax frauds. But there were tens of millions in legal, if loopholed, investments.

To his followers, Rowlands was the man God personally chose to fight the pestilences of our times—Communism, the breakup of the American family, and lately, AIDS, which he saw as God's final warning shot before Armageddon.

The more cynical might say that the man had a good sense of the business of religious broadcasting. One way to rake it in is to terrify the bib overalls and missing front teeth crowd.

Hammond had forged checks drawn on a cash management account in Rowlands's name, then sent his brother, Roger, into a small New York bank run by a third world country to open an account with the bogus paper. The FBI guesses that the plan called for a transfer of all funds to Switzerland, where it would flow into a number of accounts under various false names. Some woud go by wire to the Cayman Islands, a tiny Caribbean resort whose banks are a haven for hidden assets.

The Duke probably figured he could pull it off because he arranged to be introduced to the bank's manager at a party given by impeccable members of the very tight financial community.

The Duke promised the bank manager some very lucrative business, dropping big names and accurate gossip as usual. He did this a few times, always "running into" the manager at the right social occasions. In fact, he had said, an associate of his, who did a lot of investing for religious broadcasters, might consider opening an account. He'd work on it.

Roger was to show up with a false identification, deposit the checks, which had the ink, paper, and codes of certified currency, and leave the bank.

It is possible that someone in Rowlands's organization, its bank in Tennessee, or both, was paid to okay the transaction, or bury it for a while. But maybe not. The cash management account was a way station for funds coming in from viewer contributions, real estate holdings, and other investments.

Certified checks use special codes, paper, and ink. They carry the authority of cash. Several of Silvers's banking contacts told him that the Duke might well have processed a certified check through the system without any inside help.

But Roger blew it. He'd been told not to get his fingerprints on the checks, but did anyway, and was so nervous that he gave the bank his real identification.

The bank manager, who almost certainly would have received Roger as the promised associate of the Duke's, was out to lunch. The assistant manager took one look at the man's seasick face and made two calls, one to Rowlands's bank, the other to the police. Roger was arrested immediately.

The probability of Sidney Rowlands not prosecuting was about the same as his taking up marijuana. Instead, he paid the Duke thirty-three thousand dollars for a written confession that disclosed an alleged "conspiracy" where, in a sworn affidavit, he named another evangelist, known to be Rowlands's archrival, as his partner in the heist. In the affidavit, Hammond explained that he chose this bank for his scam because of a personal prejudice: "They are an ignorant people," he said, "with a long historical reputation for being bad with money. I believed they would not take the standard precautions. I still believe that."

The rival minister hotly disclaimed any knowledge of the Duke and threatened several big lawsuits of his own. But he had been scalded by the publicity and that, Silvers figured, might have made thirty-three thousand dollars an inexpensive investment for Rowlands. There were other figures named in the affidavit, and, by Silvers's reckoning, probably a dozen private cops tracking the Duke along with an army of law enforcement people.

Thomas Magnum would have interviewed Rowlands in a scene that began with his Ferrari pulling up to the gates of the ministry. Next, a jowly man flanked by two clean-cut goons would have received him in a palatial office and had a little chat—like he was just dying to meet a private detective with an unnamed client, so he could spill his guts at last. He would have said, "Son, I know what's come out in the papers about some of my brethren, but I run a clean ministry here and I'm about to prove it to you . . ."

Barry Silvers never met with Rowlands. He did exchange some information, on the okay of all clients, with the P.I.'s hired by the minister. There were at least five lawsuits and criminal investigations on the local, state, and federal levels from this single afternoon in the Duke of Audley's life. While not as colorful as Magnum in the parlor with the evangelical kingpin, Silvers made some new friends and picked up some information about Hammond's patterns.

They knew that the Duke was born in Liverpool and raised by an aunt in London. His education stopped before the end of secondary school, but all of his jobs—from waiter and bartender, kitchen worker, grounds keeper, and laborer—were around the privileged. He got his first white-collar job at twenty-one when he used someone's name and Oxford education to con his way into a brokerage house.

After that, he simply picked the best name and education he could to get what he wanted. But his gift for larceny also began surfacing and, after a few run-ins with Scotland Yard, he headed for Paris. The trail ends there, but Paris police did question and release a young British nobleman whose address and title did not ultimately check out.

Hammond, separated from his wife who refused to talk about him, was known to favor very attractive women and his tastes reflected his social context. When he sailed, went skiing, deep-sea fishing, or on gambling junkets, he favored unchallenging bimbos. But when he moved among the wealthy, he always did so alone or with very well-educated, connected women. He was not known to have had any improper affairs in these circles.

Silvers toyed with more official documents saying, in effect, the government is very pissed off because Richard Peter Hammond jumped bail after promising he'd show up for court on the Rowlands case. More warrants attested to the Duke's next sting, a wealthy Frenchman. The United States of America charged this time that Richard Peter Hammond did (1) "devise and intend to devise a scheme and artifice to defraud and to obtain money and property by means of false and fraudulent pretenses, representations, and promises, namely, he did devise a scheme to obtain an advance fee of $950,000 from one Eugene Belliveau for purportedly obtaining, in the future, a loan of $95 million from Swiss interests; and that in connection therewith did place and cause to be placed in an authorized depository mail matter, all in violation of Title 18, United States Code, Section 1341; (2) did devise a scheme and artifice to defraud and to obtain money and property by means of false and fraudulent pretenses, representations, and promises, namely, to obtain the aforesaid advance fee, and to obtain monies from an escrow account of a corporation in which Richard Peter Hammond was president; and in connection therewith did transmit and cause to be transmitted by means of wire communications in interstate and foreign commerce . . ."

The sentence dragged on for more than twenty lines. It said, fundamentally, that the Duke offered Eugene Belliveau $95 million dollars at 8 percent interest when the prevailing rate was close to 20. Belliveau, who had made millions in resort real estate, bought the package because he had met the Duke socially, played tennis with him, played some serious baccarat at Monte Carlo, and had met several celebrities through him.

The two men shared a passion for Porsches, Rolex watches, clothes so richly textured as to be fashion souffles, soft leather shoes, tennis, polo, and sailing. They also liked women a lot. The Duke speaks seven languages, Belliveau five. Only after several weekends in Boston, the French Riviera, and St. Maarten, did Hammond intimate that an amalgam of Swiss financiers had authorized him to spread around over a billion dollars. He told Belliveau that the money came mainly from wealthy Central and South American families who were worried about the Sandinista military buildup and feared more Marxist revolutions. He also claimed to have oil connections in Kuwait, as many Londoners do.

Belliveau, who had been looking for cheap money to build a hotel complex and casino in Aruba, fell for it. There would, of course, be a $2 million returnable finder's fee, payable to a corporation in Switzerland. The Duke, it would turn out, was president of that corporation and as far as anyone could see, the only real officer. His brother Roger was an officeholder as was a woman who would eventually answer lots of questions by law enforcement people, but who seemed to be just a name on a piece of paper.

The $2 million was due only after Hammond delivered the loan by certified check, but a good faith deposit of $950,000 would be needed to close the deal. Belliveau transferred the money to the Swiss account. It was wired to a Cayman Islands account in the Duke's name the next day.

As remarkable as Silvers found the rip-off itself, what the Duke did next was enough to make Silvers look over his shoulder to be sure this guy wasn't in the same room, the way a kid hides under the blanket the night he sees a monster movie.

Belliveau does a lot of business in California and keeps a house in Bel Air. The Duke met him there, with two very attractive women, to celebrate the "deal." The $950,000 was already in the Cayman Islands by this time. They took a chartered private jet to Las Vegas where they were met by two stretch limos, one for the two couples, one for their baggage.

They spent the weekend gambling, and pretty much broke even, give or take five thousand dollars, depending on which report Silvers read. Hammond wanted to buy two of Belliveau's half dozen Porsches that he keeps stashed at his various houses.

"My friend, my friend," Belliveau said, "take them. They are yours."

The more Hammond protested, the more Belliveau insisted that he take not only the Porsches, but a ten thousand dollar Rolex watch and twenty thousand in cash for "expenses." A very red-faced Eugene Belliveau would later tell authorities that gentlemen understand gratitude. Hammond had expressed admiration for the cars and Belliveau had turned them over as a discreet, unspoken, additional finder's fee for the Duke's part in arranging the cheap money. The next day he called his attorneys to insist that shipment and paperwork be expedited immediately.

On the third day of their junket, Belliveau received a call from the concierge. The Duke had left a note saying that he had urgent business in New York, but that he would be back in a day or so. Meanwhile, he was sure a robust Frenchman would have no trouble keeping both women amused. The hotel and gambling markers would, of course, be on him.

The Duke did not return, the cars were shipped and picked up long before Belliveau knew he'd been had, the hotel bill and gambling markers were not covered, and there was a very concerned All-American type from an air charter service looking for the five thousand it had cost to fly four people to Vegas in a Cessna Citation, including Dom Perignon and Beluga caviar.

There seemed to be a problem with the certified check Mr. Hammond had given them as a deposit.

But Belliveau was still not concerned. His friend would settle with him later. He leisurely finished his holiday, concluded a few stateside deals, paid the bills, and returned to Paris. When he checked out the loan, he recognized the sting.

Silvers also had paperwork on the Duke's forged passports. He seemed to mint them. A couple was indicted in New Jersey for receiving "assorted jewelry and watches and two gold cigarette lighters together valued in excess of seventy-five thousand dollars, the property of Chez Oren in St. Maarten, Netherlands, Antilles, knowing it has been stolen or believing that it is probably stolen." There was also a gold-plated derringer pistol, all traceable to the Saturday night the Duke talked Oren Deiter, the shop's owner, into opening so he could surprise his girlfriend with a few gifts. He paid by check.

In Rio, Hammond was something close to a national scandal. He had spent several weeks charming people and putting together deals. Down there, he had used what Barry came to know as the Sandinista sting, convincing people of his authorization to spread large sums of money from wealthy Central Americans eager to get their cash into stable economies.

Silvers had newspapers from Rio translated from Portuguese to English:

PHONY BRITISH DUKE LEAVES HOTEL BILL UNPAID

DUKE OF FRAUD LEAVES RIO IN THE NIGHT

PRINCE CHARLES'S 'POLO PARTNER' EXPOSED AS FAKE

Rio was the natural turf of the Duke of Audley. The wealth, excess, and severe social structure was ripe for the arrival, in a borrowed private jet, of a consort of British royalty. The Duke got himself into the top rungs of the social pecking order by using contacts in the British Embassy. Soon, he was a daily item in the society columns as a polo-playing buddy of Prince Charles who fed the press's constant hunger for Royal Family anecdotes. He described Diana as "temperamental but a wonderful dancer" and Lady Sarah as the "funniest lady I ever met, a lot more fun than Diana." That the Duke of Audley had been no closer to Eton or Oxford than the average Queens bus driver, had probably never exchanged a word with Charles, and certainly had not flown with Prince Andrew in the Falkland Islands War—a piece of the résumé of great interest to local reporters—would not be known until after he left.

The Duke didn't limit himself to the extremely wealthy. A smaller version of the Eugene Belliveau sting took place in West Palm Beach. This time, Hammond had promised a gas station owner a $750,000 loan at cheap interest for a muffler franchise. All he wanted in return was a $25,000 finder's fee plus a Porsche the man owned. He showed up on a Friday, collected his finder's fee in cash, gave the man a certified check for $750,000 too late in the day for any banking transactions, and sold the Porsche. The gas station owner had a very bad, very long Monday.

Then there was the case of Mrs. Sagamore and her jewels. Amanda Sagamore had spent her life among the very rich, rarely looking up to, or down on, anyone. The sixty-two-year-old widow kept homes in New York, Los Angeles, and Palm Beach. She knew everyone.

She had met Hammond through a friend of his, a genuine earl whose family she'd known all her life. One night Hammond had invited her to dinner in New York to discuss a deal he was putting together, a plan that he'd promised would return 50 percent on her investment in less than a year. Having never quite believed this so-called Duke of Audley, Mrs. Sagamore brought along a male friend. Hammond hadn't liked that, but behaved graciously enough through dinner and later in the VIP Room of one of the hot downtown clubs where there were no celebrities that night, but plenty of well-heeled young hangers-on who greeted the Duke like he was Mick Jagger himself.

Back at the hotel, there was a sticky moment when Hammond insisted on accompanying Mrs. Sagamore to her suite where the two would finally sit down to talk about the business "opportunity." The male friend came along even though the Duke insisted that it was a confidential matter. Once inside the suite, three masked gunmen came from the bathroom and tied them up. They took about 750,000 worth of jewelry from a box that Mrs. Sagamore had decided not to leave in the hotel vault. They also broke the wrist of the friend as they handcuffed him to the bed.

The Duke, also handcuffed, took command of the television reporters when they showed up, issuing terse "no comments," and saying that they would have to speak to their attorneys before any statements could be made regarding "our losses." Mrs. Sagamore was convinced she was set up by Hammond and now wanted her jewels back. They had never been adequately insured. She was paying $100,000 for their safe return. Mrs. Sagamore had her own private investigator on the job. Silvers had met him on the trail of the Duke and they'd arranged a swap. Mrs. Sagamore's P.I. would interview Barry's client and he would go to Palm Beach to see the wealthy socialite. Both clients had, of course, agreed to the arrangement.

Silvers will say only that his client is very wealthy, and was stiffed in a royal style consistent with the Duke's MO. He wanted Silvers to go where the Duke went, talk to as many of his victims as possible, cooperate with the battalion of police and P.I.'s already looking for him, and dig up as much evidence as possible.

The client did not care if the Duke went to jail for attempting to swindle Sidney Rowlands, for stealing Mrs. Sagamore's jewels, for ripping off the gas station owner, or for stinging the jet-setters in Rio. Silvers could, as far as his client was concerned, turn up or fail to turn up anything brand-new on the guy.

The client wanted Richard Peter Hammond in jail, period. That would take some doing. Aside from scrapes with Scotland Yard when he was a kid, the Duke had not, as far as anyone knew, even seen the inside of a precinct house. But he has plenty of time, Silvers thought. Richard Peter Hammond, the Duke of Audley, was not yet thirty-two.

12

Detectives, police and private, hear the tick of a weird clock. It runs on adrenaline. When a work alarm goes off, they answer. Time, as the rest of us know it, means nothing until they finish the case. They are up for days, then not at all. They miss dinner, prom pictures, anniversaries, birthdays, and even the IRS can wait if they're on a hot case.

They need the sanity of the civilians they marry or live with. It's reassuring that someone near them gets to bed at the same time every night and knows what the next day will be like, because they sure as hell do not. It's part of the rush. They need stability around them a lot more than their loved ones, who nevertheless take the chimes of the adrenaline clock as a threat close to infidelity, and who do not need the bullshit of their loved ones running off like firemen with their pants at half-mast to look after someone else.

Louis Gloskin called Vinny the afternoon after their office meeting. Sarah had told him she was going shopping that night and would he mind watching the kids.

"I'm just closing up here, Louis," Vinny said. "If I can find someone to go with me, I'll pick her up, but you don't want to ever do a car surveillance at night without someone with you. Ideally, we should even have two cars. What time is she leaving?"

"Eight o'clock. Right after the dinner dishes are done."

"You home now?"

"Yes."

"Where's she? She can't hear you, I hope."

"No, she's upstairs."

"Okay, but I'm not going to call you until later, after she leaves. We'll see what she does."

"If you can't find someone to go with you?"

"I'll call you either way, Louis."

He hung up and dialed Maximum Security's extension. No one there. His own field people were gone and he was about to give up when Marla Paul stopped in after a field assignment in New Jersey.

"Marla," Parco said. "Remember Louis, who was in here yesterday?"

"Of course I remember, Vincent. It was only yesterday."

"I need you to go with me on a night surveillance."

"Tonight? I have a date."

"Any way you can tell the guy you'll meet him later. It shouldn't take long."

"How long's not long?"

"A couple of hours."

"Okay," she said. "Since this is my case anyway." The adrenaline clock ticked again.

Old-timers remember the forties and fifties when a divorce case *was* adultery and meant giving the desk clerk at the motel a five for the master key or actually kicking the door in as soon as the panting and gasping told them the time was right. Then, as the woman screamed and the man danced toward his pants, the team of P.I.'s, often three strong, bombarded the couple with flashbulbs. There was usually one big guy in the party whose job was to carry the equipment, hand his cohorts fresh flashbulbs, and kick the man in the groin when he charged the cameras.

The little makeshift darkrooms that served the trade often printed out extra eight-by-tens that the P.I.'s used to amuse their friends. Crotches, breasts, the man running for his pants, and the woman screaming were always good for a howl at parties, or just when guys got together for a belt at the end of the day.

The no-fault divorce law that New York State passed in 1980 was supposed to eliminate the keyhole peeping and the humiliation of adultery as grounds for divorce. But with no-fault came the equitable distribution statute that grants a less solvent spouse a shot at half the total assets accumulated during the marriage.

Contested money usually means a contested divorce for which there must be grounds; cruel and inhuman treatment, abandonment, or adultery, the easiest of the three to prove. All the court really needs is proof of opportunity and inclination for infidelity. The judge doesn't need the old-style horror shots, but it helps to have pictures or video of a couple going into a motel and coming out a couple of hours later.

Parco knew that the adultery cycle was on his side. Joel and Sarah were in what he calls the "prebullshit, hunky-dory stage," and more apt to run directly to a motel. If they stuck together, the affair would eventually take the form of a minimarriage with all the aches, pains, and complaints of a human relationship. More than once in a while, a matrimonial surveillance, at a hundred fifty or more an hour for a team, turns into sitting in a restaurant and listening to two people demand more from each other.

"And the only opportunity and inclination we're going to see on one of those nights is the opportunity and inclination for two people to be a pain in the ass to each other," Parco says.

"Sometimes they even realize that they're better-off at home, especially when they find out they might have picked an even bigger jerk to screw around with than the one they were with in the first place. We see a lot of that."

Speaking of relationships, he thought, it was time for something even harder than a night car surveillance alone. It was time to tell his wife he would be late again.

He dialed his home number and winced as he said, "I have a last minute matrimonial, honey. There's no one around to do it."

He waited and moved the receiver a little away from his ear. Carol Parco was having periodontal work done and the news that her husband would be out for the third night in a row was not welcome.

"Carol, if there was anyone here who could do it, I'd say, 'Hey, you do it,' but it's me. It's right around Whitestone somewhere, it shouldn't take me any time at all to do it. Listen, I'm already running late . . ."

He hung up and figured he'd make it up to her tomorrow night, maybe surprise her with flowers. Matrimonial cases make detectives painfully aware of the vulnerabilities in their own relationships.

Marla followed Vinny's 1985 Buick Riviera in her 1979 Chevrolet Monte Carlo, known around the agency by various names including "the Dumpster On Wheels," "Marla's Dream," and, most commonly, "the AntiCrime Unit." Paul is always meticulously dressed, coiffed, and made up so carefully that a smudge would be taken by those who know her as a sign of something seriously gone wrong in her life. The AntiCrime Unit, however, seems to function as an alter ego.

The ashtrays flow so far over their rims that every bump produces a shower of cinders and lipstick smudged filters. In the backseat are coffee cups, panty hose, a briefcase, copies of deeds, election rolls, real estate surveys, and other documents from her constant trips to the outer boroughs and New Jersey to mine the bureaucracies. Vinny Parco thinks Jimmy Hoffa is back there somewhere trying to find his way out.

He gunned the Riviera through the last of the rush hour traffic, weaving the big car through small spaces with the grace of an Indy pro. He knew Marla Paul would not have a problem following him. Like the little Nash Rambler that followed a Cadillac all the way to 120 miles an hour in the 1950s song, the faster he went, the easier it seemed for her to keep up.

Parco found Louis Gloskin's house in Whitestone without much trouble. The house was a white colonial with black shutters. Parco passed the place, turned the corner, and parked on the next block. Marla pulled in behind him. He got out, walked over to her and said, "Let's ditch this, this . . ."

"AntiCrime Unit," she said.

"Yeah, right. Let's hide it before it gets us arrested. I'll wait. Drive around and park it somewhere with other cars on the street."

"What if she leaves? We'll lose her."

"We won't lose her. She's not leaving for ten minutes, at least. Louis's going to keep her there till eight. Go."

She found a street with a lot of cars on it, parked, and was back in five minutes. She and Vinny parked on a side street where they could get a view of Sarah Gloskin's car as it passed, but under a tree where she would be unlikely to notice them. They could see the Gloskin's driveway if they craned their necks.

"Nice house," Marla said. "I forget what this guy does."

"Plumbing supply, makes a nice living, Marla. He should be on the market pretty soon. Nice young Jewish guy, Marla."

"Sorry, not my type."

"And what's your type?"

"Handsome, extremely rich, and Jewish. I can live without the handsome and Jewish if I have to."

"Here we go."

Gloskin's garage door opened and Sarah's Grand Am backed out.

"That's our lady," Parco said. He waited while the car passed, stopped at the corner and turned before he hit the ignition. Then, with a screech of rubber that could be heard all the way back in Manhattan, he floored the Buick. Adrenaline, the biggest high, and maybe the biggest hazard of the detective business, was doing its thing.

Vincent Parco, no fan of car surveillance, did not like what he was seeing. Sarah Gloskin was driving a zigzag pattern through her own neighborhood, up one street, down another. If Parco followed her, she'd make him.

"I don't care for this at all," he said, more to himself than Marla. When Sarah turned a corner, he'd wait, inching the Riviera up the block and turning slowly as her taillights disappeared around a corner. Then he'd gun it up the block so fast that his car reared up like a horse, slowing down again to creep around and see what the hell was going on.

"Screw this," he said. "You either do these things right or you don't do them at all. If she keeps dicking around, we go home."

Clients don't like to hear about doing it right because it's expensive. They think tailing someone means wearing sunglasses and following the target a couple of car lengths behind or a little to the right in the driver's blind spot. What it really means is having two vehicles and two teams in contact by mobile phone, and it doesn't hurt if one of them is a van, a truck, or a station wagon with grandma and the kids in it. One team stays ahead of the target car, one hangs back, and they switch off.

Agencies that do a lot of night tails use cars or vans with custom switch panels that can turn any outside light on or off. Cars with a single headlight become fully functioning vehicles with all lights intact. Up front, a car with a single taillight disappears and reappears fully lighted. In daylight, the teams wear wigs, sunglasses, baseball hats, or any kind of uniform. Priest and nun outfits are not unheard of.

One of the agency's bumper beepers would help right now too, Parco thought, but their use is restricted in New York State. A bumper beeper, or vehicle locator, is a battery-powered transmitter with a huge magnet that bonds it to the underside of the target vehicle and sends directional signals to the chase car. From a mile or more back, the team can see a digital readout of the target's direction and speed. When he parks, they can usually home in on the signal at their own unhurried pace.

The shrewdest surveillances, be they foot or vehicular, occur in front of the target, which is why P.I. try to know the moves of their subjects well ahead of time. People are creatures of habit. If a target stops at the same newsstand every morning, it makes more sense to pick him up there. If he takes the on-ramp of a parkway at 8:15 and passes a rest area at 8:18, the detective will be there at 7:30. When the target is lost, the operative simply hurries to the next way station on his route. Even the most suspicious do not expect to be tailed from the front.

Parco shook his head. He had set out to follow an Orthodox Jewish housewife and ended up playing Smokey and the freaking bandit. He wasn't, goddamn it, going to risk getting caught by staying behind her.

"I'll pick her up out on the boulevard," he said, as he sped up and backtracked through the development to Queens Boulevard where he stopped outside a liquor store. If his instincts were correct and her eventual destination was one of the motels out toward the airport, she would pass this way in a few minutes. He was right. The Grand Am came down the boulevard leisurely, and Parco was ready to bet that Sarah was confident that she was not being followed.

"We've got her ass now. She doesn't think anyone's on her. Look at her. My mother drives faster than that."

Parco passed Sarah and stayed two car lengths ahead, where he could see the Grand Am in the mirror. Marla watched too, with an occasional glance over her shoulder. When they slowed for traffic at a red light, she passed them and turned into a parking lot near a Caldor's store.

"Vinny, she's turning in," Marla said.

"I see her, no problem," Parco said. He made no effort to pull into the lot, but turned left into a Burger King on the opposite side of the boulevard, and parked the Riviera next to a large recreational vehicle for cover.

"Watch the road," he said as he threw open the door. The chase was over for tonight. Parco, like most P.I.'s, adheres to the principle of progressive surveillance, where the investigator follows the target in graduated distances on different days, never too much at one time. It looked like he'd found Sarah's rendezvous point without being spotted. He'd pick it up from here next time.

He could see Sarah's Pontiac stopped way off to the side with a vantage point of the whole parking lot. No other cars were parked near her. If he'd followed her in or stopped to look for her in there, she would have been able to see him. Score one for me, he thought. But what made this bitch so suspicious?

About five minutes later, a Toyota showed up, she got in it and they sped off. Parco couldn't get a look at the license plate or the driver, but it didn't matter. He probably already had all of Joel's vehicles in the file.

Inside the Burger King, Marla ordered a Whopper and some fries and Vinny gloomily picked at salad.

"Screw this," he said. "I want a Whopper."

"Get one," Marla said.

"If you insist. I'll be right back." He was a much happier man when he returned with the huge burger, fries, and a milk shake.

"So, Vinny, how come she was driving so paranoid? Are people always that suspicious?"

"No, they're not, so you know what I'm thinking, don't you?"

"Ray?"

"It may be nothing, but we've got to check."

It was happening more and more in Parco's practice and, at the monthly meetings of the SPI, the Society of Professional Investigators, people said that it was happening all over the business. Louis Gloskin, who had taken the step of hiring a detective agency to watch his wife, was possibly the target of a surveillance himself. And Vinny Parco was starting to think it wasn't a legal one. Sarah was driving as if she expected to be followed. Vinny would have to ask Ray Melucci to check Louis's house and office for bugs.

13

It was time to bring a rapist home. Wherever Everett Thomas Lang was, he was probably settled, and that was good for Peter Castillo. Comfortable is complacent and complacency is a bounty hunter's best friend. Not so wonderful was that he was somewhere out of state, unlikely to be using credit, getting mail, or driving in his own name. But Castillo knew he'd get him. Like all good P.I.'s, he knows the ABCs of missing-persons work.

The term itself is impressive cocktail party fodder. People move closer to eavesdrop when they hear, "I do a lot of missing-persons work." However, there is no cloak, dagger, or call for mystique if missing-persons work is done right. It is a painstaking, molasses-paced game of chess that would never play in prime time.

Broadly, the missing-persons field divides into two categories. There are those who don't mind being found and those who do. The high school flame now living in a three-bedroom ranch house in Joplin, Missouri, after a hippie period, a stint in the Peace Corps, and two years in Paris is the easy kind. A productive hour could do it. The other category—the skipper who left because of bad debts, the bail jumper, or the runaway spouse living under a new name—is trickier. Finding that person is called a locate, or skip trace.

Criminals are canny survivors. That's one point for them. But they give back that point because they tend to be acutely unhappy in unfamiliar surroundings. They don't easily drop into a new community and they have a hard time staying away from other criminals. When they skip, they get caught because they head right for a friend, girlfriend, cell mate, or relative. Vinny Parco puts it another way. "They're stupid," he says.

Like the bounty hunters of the old west, Peter Castillo knew his quarry well by the time he was ready to start the chase. He'd studied Lang's family, checked his mother's maiden name, tracked the married names of sisters, and kept a careful watch on Lang's friends.

The friends were mostly uninspired, uninspiring working guys in their midtwenties who smoked pot, lived with their parents, hung out at bars. A couple had minor criminal records. Castillo did not try to gag or interview them directly, preferring instead to move among them freely in quiet corners of their hangouts, watching as they shot pool and played video games.

He knew that Lang's nickname was Tommy, an easy name to listen for in the noise of a bar. A television investigator would probably say, "Hey, where's Tommy been keeping himself?" or "Where's that ole slimeball Tommy? Guy bet against the Redskins and I want my twenty bucks." Instead, Castillo just blended into the bar, probably never even noticed in the dim light. He didn't hear much.

On a television show, Castillo's problem would be milked for its drama. One good man looking for one bad man hidden somewhere out there in the fifty states, who knows where? How would he, how could he do it, when the odds were two hundred million to one?

In fact, Castillo had fifty or sixty good options, and at least a thousand other tried and true skip trace techniques. The hunted is the one up against the bad odds.

Castillo chose an old and very reliable investigative trick that delivers financial data, listed and unlisted phone numbers, clues to sex habits, personal tastes, alcohol consumption, employment information, indications of prescription and illegal drug use, income, and hundreds of other leads. It was Monday night, garbage night at the Langs.

From Jack Anderson, who tweaked J. Edgar Hoover by reporting the contents of his trash coast to coast, to the CIA, everyone who investigates anyone knows that a Hefty Bag on a Monday night can produce more good information than bales of night vision lenses, surveillance vans, informants, infinity bugs, and all the other exotica that feed the mystique of the private investigator.

A garbage bag is a vivid, if soggy, résumé. If there are three used condoms, there's a piece of the sex life. An empty Valium bottle or a Baggie with twigs and seeds is a signpost to drug use. A check stub tells how much Dad gets paid. People throw away their Mastercard and Visa information, complete with the right toll-free number in case the P.I. has any questions about the charges. American Express, Diner's Club, and Carte Blanche are even nicer. They print it all out in letter quality.

If garbage is curbed, searching through it is legal. On May 16, 1988, the Supreme Court ruled that the police may freely search through garbage bags and other refuse containers that people leave outside their home for collection. The decision reinforced the rulings of lower state and federal courts. In his opionion for the majority, Justice Byron R. White held that the privacy of garbage bags is not protected by the Fourth Amendment because there is no "subjective expectation of privacy in their garbage," because, "it is common knowledge that plastic garbage bags left on or at the side of a public street are readily accessible to animals, children, scavengers, snoops, and other members of the public." Searches, claimed the court, can be conducted without a warrant and without any reason to suspect criminal activity.

In this instance, it was both curbed and legal. Castillo looked up and down the block until he found a neighbor who had put out a bag matching the Langs' in bulk, texture, and color. He slowly walked to the neighbor's house, picked up the sack, made his substitution, and took the Lang's garbage home.

Missing-persons work, like everything else in the investigative business, is a superhuman focus on the obvious. The answer, the big eureka, is probably right in front of the investigator, but the obvious clues are the hardest to see. The novice finds the work similar to searching for something in every old trunk, every dark corner of the house, only to find that it's been on the coffee table all along. A professional trains himself to start at the coffee table.

The freewheeling, and largely unchecked, passage of data from one source to another and the use of that information, especially in the private sector, raises major questions that many believe to be the twentieth century's last great constitutional battle.

The typical American citizen appears in thirty-nine federal, state, and local data bases and forty private sector files. On any given day, every individual in the United States can expect his name to pass from one computer to another five times, despite the Privacy Act of 1974, a post-Watergate remedy enacted to restrict access to our government files.

The Privacy Act is weighed down with loopholes and exceptions, from the CIA and congressional access, to Freedom of Information Act requests, and the Reagan Administration's generous use of its "national security" stamp. It is also so far behind the technological explosion that followed its passage that it now has the teeth of a "do not remove" tag on a pillow.

The labyrinthine federal telecommunications network feeds, and intersects with, a fiber-optic interstate system of data traveling at the speed of light to God knows who and where. In her 1987 book, *Crimewarps*, anthropologist and journalist Georgette Bennett points out that the Congressional Office of Technology Assessment has identified eighty-five computerized law enforcement investigative and intelligence systems which hold 288 million records on 114 million individuals. The FBI's National Crime Information Center computer services sixty-four thousand criminal justice agencies and processes about 400,000 information requests a day.

There are 20 million names in police computer files and another 40 million listed manually. This information is officially not available to P.I.'s, but, since most of them are part of the cop fraternity, it's no big stretch.

The NCIC data base and its interfacing cousins in other agencies are notorious sources of computer age horror stories. A woman couldn't get a government job. When she pressed in for the reason, she found out that a teacher in the fourth grade had conjectured, on the basis of hearsay, that the woman's family was "crazy."

Shirley Jones of New Orleans applied to become a foster parent and got arrested twice because the computer said she committed theft and forgery, which she had not. A California man was arrested and hauled back into the Marines who said he was absent without leave. Seven years after he was legally discharged, he spent five months in custody before the mistake was corrected.

Excesses such as these are legion and certainly not philosophical battle lines. No one wants them, or even wants to think of them as an acceptable side effect of progress.

The social security number, or SSN as it is called, has become what the founding fathers of the Social Security Administration feared most. It is an emblazoned brand on our hides, a national tattoo that never goes away once in place. It is a military ID, a student number, a medical insurance number, a credit and tax number, a criminal file number, a department store charge number and, by the end of the century, it may even be a phone number. It will certainly continue to be the prime unit of American identification, and available to anyone with access to a legal data base.

Information processors sell P.I.'s a computerized "social scan," which prints out employment, medical, credit, and other information glued to the social security number. A social scan, which costs a client between seventy-five and five hundred dollars, is one of the big legal bargains in the information marketplace.

We may not give out our phone number or our home address, but we usually accommodate anyone who asks for our social security number. Every time we scribble it on an application or questionnaire, or unconsciously hand it over to some anonymous source, the SSN gets printed out and stored where a thousand faceless clerks swarm over it like bugs on spilled food. The target has no idea of his visibility through the SSN, but the P.I. looking for a missing person follows its trail as easily as he reads the morning paper.

The number itself is often a giveaway. SSNs are coded according to the locale of a person's application. If the first three digits are 001-003, the target once lived in New Hampshire. If it's 577-579, the person first applied for his working papers in Washington, D.C. There's probably a wealth of paper and old friends in the region.

A social scan will lead an investigator to his target's occupation. Even drifters tend to do the same thing from state to state. People may run away but they don't like to enter a new line of work. If a target worked construction in New York, he's probably going to do it in Idaho. If he's a union member, he'll keep his card. Executives are found in executive guides, lawyers through bar associations. There are thousands of trade and professional journals, directories, executive guides, various *Who's Who* publications. Most investigators who do missing-persons work are familiar with the thousands of listings in the *Directory of Associations,* or the *Directory of Directories.* P.I.'s frequently get requests from adults who want to see old teachers. They're listed with the National Education Association or state teacher's organizations.

Virtually anyone with any skill is trackable through his professional or trade group.

From registered nurses to registered airplanes, there is a computer service for every purpose under heaven. Court records, credit, professional associations, what's what in fluid engineering, yellow pages ads—there are five thousand data bases available to anyone with the subscription or processing fee. There are research services, such as Disclosure Incorporated of Washington, D.C., which are so thorough that they start punching up the answer before the client even finds the phraseology for the question. When decades of accumulated information is available at the tap of an access code, the layers the target thinks surround him turn out to be as make-believe as movie props.

High school, that mushy emotional core where we treaded into the dangerous waters of adulthood for the first time, is Disney World to a skip tracer. Yearbooks can be found in any library, complete with a whole italicized rundown of young Bobby's passions and activities. There's a wonderful chance the reunion committee knows exactly where he is. College alumni associations, in business to keep up with graduates, are also a big help in tracking missing persons.

Mediocre detectives look like miracle workers to their clients because they can pull off a sleight of hand with public document searches. They can watch a blonde hop into a car, dial up the agency, and, if she owns that car, come up with her name, address, phone number, who owns the property where she lives, where she shops, how much she spends a month, and when her license will expire.

They can call for this information from a car phone at a red light and, if the apparatus of the agency is oiled, have it all by the next red light. The "magic" is a routine motor vehicle check done with a DMV data base, a property scan from another computer, and a credit check.

Once they find a phone number, P.I.'s can come up with a whole song and dance about its owner in seconds by using the Big Daddy of cross reference publications, *Cole's Directory. Cole's* is a telephone directory in reverse. The P.I. looks up the phone number and gets his target's name and address. If the only information available is a street address, *Cole's* provides a name and phone number to go with it. *Cole's* also provides a thumbnail economic rating of the target's neighborhood, a listing of other tenants at the same address if a target lives in an apartment, and a listing, plot by plot, of the whole street, who lives on each parcel of land, and the year they probably moved in.

If a *Cole's* client—a P.I., librarian, telemarketing firm, bank, or whatever—needs information from another region, he or she can call the company's toll-free number and an operator at the company's Lincoln, Nebraska, headquarters will look up the information either as part of the annual subscription or for a nominal fee.

There are many good cross reference directories, maps, old phone books, and surveys which a sharp public document diver can use to recreate any community a target lived in at the time he lived there. Somewhere on the trail, probably in a dozen or more places, is a date and place of birth. Once a P.I. has that, he need only head for the county clerk's office for a copy of the birth certificate. Anyone can do it.

Birth certificates list mother and father, occupation of each, and the doctor who delivered the baby. He probably grew up in one town, and spent the bulk of his elementary school years on a single block where there is almost always some very elderly and talkative individual who not only remembers the skipper, but what he wore on the first day of school.

Marriage certificates, also available for a small fee at the county recorder or county clerk's office in most states, reveal a woman's maiden name, along with the date and place of birth, occupations, and blood types of the happy couple. They also provide witnesses who are, often enough, good friends who are still in touch. Chances are, there's an article about the wedding and the reception mentioning the names of the whole wedding party.

Newspaper microfilm, not one of the big draws on television, is gold on a missing-persons case. Everyone makes the paper sometime. Once a P.I. isolates the place where the target grew up, there's usually a cooperative person in the paper's morgue who will help find the little telltale squibs that can close a case.

Hobbies and quirks pay big dividends. Castillo was once able to find a missing child because the kidnapping parent had only one possession that he treasured, a 1957 Chevrolet. Having owned one himself, Castillo knew that the car would not be very far from the parent, even if the parent changed his name. Through the car's vehicle identification number and a search from a commercial firm, Castillo tracked it to Peekskill, New

York, where it was registered under the new name of the parent and child.

Magnum would find the target washing the Chevy one Saturday. Castillo drove by it at least a dozen times as he cruised Peekskill. The car was garaged and covered, but the child was in school, and the father back at his old construction trade, doing what he always did. Castillo found the missing child in the school nearest the job site.

In most states, Department of Motor Vehicle records are public. They provide the most recent address of an individual, plus some important physical information such as eye color, hair color, height, weight, and whether the target needs glasses to drive. Alcohol and drug problems often show up in a person's driving record. If they have several suspensions for driving while intoxicated or impaired, there is a clue. The DMV may solve more missing-persons cases than any other source.

State motor vehicle departments keep track of 126 million registered automobiles and 152 million licensed drivers. Most of this information is legally up for grabs and is a source of revenue for many state governments.

Besides P.I.'s, who thrive on DMV information, the Selective Service goes to the state motor vehicle well to check for males between eighteen and twenty-four who have not registered for the draft. Private list brokers and market research firms often find it a lot cheaper to buy DMV lists than to update their own. Consumers, after all, are far more honest about their whereabouts when filling out a form for a state agency, then they would be if questioned by a private firm, especially when they think the state is above peddling their names to commercial interests.

If Tommy Lang had had a history of motor vehicle violations, Castillo could have checked him out through the National Driver Register Service, a data base maintained by the Department of Commerce to keep tabs on drivers who have lost a license in one state, then applied in another. The information is public.

The IRS purchases professional marketing lists of upscale households to match against the economic information on their own taxpayer rolls.

Medical information—detailed accounting of our most private health matters—is an open book to anyone who wants it. The insurance industry, the main employer for P.I.'s, maintains detailed medical files on 12 million individuals, listing hospital stays, doctor visits, illnesses, surgery, and injuries.

In the unlikely event that a P.I. could not get medical information from insurance sources, there's always hospital personnel. In 1984 a physician at the University of Chicago's Billings Hospital was confronted by a patient upset at the number of employees with access to his chart. The doctor decided to count, but gave up when he got to seventy-five employees. The only way to avoid this warehousing of our most intimate health affairs is to check in under an assumed name and pay in cash.

If Lang was foreign-born, Castillo could have traced him through the Department of Immigration and Naturalization which provides good information when the P.I. knows the language of the system and how to fill out forms.

Postal clerks may scowl, but they have to provide forwarding addresses which are kept in a binder called the "removal book" for two years. After that, only the most persuasive P.I.—preferably one with a discreetly folded bill—can get a clerk to dig out the record, if, indeed, it still exists.

The United States District Court is packed with records of mail fraud, stock listings, bankruptcy, tax liens, and other government action. The Securites and Exchange Commission is a valuable pocket of information on public companies, complete with biographies of their principals. Regulatory agencies, such as the FCC and FAA, have their own exams and licenses that people don't like to see expire. A commercial pilot with instrument, multiengine, and jet ratings, for example, has a license of such value that he's likely to keep it current.

Voting records are public. If a person votes, he is listed by address and party affiliation. This information is a big part of Vincent Parco's practice where so much of the work is proving or disproving residency.

Parco also makes extensive use of the Uniform Commercial Code. A UCC filing includes home improvement loans, liens against property, car loans, and other data. The filing provides a name, address, the name of a bank, and data about big ticket items such as boats.

P.I.'s don't like to talk about it, but they can also find someone's tax information. Returns, those sacred pacts between citizen and government, couldn't be more public if they were published in the *New York Times*. Rare is the P.I. who would bribe an IRS or state official for tax information, but rare too is the P.I. who doesn't know where to look if he wants an unofficial peek. If someone on public assistance needs psychotherapy, the fee is probably based on a sliding scale according to income. If the client wants that therapy, or medical help, dental treatment, prescription drugs, food stamps, or a hundred other items, he must provide a tax return. No return, no benefits.

A self-employed individual shows his tax return when he takes a mortgage or applies for a credit card. Lending institutions also require it to prove that the joint income of a married couple is enough to pay back the loan on a condo, whether they are self-employed or not. Returns are Photostated, stored in computer banks, filed in unlocked drawers, left on top of desks, and passed from committee member to committee member all afternoon long as the fate of student loans and scholarships is decided. The tax return is in the hands of a thousand clerks, and is therefore vulnerable to unauthorized scrutiny. The IRS itself is bound by law to share information with thirty-eight government offices.

As Castillo went through the Lang's garbage, he put aside a monthly phone bill, a pivotal document in private investigation. One of the first items a detective gets when he is hired by a spouse is a printout of toll calls. He then tells the client to request a documentation of all local calls, which a spouse, whose last name is on the bill, can do legally. Calls tell so many tales that the investigator can almost hear the conversation as he scans the monthly bill.

Every number is a story—a business call, a call to a doctor's office, a long-winded call to a member of the opposite sex who is not a spouse. With a call and its length, the P.I. can plug a lot of holes in a case.

Unlisted and unpublished numbers are in constant demand from clients. Such requests are often nothing more than a seedy power trip that even the most marginally ethical P.I.'s despise. An estranged spouse or lover wants to be free of some creep, so she changes her number to a nonpub. That night he's on the phone. She changes it, he's on the phone again. She calls the phone company, they say they'll investigate, and that night . . .

There are two types of confidential phone numbers. Unlisted numbers show no acknowledgment of service. Where most phone company employees are concerned, the target doesn't exist. Directory assistance will not show it. Unpublished numbers are listed, but not given out. The techniques for getting these numbers are like one's recipe for chili; everyone in the business has some secret way of doing it that he'd rather die than share. Some, but not all, methods, are illegal.

Primitive as it is, there is bribery. Where there are employees, there is greed. Graft will probably always be there, especially in the new companies whose security apparatus is not as sharp as AT&T.

Illegal trespass where an operative pretends he's in the phone company, is common. The game is played like a kid's novel with the phone company as the huge cave, illegal information as the treasure, and the operative as the Hardy Boys or Nancy Drew. There are dozens of secret entrances and exits in the form of provisions for passing information from division to division, and employee to employee: "Hi, DeePac [the installer's private data base], this is Sacramento CNA [Central Names and Addresses]. I need one [a telephone number] on a 202 [Washington area code]. That's you, right? Name is Thomas, R.D., 492 Central."

The network is too huge to keep its inside numbers and access codes a secret. The breakup of AT&T resulted in a nightmarish disbursement of confidential numbers into smaller, and far less secure, phone companies. Resourceful information thieves can leapfrog over the elaborate AT&T security apparatus and pluck unlisted numbers like berries from offices of the smaller firms. They pretend they're installers, repair personnel, customers, or others with a need to know. If they call for information on an inside number, supposedly known only to employees, the operators will cooperate. It's not legal, but it's done.

A safer, legal, way is to take a very large sponge to the many places where people spill their numbers. Necessity dictates giving them to friends, physicians, schools, and other places P.I.'s know how to find. One simple subterfuge is to use *Cole's* to find a neighbor, then call with a gag.

"Hey, sorry to bother you. This is Gary from I. Leonard Furriers, and Mrs. Burton gave you as an alternate number in case anything happened with her mink. I'm afraid I have some bad news . . ."

The true art of subterfuge is not extracting information but getting someone to beg you to take it.

Some P.I.'s get their numbers from security itself. The P.I. is probably a former cop. So is the security person. Many cops and former cops have friends in the phone company. Enough said.

Any phone company must provide the name of a party whose number appears on a customer's bill. If a P.I. has a number known to be unpublished, he can call it on his own phone. If he can't talk the person he calls into disclosing his or her name, he can wait until the end of the month and the phone company is obligated to tell him. It's legal.

Whether they use legal or illegal means, P.I.'s can always get unpublished numbers. So can organized crime, the police, government agencies, debt collectors, con artists, journalists, and anyone else who wants to call up a target.

Seven commercial credit bureaus hold files on 150 million private citizens. The Fair Credit Reporting Act of 1971 was set up to protect the rights of access to a credit file, the right to correct errors, and present the consumer's side of a disputed issue. A check and a letterhead are all it usually takes to get information whose accuracy is always an open question.

TRW, one of the largest repositories of credit information, maintains files on more than 120 million Americans. Retail Credit Company, Inc., with over 50 million files, supplies back fence gossip with its credit ratings. If one or two neighbors tells one of its six thousand or so field investigators that someone smokes marijuana or drinks too much, it can easily creep into a report. Employers frequently use credit reports, especially those with a little gossip, to assess a job applicant.

The use of credit reports by detectives is a sketchy area. Some credit bureaus consider P.I.'s competition and don't take them on as subscribers. In New York, P.I.'s are kept away from credit reports except where there is a probability of litigation. They also are not permitted to act as collection agents, which is not the case in many other states.

Of the 4 million people who ask to see their TRW reports annually, 350,000 challenge the reports and either get them changed or make notations in their files. The credit reporting agencies, according to Robert Ellis Smith, editor of *Privacy Journal* "have a poor reputation for maintaining the accuracy of their information."

The unchecked proliferation of personal information is a growing source of alarm to all philosophical factions. The American

Civil Liberties Union and the National Rifle Association have both been vocal on the erosion of privacy in the computer age. To now, the gap between exploding technology and snail-paced legal progress has given P.I.'s and security people a wide berth to operate without breaking the law. But civil libertarians, after a long public eclipse in the Reagan Era, are tanned, rested, and ready to change the laws and draw blood over privacy issues. The nation's private cops, and the sworn officers as well, have a little rain coming on their parade according to Richard Emery, a ten-year veteran of the New York Civil Liberties Union. He sees privacy challenges as *the* major issue of the 1990s as legal battles over information usage heat up.

"Privacy will be redefined in the next decade," he says, "and P.I.'s are right in the center of the most crucial domestic legal issues of our time."

The information war will be fought in the leathery chambers of state legislatures and the Supreme Court, issue by constitutional issue, as the very definition of privacy is redrawn for a new century.

The Constitution does not even mention the word. Articles IV, V, VIII, and IX of the Bill of Rights address various implications of privacy, such as unlawful search and seizure, but those amendments were drafted in an agrarian, home-centered culture. The only public documentation of our lives two hundred years ago was birth, death, marriage, and property records.

Today, we do all our business outside the home, and the Fourth Amendment, adopted to protect us from unreasonable search and seizure, does not, under current Supreme Court interpretation, cover medical records, credit, insurance, school records, and data bases.

The High Court has also held that we have no reasonable expectation of privacy on land surrounding our homes. The police on official business can trespass, and P.I.'s can shoot video at us from inside a van as we sip beer in the front yard. Outside is up for grabs. If we're on the street, be it going to the office for a day of honest work, or into a motel for a tryst, we can expect no help from the law if we don't like being followed or photographed. It is the P.I.'s prerogative once we leave the house. Emery feels that the garbage that we must discard for sanitary and civilized reasons, should not be considered public property.

"Garbage does not belong to a P.I. once someone throws it out anymore than urine is theirs once it goes into the toilet. But that's how basic the problem's become. We have people following us around, examining our waste products and bodily fluids without our knowledge or consent," he says.

However, the Supreme Court has spoken. Garbage, once curbed, usually belongs to anyone who carts it off. "We can only urge people to be more paranoid about it right now," says Emery. The attorney would also like to see more standardized regulation and disciplinary measures for private investigators. They do not exist.

In New York, P.I.'s must have no criminal record and three full years of investigative experience. The Department of State hears complaints and takes action if a P.I. has strayed from the law. By many accounts, it is a prudent, though slow-moving, regulatory body where field investigators personally check out each applicant and the documentation for the three years of investigative time is carefully verified. However, the Department of State is a business licensing agency whose priorities run more to the task of smooth administration than codified disciplinary action.

"P.I.'s need a disciplinary body to monitor their practices and make decisions on the ethics of their conduct. Otherwise, the temptations are too great," says Emery. "They're paid to snoop but someone has to put a lid on what is and is not appropriate beyond the strict interpretations of the law. They badly need this and don't have it."

In Iowa all it takes is a shingle, a surety bond, and two hundred dollars to become a P.I. In Alabama, Louisiana, North Dakota, Oklahoma, Rhode Island, Tennessee, Utah, Wyoming, Alaska, and other states, licensing requirements are largely nonexistent. Three years of full-time investigative experience appears to be the emerging norm. New York is expected to pass legislation that will increase the apprenticeship to five years.

Subterfuge is a thorny issue considered by P.I.'s and working cops to be a tool so valuable as to be nonnegotiable. They understand the need for limits, but feel capable of keeping their own counsel. But information is power and there are probably long court fights to come over the determination of its worth, how it is obtained, and what should happen to people who take it under false pretenses.

While it is clear that no one can steal blueprints and trademarks, or listen in on someone's telephone calls, the line between subterfuge to a justifiable end and lies that cause irreparable damage is unclear. For now, Richard Emery acknowledges the technical legality of subterfuge in many cases, but he is not pleased.

"It's probably true that it is legal in the strictest sense," he says, "but it is an unethical, inappropriate, and improper intrusion into people's lives and one that, in many cases, strays into illegality."

Many, one would guess most, working P.I.'s feel that subterfuge stands little chance of being legislated out of the work. "With lawful guidance," says Vincent Parco, "subterfuge is valuable to the client and the P.I. It's a little hard to go up to someone and say, 'Hi, I'm Vinny Parco. I represent the wife you're planning to shaft and I'd like you to tell me where your money is hidden.' Or 'Hey, dude, Citibank thinks you ripped them off for a hundred fifty thousand. How about you tell me so I can put you in jail for fifteen years?' "

But even Parco is suspicious of P.I.'s who are too gag happy and use lies as a substitute for documentable evidence. Regulation, he feels, is a nuisance that he can live with.

"I won't break the law," he says. "But I will stretch it as far as I am permitted. When the Department of State tells me I can't do something, I absolutely won't do it, but we're not about to run around like choir boys making moral judgments all the time. We know what we can and cannot do and we sleep just fine at night."

The workplace and corporate security can expect a lot of scrutiny in the 1990s. The ancient doctrine of employment-at-will gives employers the sweeping right to fire, and to threaten to fire their employees. Corporate security is within its rights to search a desk or a locker and conduct an extensive interrogation without Miranda or other constitutional safeguards. The Bill of Rights exists to prevent abuses of citizens by their governments. An employer is not a government. If the company plans to prosecute, they have to call in the police and go through due process. If the investigation and the action based on its findings is internal—i.e., firing the employee and canceling his pension—there is no need to worry a whole lot about the Constitution.

Under the very broad umbrella of settling matters outside the legal system comes interrogation without the privileges of counsel, polygraph testing because an employer says that's the way it's going to be, mandatory drug or AIDS testing, and other intrusive practices forbidden in the culture at large. Some feel employment-at-will, thanks to technology, has become tyranny-at-will and only a protracted legal fight can cure the excesses.

Public documents are here to stay. We'll always leave traces of our existence in municipal buildings. The hall of records is a Technicolor movie of a target's life and a P.I. will never have to tell a fib to get at it.

Civil libertarians will certainly gain ground, but the staggering white collar crime rate, epidemic use of drugs, barbaric assets and custody battles in divorce, and scams that haven't even been invented yet will give the private cops plenty to do. When the headlines scream of marijuana in the system of the train engineer who killed twenty people, or cocaine in the police ranks, employee theft running as high as 75 percent in some fields, the private cops won't be shackled. Privacy, its definition and resolution, will give all sides something to do in the 1990s.

For Peter Castillo, the garbage he legally carried away from the Lang's curb on a Monday night contained the answer he sought for weeks. He found a discarded blue and white Western Union envelope with a one-line confirmation that a money order had arrived at the home of his father's sister, Margo Whalley, who lived deep in the mountains of Kentucky. Maybe the senior Lang just loved his Sis to bits and sent her cash all the time, but Castillo didn't think so. He guessed that a dutiful father was sending money to a problematic son. He left for Kentucky that night.

14

"Morning, Eddie," Joe Howard said. "Sleep well?"

It was a little after twelve when Eddie Gingras left his building, probably to catch first call at the nearest bar, by the looks of him, Howard thought.

Gingras was about thirty-five and any muscle he once had was gone to flab from one night too many with the booze. He looked at Howard and Meehan through dull blue eyes that were almost obscured by pink fleshiness.

"Who the fuck are you guys?" Gingras asked.

"I'm Joe Howard and this is Marty Meehan, retired New York City detectives, here working on the break-in over at the Calgary."

"Funny," Marty said, "we kind of thought we'd have met you already being that you're—head of security, is it?"

"Yeah, that's right. So what have you two hotshots from New York come up with?"

Joe Howard gives a punk fifteen seconds not to be a punk. From years on the street, he knows that you take control or you don't in the first half minute. Eddie Gingras's time was up.

"You're not talking to a curator now, fucko," he said. "You either give me some answers or I'll throw your fat ass across the street."

"How's your cold, Eddie?" Marty asked. "Or is it a head wound?"

Howard's eyes emitted a laser that seared directly into the flesh. Eddie Gingras started to shake.

"I—I don't have to tell you nothing. You guys can't do shit to me."

He was right. And wrong. They lashed at him with question after question about keys and who had access to them, about missing art and where it went. Gingras said he'd have to talk to his lawyer before answering any questions.

"You're giving those nice men quite a fucking over there, Eddie," Howard said. "Was it blackmail or did you just beat the shit out of them with your friend Onari? By the way, he's on his way back to Turkey. Maybe you're going somewhere yourself," Howard said.

By the time they finished with Eddie Gingras, he was a trembling mass, saying he had to go to the bathroom, and insisting that he wanted his lawyer. He didn't know what happened to the keys, a lot of people had keys, it could be anyone who got in.

Howard had been in telephone contact with Joe Chapman since they'd gotten to Philadelphia. Now he called, told his friend about their interrogation, and said he would put it all in writing.

As a cop, Howard would have enjoyed the thrill of a nice long chat under the lights and, Miranda or no Miranda, this worm would have begged for relief and told all—where the goods went, how much Bongarten and Buehller knew, how much he terrorized them—and maybe he'd have done a dime or so, ten big ones for you asshole, as his social debt.

But, as a subcontracted P.I., Joe Howard's job was to file a report and go home.

"I tell everyone who works for me," he says, "that you're not on the job anymore. You stop when you're told to stop. Period. It's the worst part of the whole thing. Do I think this asshole was blackmailing those poor bastards? Yes, I'd bet on it. Can I prove it? No. Was he stealing them blind? Yes. Can I prove that? No."

Eddie Gingras never went back to the Calgary. He also never went to trial or jail. It was Joe Howard's job, as it often is in private security, to remove a malignancy. Howard assumes that Gingras won't resurface in a museum, but that he will be dumb enough to try something similar in a large corporation. Should he do that, Eddie might find himself smartmouthing a few soldiers in that sparsely regulated army of corporate security people who range from tweedy career FBI and CIA alumni with graduate degrees to bikers with a yen for raw flesh.

The odds of minimal consequence are clearly on the side of the Eddie Gingrases. Corporations don't want the hassle of a court case, so they trade prosecution for a signed, often videotaped confession, and send the criminal away with a warning to stay out of their path. But not always.

Eddie Gingras might not be able to recognize a mob business where "security" means goons fully licensed as P.I.'s who would get their information by cuffing him, smearing his genitals with raw meat, and bringing on a pit bull. Where'd you say you fenced the stuff, Eddie?

Or, he might just find himself in a room without witnesses being kicked from wall to wall by some old-time cops no longer troubled by public sector niceties and scrutiny. He'll name names, tell exactly what he did, take a lie detector test in lieu of prosecution, then confess on videotape to this crime and every job he ever pulled, all the way back to the Gilligan's Island lunch box he stole from Woolworth's when he was seven. He'll walk, but only if he can still move his legs.

On the high end and the low, security exists to solve problems discreetly. The Eddie Gingrases of the world sometimes confuse the impotency of due process with the pragmatic, sometimes goon-driven, often litigious solutions of private security.

But if he's dumb enough to steal from IBM, or a hundred other major corporations where security is an executive priority right up there with marketing and sales, Gingras will find himself surrounded by polite pros who'll call him "sir" for the first time in his life, in carefully worded interrogations that cover all legal bases.

Eddie's cocky threat that he'll have to speak to his lawyer won't exactly be Fright Night to these agents. They'll bring in the highest priced legal talent, or maybe even hire an especially flamboyant criminal lawyer to blend his skills with the full weight of the company's community influence and public relations apparatus to hang Old Eddie from the nearest elm. As he climbs into the prison bus in irons, he'll wonder why he's doing a decade when all his street buddies said, "Don't worry, they never prosecute these things."

As it turned out, Eddie Gingras just didn't go back to work. He talked to his lawyer, who advised him that, given his police record, he'd best cooperate with Joe Chapman to trace the stolen art.

The trustees nodded solemnly as Theodore Hill reported that the detectives from New York had eliminated a piece of the problem. Chapman and his resources in the art community would talk to Gingras and eventually recover some of the larger missing pieces.

Bongarten and Buehller had a discreet session with Theodore Hill and the trustees. They kept their jobs. Everyone decided that the detectives from New York were miracle workers and said so to Joe Chapman. The miracle workers were on the next train out to New York.

15

Barry Silvers caught a bumpy commuter flight to Providence's Green Airport where he picked up some maps and local history. He learned that it is a heavily Catholic city going all the way back to colonial times, that the region has long been host to a number of Navy and Coast Guard personnel as well as the gateway to America for thousands of Portuguese who continue to settle near the fishing industry.

Karen Girard had called him after the meeting to thank him for his tactfulness in dealing with her husband. Jeff's coming to accept the idea, she said, but he'll probably never come out and say so. The issue of confronting the mother, should Silvers find her, continued to loom, but right now the investigator was not worried about it. The odds were not good, especially since it was clear that Jeff would not ask his adoptive mother to fill in gaps.

Karen had also said that the doctors were now beginning to focus more on a middle ear infection as the medical basis for little Laura's problem and she was feeling more reassured about that.

"But I'm a worrier, Barry," she said. "Even if that's the problem and everything's okay, I want to know her medical history. I wish I could help that, but I can't."

"I understand, Karen," he said. "But for now, let's focus on the real search. We'll all be lucky if we get far enough to know who Jeff's mother is."

She'd never let go of that, Silvers thought, but it was something for her to work out with Jeff, not him.

The birth certificate itself would be needed to verify Providence as Jeff's birthplace. It would be in his name and it would not be hard to find.

There is always a birth certificate in a natural parents trace, a duplicate of the original that substitutes the name of the adoptive parents for the biological mother or parents. The original is sealed, but any adopted child has access to the duplicate. Barry Silvers had gotten a notarized authorization for the release of Jeff's duplicate by the Rhode Island Bureau of Vital Statistics.

It wouldn't do him much good if Jeff Girard wasn't born in Rhode Island. Sometimes these cases involve a state-by-state sweep of birth records, with so many false leads that only a Kuwaiti sheik could afford the investigation.

In most cases, the client knows his date, time, and place of birth, if not the hospital itself. Unfortunately, this was one of those charged exceptions where the nonbiological parents are so threatened by an imagined loss of their adopted child that the information is kept hidden, even when the child becomes an adult.

Silvers believed he had the right date of birth for Jeff Girard. He'd never seen any misinformation about a birthday in one of these cases. He was also convinced that he had the right city. His conviction was based only on hunch, but he felt it strongly. Now he needed the hospital.

Before he left New York, Silvers jotted down the names of three Providence investigators from the directory of the World Association of Detectives. The directory provides a picture, a list of specialties, and a brief résumé of investigative experience of a detective. Silvers does a lot of business through WAD and finds himself calling on brother P.I.'s all over the world to help on cases. But he knew what to do well enough so he didn't think he'd have to add five hundred dollars or more to the budget by bringing in local talent on this trip.

If he needed them, he also had the names of several lawyers. Near the political machinery of any city are law offices that a wise P.I. working way off his turf makes it his business to know about. These attorneys are set up to grease the municipal skids. The partners are always local hotshots—mayors, former mayors, councilmen, aldermen, state legislators—who can change uncooperative bureaurats into Welcome Wagon hostesses.

By the time he got in from the airport, it was too late to start working Vital Statistics. He doubted that Rhode Island's health department, where the records were kept, was any different from anywhere else in the world. He'd never get anyone's cooperation near closing time, so Silvers checked into a Ramada Inn and headed for the Providence public library where he needed to make a friend.

Silvers believes that the further you get from New York, the more open and trusting people become. Subterfuge, therefore, is less necessary.

"I'm looking for some help," he said to a librarian, flashing his credentials. The detective license is adorned with "State Of New York" and, because the Department of State regulates P.I.'s, there is a diplomatic ring to the credential, a sense that Henry Kissinger is your partner. Former law enforcement officers sometimes improve their chances of cooperation by placing a small plastic replica of their badges next to the laminated P.I. ID in a smart leather case. They have long experience in snapping their credentials, called "flashing your tin," authoritatively. The tin with the "State of New York" and "Department Of State" officialdom, plus the world-class snap of the case, creates an air of mystique.

"I'm a licensed private investigator from New York working on an investigation involving medical history," Silvers told a young librarian. Within five minutes, he was chatting with the head librarian, a pleasant woman his own age named Mrs. Burgo.

"It must be fascinating work," she said to him. "How may I help you?"

Being liked is everything. The smart P.I. knows when to be nice. Silvers sold himself to Mrs. Burgo fast, assuring her that all New Yorkers aren't abrasive or otherwise malignant and that the media image of the Big Apple was true enough, but it was a half-truth.

"Beautiful area," he said. "I wish I could stay around longer. What should I see while I'm here?" He listened while she told him about the mansions at Newport, the beaches to the south, the Cape to the east, and Boston to the north. Move slowly toward your critical information, backing in, and treating it like it's just an aside, something that, hell, anyone could answer for me, but since we're both here . . .

"You from around here?"

"Oh yes, born in Winsockett, which is," she thought for a minute and pointed, "that way, but I've lived and worked in Providence since I was a kid." She was a nice-looking woman who seemed to keep herself in good shape and wore stylish clothes. No severe gray dresses, no hair in a bun. "Why, do you want to interview me for your case?"

"In a way," he said. "I'd like to know if you can tell me anything about hospitals in 1956. Not that a young woman like you would remember 1956, of course—"

"Of course."

"Me too. But say someone around our age in 1956 got pregnant and was unmarried, say an unmarried girl without a lot of money, which hospital would be the one where she delivered a baby?"

Mrs. Burgo frowned. "I see. That kind of medical investigation."

"Afraid so," he said.

"Well, I would guess Providence General, myself, if she was on public assistance of some kind. And there used to be the St. Luke's Infant Asylum where a lot of unwed mothers went during the war, but that's not there anymore."

"Any idea where the records would be?"

She called an extension in the library and came back with half an answer. "That would now be part of either Roger Williams or Mount Hope, I'm not sure which."

Silvers thanked her and started to leave, but she insisted on calling the medical records departments of both hospitals for him. "It's neither. The records are part of Providence General, but you'd have a hard time getting them. They're locked up."

As always, he thought, thanking her with a warmth that celebrated her decency as much as the information she had given him. I should only be so lucky as to have what I need locked up on the premises. Barry Silvers learned to chase paper in the late 1950s and early 1960s when he was an investigator for the President's Organized Crime Task Force. He once spent weeks hand sorting thousands of canceled checks to prove that a golf course was built by the mob with misappropriated union funds. He has the public record searcher's most essential gift, patience.

His new friend, Mrs. Burgo, would be far more valuable to him if he had to go the long way on this case, if he had to trace Jeff Girard's identity without the shortcuts.

The library kept old voter rolls on microfilm, and high school yearbooks in the stacks. It also had bound issues of the Providence City Directory, old phone books, and other documents that would enable Silvers to do some serious tracing once he corroborated Providence as Jeff's birthplace.

When the doors to Vital Statistics opened at eight-thirty the following morning, Barry Silvers was outside waiting to do the real work of a private investigator.

His first obstacle was a clerk no older than nineteen. She chewed gum and cracked it as he explained that he had written authorization from Jeff Girard to examine his adoptive birth certificate. The clerk started to shake her head as soon as Silvers took out his notarized letter. The more adamant the shaking head, the more she cracked the gum.

"You'll have to talk to Mr. Driscoll about that," she said, "but he's not here today. He's on vacation."

Without pausing, she looked over her shoulder to another clerk, a woman in her sixties with a blue tint to her gray hair, and said, "This man wants to see someone's 422."

The blue-haired woman shook her head too. "And he's not the adoptee?"

The young clerk said no, he was not the adoptee.

"Never," said the older clerk. "We release that information only to the adoptee. It's policy. I don't care if you're President Reagan." She returned to her seat and the gum-cracking girl looked past Silvers to the woman next to him at the counter.

Silvers anticipated the reaction. A civilian would begin to fume, then assert himself, raise his voice, threaten to write letters, raise his voice again, now in an incoherent babble about taxes and rights, and ultimately be kicked out. But the private investigator knows that the secrets he wants are guarded by low-level bureaucrats and corporocrats who learn by their second day on the post that their job is to say no to everyone they meet.

After twenty years in government offices, Silvers wasn't about to be intimidated. He understands the importance of that pension. He also knows that "no" is not an answer but the reaction of a guard to a presumed trespass.

"Excuse me," he said to the gum cracker.

She looked over at him and said, "Yes?" in a way that defied him to have the audacity to bring up that adoption thing again. The woman at the counter, who was filling out a form to get her birth certificate, also looked annoyed at this person who had had his turn and was trying to horn in on her time.

"Miss," he said, patiently. "I know you're busy, but this is a serious medical matter and I've come all the way from New

York. There must be someone I can talk to about getting the information I need."

"I told you, see Mr. Driscoll. Come back Monday."

And if he came back Monday, it would be Tuesday.

"I'm afraid it can't wait. I wouldn't trouble you if it could."

Always get a bureaucrat to pass you off. Eventually you get passed to the person who will help. As Silvers persisted, he did his dance again with the blue-haired lady whose name was Emma. Then he was on the other side of the counter, getting there. Then Emma took him through another door, where he was now safely beyond her, and to the desk of the senior person, who was a black man of about thirty and one of the youngest people in the room. The name plaque on the man's desk identified him as Randall Blaine. His face was alert, not yet stomped by years of gray desks and green walls.

"I know what you're saying," he said, "I hear you, but I still can't release that abstract to anyone but Mr. Girard himself. He has to be here. Bring me Mr. Girard and you will walk out of here with the certificate. No Mr. Girard, no certificate."

Silvers said, "I can bring Mr. Girard here, but let me ask you this as one career government person to another."

"Oh, right," Blaine said. "One government person to another. I can hardly wait."

"Since I'm in Providence anyway today, would you pull the file and acknowledge if I'm right or wrong on certain information? Unofficially, of course."

Blaine sighed and shook his head. "No, I won't do that," he said. "It's against the *rules*, you understand. The *rules*. But let me just take a stroll back into my files because I need the exercise and I just love to put my whole career on the line for some guy from New York I've never met before."

In a few minutes, he returned with Jeff Girard's files. Silvers felt his pulse quicken at the the first official confirmation that a baby known by the adopted name of Jeffrey Allen Girard was born in this city. Until now, there had been no such link.

"What is it I'm not going to answer?"

"Date of birth," Barry said, trying not to let his nervousness show. "8-10-56?"

"Confirmed."

"Is the hospital Providence General?"

"No."

"St. Luke's Infant Asylum?"

"What the hell's that?"

"It's where a lot of unwed mothers went to have babies around this time."

"Well, it isn't where Mr. Girard was born."

"Mercy?"

"Amen."

Now for the information he needed most.

"Time of birth. I really need the time of birth."

"I like to take my lunch hour at 12:24. We government people are very precise."

16

When it comes to public document searches, Barry Silvers is Sir Edmund Hillary taking one more shot at Everest in 1953.

He took to that phase of the work early on. As a college student in the mid-1950s, he enjoyed writing papers and pawing through libraries. When he graduated as a business major in 1958, he considered corporate research, graduate school, and, finally, at the urging of his father, an agent with the department of Treasury, the government. The recession, plus a desire to settle into something secure, led him to go for a civil service job which, he points out, was a pretty reasonable thing to want in the 1950s. He went to work for the President's Organized Crime Task Force as a trainee.

Silvers never caught crooks with the street swagger of Joe Howard, but he got quite a few big-timers locked up, often through the painstaking trace of their paper. He did a lot of organized crime and union graft work in the years when Bobby Kennedy was Attorney General and Jimmy Hoffa was an administration priority. Despite his talent with the inside work, Silvers spent his twenty years as a field agent. Sometimes it got hairy. While investigating the Teamsters, one of Hoffa's men told him that he should really consider backing off because things happen to people who don't. Bad things.

He learned in those days that public documents aren't always so public. Even with the Freedom of Information Act, and the guarantees of the law, the bureaucratic guard dogs are trained to hide information forever. The law, as usual, is murky. Information that is legal in New York is illegal in Florida. And legal again in New Hampshire.

Barry Silvers does not share his trade secrets with underlings.

When he finished with Randall Blaine, and headed for Mercy Hospital that afternoon, he knew what he needed. He didn't wait to be escorted to maternity, or to try to talk his way through the hospital's records department. Hospitals are sued so routinely that their first line of defense with records is, "Sue me for them, you bastard, I hate you." Then they get really nasty.

He entered the hospital with the right expression, a deliberate walk and countenance that made him look like a surgeon in a hurry. He passed through the front offices and the security guard practically saluted him. When he got to the maternity wing, he lingered at the nursery window, where he could have been a new grandparent ogling his namesake through the window.

He was not there to look at babies, however. Silvers studied the layout of the floor and watched the faces of the staff. He needed the right kind of person because he was going to talk his way in with one of the most forceful pitches a detective can use—the truth.

The nurse in charge was too much of a power tripper, so he watched the doctors. Not this time. No one struck him right, so he left.

He came back on the next shift and found the person he needed. Elaine Roux was obviously in charge, but seemed to run her shift with the mix of compassion, urgency, and wisecracking irony that made her an ideal choice. He took a deep breath, stomped on his simmering emotions and walked to her desk.

"Hi," he said. "I think you're the one who can help me."

Ms. Roux was making fast notes on a clipboard.

"That's what they all say," she said. "Who are you and what do you want? I hate it already."

"I'm a private investigator here from New York on a medical investigation that my client thinks is an emergency," he said, presenting his laminated license.

"What?"

"Well, like I say, my name is Barry Silvers and I'm—"

"Yeah, yeah, a private investigator from New York," she said, finally taking the license from his hand. "I got that part."

She looked at the license carefully, turning it over, then handing it back. "And what makes me so lucky? You probably should be talking to someone else."

"Yes, I probably should, but I picked you because you're the one that I think can help."

"Oh, Jesus."

"Is there somewhere we can talk privately. I can wait."

Fifteen minutes later, nurse Roux was on break listening to Barry Silvers.

"So what do you want me to do here? Nothing illegal I hope."

"No, nothing illegal." Silvers's heart was beginning to pound. "I would like you to get the delivery room log from August 10, 1956, and look up a boy born at 12:24 P.M."

Elaine Roux was sipping her coffee when he said it. She made a noise through the sipping that sounded like she had jumped into the plastic cup and was drowning.

"I mean, you don't want a hell of a lot do you? Just go back to 1956, just saunter into medical records and say, 'How you doing? Don't mind me, I'm just here to get the delivery room log from 1956.' Shit, Barry, you really know how to show a girl a big night."

Silvers did his best Columbo sheepishness, holding up his hand and saying, "I know, I know. I feel terrible asking you to do this."

"Those records, Barry honey, are on a need to know basis. Now you tell me how an RN needs to know about a delivery in 1956."

"What year were you born?"

Elaine Roux thought about it and nodded. "That could be a way to go if I wanted to do it. I'm not saying I'll do it or anything, but I could go in there and say I'm looking up my own birth. Listen, when do I have to decide if I want to do this? I'm a single mother, you know? It's a little, you know, bending the rules."

Know when to push and not to push, Silvers thought.

"Time is important to me, is all I can say, but I really don't want to push you."

She winced. "Well, I couldn't do it tonight anyway, Barry. It's just not a good time. When's the next time you're coming back to Providence?"

"I'll be honest with you, Elaine. I'm coming back to Providence when you call me in New York and say I'm coming back to Providence. Right now, you're one of the most important people in the world to me and to my clients."

"You had to put it that way. Okay. Go back to New York and I'll think about it. But if I do it, I've got to do it in my own time.

I know you're in a hurry and all, but I'm going to do it my own way."

Barry Silvers went home.

Elaine Roux called two days later. "Get your buns up here, honey. You are not going to believe this. You know what a delivery room log looks like, right?"

Silvers's hands were trembling. "A big ledger, right?"

"Big ain't the word, hon. Huge. Page after page after page. It's on this huge table and they've just kept adding pages to it. Barry, that thing goes all the way back to 1953. That kid you're looking for, he's still in the delivery room, as far as the log goes."

Silvers didn't call home and say he was going. He didn't care about the Duke or the stolen credit cards, his staff, or the paperwork. He just went flying out with a hurried, "I've gotta go, I'll call, bye." He almost hit the parking booth at LaGuardia and, when he got back, he would take forever to retrieve his car because he stuffed the ticket God knows where. One minute he was out on Long Island. The next, he was in Providence speeding toward Mercy Hospital.

Elaine Roux was waiting for Barry Silvers in the lobby of the hospital. So was the head of security. And the hospital administrator. They asked him to step into an office on the first floor.

The head of security was a tall man with a crew cut who looked like an older, less amusing, version of Richard Moll on "Night Court." He stood by the door, folded his hands, and glowered. Silvers took him for a retired beat cop, probably way out of his depth with anything more sophisticated than an employee running off with a bottle of Valium.

"What are you doing here, exactly?" the hospital administrator asked. Behind him was a metal table beneath a large, very worn black ledger with a heavy steel binding. Silvers knew it was the log. He also knew they weren't happy to see him.

Silvers looked toward Ms. Roux. "She can't tell you what you're doing here, pal," the head of security said. "So, how about you answer Mr. Talbot's questions?"

Talbot, the hospital administrator, was a redheaded man in his early forties. He didn't look menacing, but he didn't look too pleased either.

"Well, as I told Nurse Roux, I am a licensed New York Private Investigator here on a case that my clients consider a medical emergency." He passed the laminated ID around. The head of security held it up to the light, wiggled it around between his thumb and forefinger, examined both sides, and flipped it back.

"What kind of emergency?" Talbot asked.

Silvers told him that he would be glad to discuss the whole issue, but he preferred to speak alone, in confidence. The security head was unhappily dismissed, muttering as he left that he would check out Barry's credentials and that Talbot should call if he needed him.

"Shall I go out too, Fred?" Elaine Roux asked.

"For now, yes, Elaine, thank you," Talbot said.

When the door closed behind her, Silvers said, "If I got her into any kind of trouble, I'm sorry. That would be the only regret I have. I've done nothing illegal."

Talbot took out a pack of Merit lights, tipped one toward Barry, and lit up when the detective declined.

"We're friends, she's in no trouble with the hospital, but I want to know more about your case, what you're doing here, and what you're looking for."

Silvers eventually found out why he had been so surprised in the lobby. While looking through the delivery room log, Elaine Roux was interrupted by the head nurse on the first shift, who confronted her and called in the head of security who, as Silvers might have guessed, was a man who looked for any excuse to magnify his role in the hospital.

Fortunately for Nurse Roux, Talbot liked her and, Silvers suspected, neither had much use for the head of security and the officious first shift nursing supervisor.

Silvers told Talbot what he had told Elaine.

"I sympathize," he said. "I really do. But I can't let you look. It's not just the hospital policy. It's my own."

"Understandably," Silvers said. "Let me ask you this. What if I asked you to look up the birth and confirm or deny any information I have?"

Talbot shook his head. "The answer is no, and you know why. Your clients, no matter what you tell me today, are going to be trouble. It might take a year, two years, you'll be long gone, and maybe I'll even be long gone, but they'll be here. It's trouble and I say no. It's a guarantee. It's also a guarantee that even unofficial cooperation is going to get us in hot water. You know what we pay for liability every year? I can't. I really can't. I'm sorry you came all this way."

"May I ask a couple of questions not about the log?"

Talbot looked at his watch. "If they're quick questions, go."

"What would be the economics of coming here in 1956? Would a poor person have her baby here?"

"God, how would I know? I wasn't here in 1956."

Silvers was more interested in selling himself to Talbot than getting the information, although the information was valuable. He felt everything inside him churning. The log was in this hospital, in this damn *room*, and he'd never see it, especially with that security moron waiting for him to try. They would probably take the pages out, microfilm them, lock up the microfilm, and destroy the originals. He had to keep the man talking.

"You wouldn't consider just looking up the birth on the log and—"

"And what? No, I'd never consider it," he said. He reached behind him and pushed the log to the side of the table. Then he went to the men's room and didn't come back for a long time.

Later that afternoon, Karen and Jeff Girard received a message on their answering machine.

"This is Barry, and I have very good news for both of you. Jeff, I know your mother's name."

17

"I want a brown or gray car with out-of-state license plates," Peter Castillo said to the car rental rep on the telephone. "I do not want Washington, Virginia, or Maryland plates. It's very important. Do you have such a car in your inventory?"

"No problem," said the customer rep.

"Really, it's important," Castillo said. "Would you check that out please?"

Peter Castillo had been to Kentucky before. It's a part of the world where the law, even this late in the twentieth century, is locally interpreted.

It would not surprise him to find that one of Tommy Lang's kin was running for police commissioner. He knew too that the rapist's cousins and uncles were of the kind of rifle rack and pick-up truck country boys who would consider it a public service to run a troublesome city slicker into a ravine. The last thing he needed was D.C. area tags.

The car rental office had reserved a red Pontiac Firebird with D.C. plates and they had a hard time understanding his annoyance. They were further inconvenienced when Castillo made the rep call the guy with the jitney bus to make a special trip to the back lot so he could shine a flashlight on thirty or forty cars and their license plates until he came across a gray Oldsmobile Cutlass Ciera with West Virginia plates.

"Perfect. I'll take it."

Castillo had packed his standard arsenal: three dark green cans of Smith & Wesson Mace, his Smith & Wesson nine-millimeter, six-chamber automatic, the big 36-round, nine-millimeter Intratec, and, for the lighter work of routine surveillance, his five-round Charter Arm .38 Undercover. The job, of course, was not to put a bullet in Lang, just to convince him that the guns work. If he wants to find out how well they work, that's up to him, Castillo figured.

Lieutenant Wayne Rojak of the county sheriff's department was Castillo's kind of cop, a big, regular, country guy with a straight arrow perspective on criminals. If they did it, they do their time. Don't try to understand or reform them, just put them in prison. If they get convicted again, put them away longer. Sooner or later, they'll get the point.

"Guess the first thing we need to do is find out if your man's here," Rojak said. "And find out quietly. You say he's staying out at Cora Whalley's place?"

"Yes, do you know her?"

"We know her all right," Rojak said. "And you got us at a good time. Her brother-in-law ran against Sheriff Hayes and lost."

Sheriff Bob Hayes was a reformer, which was also good. For years, the county sheriff's office had been tainted with corruption, cronyism, kickbacks and other pollutants of democracy. Hayes got elected because he said it was time to "clean up."

"Come on with me," Rojak said, "and you'll see how literally we take the term." They drove ten miles up a quiet, single-lane road surrounded by heavy woods. The pavement stopped part way in and turned to dirt, and Rojak kept driving.

"They still run a lot of hooch, you know, moonshine, through these mountains," Rojak said, "but now we got a new generation of bootleggers. They're into much bigger leagues."

"Cocaine?" Castillo asked.

"You got that right. Coke, pot, all the good stuff. Keeps us real busy."

They came to a clearing where they found a convention of police cars, two wreckers, rescue vehicles, and small trucks.

"What is this?"

"You won't believe it," Rojak said.

They stood on a rock formation looking up at some high cliffs that dropped straight into a spring-fed pool. On the other side, a red Pontiac Trans Am was being hoisted out of the water. It dangled from a tow truck like a fish on a line.

"This quarry's about bottomless," Rojak said. "The drug runners buy these cars, take them on a few runs, and roll them right over that cliff over there."

"Get rid of them before they become too familiar, right?" Castillo asked.

"You ask me, it's just a way of giving us the finger," Rojak said. "But yeah, that's pretty much what they do. Run them and throw them in the drink. But we're starting to make believers out of them. This time, we got the guys just when they put their little toy over the ridge. Lots of fun."

Rojak introduced Castillo to Sheriff Hayes, who kept one eye on his excavation as they talked.

"Sounds okay to me," he said as Castillo showed him his warrant. "Wayne, you got it. Give this man what he needs. You want any of the specials? They'd probably be a good idea."

"We'll see. I think I just want a few of the regulars." Rojak didn't want to offend his boss, but he took a dim view of the special deputies the sheriff brought in for the salvage operation.

"See those guys over there?" he asked Castillo, when they were out of the sheriff's earshot. "Those are the esteemed special deputies up from Louisville. Experts."

Castillo had noticed that four or five men on the salvage crew seemed to be in love with their own voices. "Experts at what?" he said.

"Well, now, those are the world's greatest authorities on bootlegging, drug running, anything you can name. They're over here to help us get rid of those drug runners. Because they're experts, see, they don't have to do or find anything. Our boys take care of that. The experts get to go on the news with the governor. Want them on your operation?"

"No way."

"Good, now let's go on over and see if we can find Mr. Lang, is it?"

"Lang, Tommy Lang, right."

Surveillance to Wayne Rojak meant driving up to a Citgo station and talking to his brother-in-law.

"Now, Cecil, this ain't for broadcast," he said. "Cora Whalley got a boy visiting?" They knew three things when they left. Cora Whalley did have a boy visiting, that boy drove a green Chevette, and he could be found most afternoons playing basketball in the school yard.

"You tell Cecil something ain't for broadcast, he'd go to his death with it," Rojak said as he keyed his radio handset to do a quick DMV check which produced the Chevette's plate number.

They cruised by the school yard, but no one was there. Castillo went back to his motel for a while. Later, he parked across from the school and waited.

At three o'clock a group of high-school-aged boys began playing basketball. Fifteen minutes later, the Chevette pulled up, and Castillo got his first look at Thomas Everett Lang.

Lang got out of the car and walked up a grassy hill to the game, where he stayed on the sidelines talking with other young men in their teens and early twenties. There was no criminal cast to his face, no deranged look. In his denim jacket and Van Halen T-shirt, he looked like any young man in an after-school basketball game. But to at least two women, and probably many more, his face was the epitome of day and night horror, a memory that would never go away.

He took off his jacket and joined the preliminary feinting, blocking, jumping, and shooting that served as the warm-up to more serious play. Good, Castillo thought. Let him get a good workout, let him get nice and tired. Castillo spent the next two hours exploring the roads near Cora Whalley's house.

On his way back, he passed a Seven-Eleven convenience store just as the Chevette turned into its parking lot. He drove by, turned around in the nearest driveway and pulled up next to Lang's car. The local police might just be spared the hassle of surrounding Cora Whalley's house. He would Mace his target right here in the parking lot. But Lang didn't come out, so Castillo, with Mace cans in his jacket pocket and the Undercover snugly in its shoulder holster, went in after him.

Lang leaned comfortably against the wall as he thumbed through a car magazine. Castillo walked to the magazine rack and picked up a copy of *U.S. News & World Report*. He didn't look at Lang, but he could feel his presence. Being so close helped him get a reading on the man and assess how much of a problem he would be outside. Spraying Mace or drawing a gun in the store was, of course, out of the question.

As Castillo approached the checkout counter, Lang passed him like a pushy motorist heading for the toll booth just ahead of a car almost there. He bought a pack of Marlboros. Castillo fell in behind him, deciding to be cool about it. There was plenty of time to get him outside. He'd stop at the door on the passenger side of the Chevette and spray. Zap. One less rapist on the street.

Lang paid for his cigarettes. Castillo bought a candy bar and walked outside where his target was leisurely crossing the pavement to his car. Castillo picked up his pace. Just as he was about to say, "How's it going, Tommy?" a car came into the parking lot and stopped on the other side of Lang's Chevette. The rapist was free for a few hours.

Castillo called ahead, then met with Rojak in the sheriff's office. County law enforcement is where Castillo did his time as a cop. He is as comfortable with sheriff's offices as Ray Melucci is with transit police. He knows the rhythm of their bureaucracy, their jurisdictional ambivalence with local police and the highway patrol.

"I'm ready any time," he said.

"Good," said Rojak. "Let me see if I can get my boys together. They got kind of upstaged over at the quarry, so I think they're ready for a good night of police work. All we need's the when and where."

Castillo went back to the motel and got a couple of hours sleep. To him, it was all but over. He'd found his target, the police were not only good, but highly competent, and not only that, but closemouthed. That left only the execution.

But while he slept, Wayne Rojak struggled with problems. There had been a leak that this guy from Washington had something going down tonight.

Everyone wanted a piece of the thing—local cops, the ambitious, reform-minded sheriff, and the gum-chewing, cock-of-the-walk special deputies Castillo had seen that afternoon at the quarry.

Rojak's fellow townsmen had it on good authority that this fellow from Washington was FBI, and everyone knew what that meant—a big, local coke bust that was going to make the papers in a big way. Everyone who had ever carried a badge in the last twenty years showed up at the sheriff's office wanting in.

Sheriff Hayes was besieged. What's going down, politicians and local cops wanted to know, and how could they do their civic duty to help? The longer the night went on, the wilder the rumors got. A terrorist camp right out there by the quarry, swear to God, Josh Simmons saw the Arabs with those funny things on their heads. The woods are crawling with Feds. You know those secret jets, the ones that can't be picked up by radar? Well, the word is one of them crashed.

Any way anyone sliced it, there was a national story breaking, and no one who wore a badge or worked volunteer fire or ambulance in those parts wanted to miss it.

When Castillo showed up for his rendezvous with Rojak and the deputies, he thought something close to World War III had started. The parking lot behind headquarters was police car heaven. The tinny hiss of CBs, scanners, and squawk boxes was so loud that a 747 could have landed without being heard. When he pulled up, he faced the expectant looks of dozens of police officers, who would later be very unhappy to hear that they had about saluted a P.I.

Castillo had the sinking feeling that everything had been for nothing, that his operation was over. Lang was probably gone by now. He had learned the hard way that small-town, part-time cops on an operation can be like Crazy Glue in a car door lock. Some joker always turns on his dome light and starts a chain reaction. They all turn them on. Then someone else hits the siren. Once they start screeching around like extras in a Burt Reynolds movie, intimidating every cow and pig within three miles of the target, forget about your fugitive and forget about your reward.

Fortunately, Sheriff Hayes also showed up, cursed for ninety seconds straight, and ordered all but the nine deputies Rojak had contacted for the operation to get on back to what they were doing and stand by. If they were needed, they would be beeped, goddamn it. Meanwhile they were to transmit nothing, make no phone calls, and not congregate down at the Whippoorwill Diner like they usually do when something's happening.

He was more diplomatic with the local police with whom he cooperated regularly and vice versa. He told them what was happening, but did not disclose the location of the target. Their chief would fillet them if they weren't present.

Rojak spoke to the deputies. "Gentlemen, this is Peter Castillo and he's from up in Washington, a private investigator here with the papers to pick up a rapist out on Route 117. You know the Whalley place. Well, this guy's related to the Whalleys and he's out there. He raped one woman, got out on bail for it, and raped another one the same day. When we get out there, we surround the house. That's it. Let's go."

They parked their cars down around a bend and walked the rest of the way to the house in the dark. When they reached the property, Castillo and Rojak walked silently to the henhouse to make sure the Chevette was there. It was. They came back and moved slowly to the door.

There was a light on in the living room and they could hear the urgent play-by-play of a football game on television. Castillo and Rojak walked to the front door. Just then, one of the deputies tripped over a crack in the cement and shouted, "Shit," as he hit the ground.

Great, Castillo thought. Now she knows there's someone out here. Might as well continue the shock, he figured. He knocked vigorously on the door until Cora Whalley turned on the porch light and opened it.

"Mrs. Whalley, we have a capius for the arrest of Thomas Everett Lang, and we're coming in to take him."

"I don't know what you mean," she said. "He's not here."

"Yes, he is, ma'am. You know he's in there," Castillo said.

"Well, I just got home," she said, hedging her bets.

"Step aside, please," Castillo said. He ran past her, through the living room, and into a hallway with bedrooms on both sides. Rojak and several deputies followed, moving slowly by each doorway. Castillo came to a half-closed bedroom door, kicked it open, and stepped back. Nothing moved.

He put his back against a wall and stuck his hand in the room, feeling the walls for a light switch, which he found and flicked on. There, in the bed, with his feet sticking out from the blanket, was Thomas Everett Lang. He blinked his eyes and Castillo moved over to him, gun drawn.

"How's it going, Tommy? How're you doing?"

Rojak came in with his gun drawn. So did four of the deputies. Lang, who had not quite opened his eyes yet, had six guns pressed to his head.

"Hey, Tommy. Listen, you talk to your mother lately?" Castillo asked.

"Yeah, I talked to her yesterday."

Even though he knew he had his target, Castillo wanted to talk specifics to be certain. A bounty hunter's worst nightmare is to pounce on the wrong person. And the absolute worst thing a bounty hunter can do is pounce on the wrong person, press six guns to his temple, chain him up, and take him out of state. Castillo always asks his targets key questions before taking them into custody.

As Castillo asked questions and Lang gave answers, Rojak reached into a closet, pulled out a pair of jeans, checked the pockets, and handed them to him. Then he found a shirt. "Tom, we're going back to Maryland right now," Castillo said.

Castillo put a pair of cuffs on him, and they took him to the sheriff's headquarters.

"Listen," Castillo said to Rojak. "I don't want to take this guy just yet. I think his kin will attack me on those back roads."

"How about an escort?" Rojak asked.

"The problem with that is you can take me as far as the county line, and I can't expect an escort through every county. I'm honored, though."

"So what are you going to do?"

"Go back to the hotel, sleep an hour or two, and I'll call you before I'm ready to pick him up. How's that?"

"Fine."

Sometime between four and five in the morning, the sheriff's office was only too happy to release Thomas Everett Lang to Peter Castillo. Calls had come from Lang's parents in Maryland, from the political connections of Mrs. Whalley, from the bondsman Ronald Grace, and from Mrs. Whalley herself. Where was Lang? When would he be released? Why was he being held?

One complication that nearly held up the transfer was that Lang had been arrested in a neighboring county for molesting a child and was due to stand trial next month. But a detective from the D.C. Metro Police persuaded the local authorities to release Lang without delay.

Castillo chained and handcuffed him and said, "All right, Tommy. Do whatever you have to do right now. Eat, piss, and shit, because once we get on the road, we're not stopping. And, Tommy, I hear even one link, one rustle of chain, and I'll split your head open."

There were no hijackings by kinfolk. Rojak had radioed the Highway Patrol that an Olds Cutlass Ciera with West Virginia plates would be carrying a prisoner and exceeding speed limits. Lang posed no problems during the trip.

18

Vinny Parco's sister Rita was working the front desk of the agency when two extremely well dressed men in their forties came in.

"Good morning," she said, "May I help you?"

"Hello," one of them said in a British accent. "I certainly hope you can. We saw your advertisement, you see, the one that said you specialized in unusual investigations?"

"Yes?"

"We have one. Is there someone we could talk to?"

Inside, Vinny Parco was sorting out applications for the Society of Professional Investigators. As secretary for the 1986–87 term, he was responsible for maintaining the mailing list, getting out the newsletter, and wading through the usual gripes and politics of any association.

"Vincent, two men would like a word with you," Rita said.

"Be right out," he said, cursing a walk-in when he was just about to leave for lunch.

"Gentlemen, come on in," he said as he shook hands with the men. "I'm Vincent Parco. How may I help you?"

"Nice of you to see us without an appointment, sir. I'm Robert Grove and this is my brother, William. I hope we're not disrupting your life."

"Disruption *is* my life," Parco said. "It's the nature of what we do. So, I gather you gentlemen are not from the Bronx."

Robert laughed. "Pretty close. London, actually, and we were about to return home empty-handed. We came because we saw your advertisement in the telephone book about unusual investigations. I'm hoping to find a father I never knew."

The men had been in New York for about ten days and had

spent thousands of dollars with another agency looking for a man named Daniel Reggia, an American serviceman who had a wartime romance with Robert's mother, Sheila, who learned she was pregnant after Reggia was shipped home in 1945. The other investigators had learned that Reggia lived in Manhattan until the mid-1960s, but had vanished after that.

"I'm not surprised there are problems," Parco said, "but give us a shot."

"Certainly, but I must ask how long a shot you need," said Robert. "You see, unfortunately, we have to be back in London."

"How about an hour?" he asked.

The gentlemen tried not to look shocked and in so trying, looked all the more shocked. They had just spent thousands of dollars on missing persons work—credit reports, motor vehicle check, voting records, a contact in the Department of Immigration and Naturalization. All the usual checks had produced nothing. Their father seemed to leave no paper.

"Tell you what," Parco said. "Make it two hours. Go have a nice lunch and when you come back, we'll probably be able to get your father on the phone for you."

Parco, now on the second week of his despised diet, brooded on the image of the two men huddled over an exquisite lunch sharing a bottle of Cabernet Sauvignon, perhaps, while he gagged through the boring salad washed down by club soda that awaited him at Mumbles. Wishing them a nice meal was the biggest lie he would tell all week, but it was the nicest, most reassuring thing he could think of to say to the men.

That other issue, the father who had been missing for forty-one years, the man no one could find, was a given. Parco knew he would be found in minutes because he has a secret. He has total confidence that he employs five of the best skip tracers who ever practiced the craft.

Parco's tracers work across the street from the town house in a windowless room that blends the exclusive aura of a speakeasy with the subterranean sleaze of a cockfight. There is no designation of their existence on the mail box and visitors have to be buzzed inside. Skip tracers don't like civilians around. Sometimes they don't even like other skip tracers around.

"Some people consider themselves skip tracers because they know how to look up a person's address and phone number in a cross reference directory, or they know how to check with motor vehicles to find out a guy's license. But they are not skip tracers. True skip tracers can find out information that's not available to most P.I.'s. They have sources that they've developed themselves, that exceed what most private investigators would know. For example, they have sources in the phone company throughout the whole country where they can get information that no one else can get—third party calls, credit card calls. They can trace these calls back to their sources. They can do it every time out, not just once or twice. We have the best skip tracers in the country. I hire only the best."

All day, every day, the skip tracers—Jo-Ann, Mark R., Jerry L., Cisco Villar, and Joe Rodriguez—dig up information thought to be inaccessible in many circles. Says Parco, "We take public documents and the data bases that we subscribe to and analyze the information for what limited value it has. Then we expand on it through innovative, and legal, subterfuge."

Legal subterfuge? "Lying," Parco clarifies. "Skip tracing is total subterfuge. Total. Everything they do is total subterfuge. But you have to do it without breaking the law and you have to know what lines you can't cross."

Parco's tracers are not permitted to identify themselves as part of any government agency including cops, tax collectors, or other officials. They can't be doctors on an emergency or clergy. Sometimes they "go in as the stiff" or represent themselves as their targets to get information: "Allo, who ees thees? Allo Carol, I am Masud Ravat. Eees thees the nomber to bahlance my check? . . . Bahlance my check. Baahlance. Baahlance. You know, baahlance. I want to baahlance my check. . . .

"Oh, yes, I am sorry. I should say check my baahlance, no? Engleesh, so easy if you know it, so hard if you don't. Who am I? I tole you, I am Masud Ravat. I spell that for you, Carol. My account number? I don't have it here. I move. How 'bout you tell it to me, then I have it all the time, eh?"

Jo-Ann Kunda demonstrated the technique for a television news crew when she uncovered the illegal occupancy of an apartment by impersonating her target to a department store credit clerk. She casually mentioned that she was having trouble getting her bills, maybe the store didn't have the right address. What address did they have for her? When the clerk read the address, it became admissible evidence in proving the landlord's case that the woman was, in effect, stealing from him by subletting the rent-controlled apartment and living elsewhere.

Parco prefers the term "paper investigator" to distinguish his tracers from the many free-lance debt collectors who move from small-time collection agency to small-time collection agency and take subterfuge to its most dangerous limits. If they don't collect the money, they don't get paid. To get to the bank account or other assets, where they can get a restraint on the assets and make as much as 50 percent of the bad paper, they will often say anything.

Debt-collecting tracers have been known to say they are doctors with a life or death need to find someone, or the Internal Revenue Service, FBI, a member of the clergy trying to reach the next of kin, or the *New York Times* thinking about a feature article. They just need to ask a couple of quick questions. There are hundreds of illegal ways to get information on the phone. The same people who barricade their doors and use killer dogs to keep intruders away from their homes, give away their secrets to an anonymous voice on the phone. Parco doesn't allow such practices.

"Not that we're altar boys," he says. "But we are professionals. I think there's one thing that keeps P.I.'s a lot more honest on the phone than say, collectors, who don't have our regulation. We can lose our licenses."

Within the law, there are enough openings for a convoy of eighteen wheelers. Skip tracers can pry financial information out of banks, wattage and cubic feet from utility companies, employment, medical, and sexual information from anyone. They can sound like a surgeon to a surgeon, a banker to a banker, a boss to an employee, a fellow bored clerk to a bored clerk.

"A skip tracer," says Parco, "is only as good as his book. You hire him for his book. If you need to gag the welfare department to find out if someone's on public assistance, the tracer will have notes on exactly what language to use, what numbers to call, and who to speak with."

And all good tracers are actors. "I once knew a white guy who could be a white guy, a gay white guy, a white woman, a gay white woman, a black man, a gay black man, a black woman, and a gay black woman," says Charles Eric Gordon, an attorney who worked as a skip tracer chasing bad college loans when he was in law school. "He could make the switch in the same conversation if he had to."

Creativity, says Parco is the one quality that predominates when he looks for a tracer. "Frankly, they're a pain in the ass to manage sometimes. They're high-strung, like pitchers or actors. You have to wait them out, or come down on them. But a good tracer is so rare. You just don't get a real tracer coming down the pike very often. When you find one, you pay him well and, if he's moody, he's moody. Creative people are."

They will not reveal precisely how they find things on people so fast, and find things that are not open to others, but creativity and improvisation seem to be a substantial part of the answer.

"The interim conversation is more important than the business at hand, getting the nonpub, getting the social security number, or the bank account number," says Cisco Villar, a twenty-nine-year-old tracer with a degree in film production. "Phone company people and bank tellers really do not care about their jobs and if they feel that they're talking to someone who's in the same boat, they'll give up anything."

Villar, like all of Parco's tracers, gets calls from other tracers and agencies, from people wondering how he does it, and how they can do it. Gags are trade secrets like magician's tricks or a pickpocket's moves, and are sometimes not even given out to fellow tracers in the same agency. But subterfuge alone does not make a tracer. The trick is in the application.

"When it comes to certain phone work, there's nobody out there who can do what I do, so everybody calls," Villar says. But he can't give them their answers because he may not know himself. There is nothing in the words that explains why there is an almost instant rapport between Cisco Villar and any bored, drudge-bludgeoned clerk he befriends.

"Hi" is modulated in gentle, caring tones. He remembers names, birthdays, children's names, that creepy sister-in-law who always insists on making the worst stuffing in the world on Thanksgiving.

"You're another person they can share their problems with. They really need that."

"It's the game," says Jerry L., a rock guitarist and musician who worked as a collector before answering an ad Parco ran in the *New York Times*. "You get addicted to the game. It's me against him and I'm going to win. I'm going to get the information and if I don't get it, I'm coming back for it."

Guarded pinstriped executives who lock their files and shred their memos are Jerry L.'s favorite opponents, and the ones he sinks best. Corporate financial investigations are his main act in the agency. He enjoys the edge, being an inch away from the lip of the waterfall and beating the plunge. He'll play hard rock in a Jersey bar until dawn, grab a couple of hours sleep and rechannel his beat into tracing. He is the consummate authority figure on the phone.

"What? Maybe you didn't quite get what I'm saying here. I didn't *ask* you for anything. I'm telling you I want that now. Give me your supervisor."

Then he'll chew out the supervisor.

When he is in an authoritative role, the soft-spoken tracer becomes a fearsome Mr. Hyde. His face turns pink, then red, then crimson, and, if one dares look long enough, probably blue. He seems to bring every slight in his life, every bad moment, into the gag until it builds to a peak where it isn't an act at all. The fury sets into his eyes which bulge and take on the look of a beast about to pounce. Veins pop out of his forehead and throb. It is a blessing that his target can't see him. His technique is enough to make Yassir Arafat say "screw it," and give up the information.

A bank robber can get ten thousand dollars on a good day. He'll be videotaped and probably caught. A white collar criminal can pick up an access code lying around someone's desk, transfer a million dollars into a Swiss account and disappear. Investigators like Jerry L. will be able to name their price as white-collar crime blossoms into the growth industry of the nineties. Without computers or any equipment more sophisticated than a phone and a headset, Jerry L. has the reputation for finding a buck anywhere someone can stash it. It's the game.

Mark R. is considered the best in the room. Since there are no skip trace tournaments or award banquets, and since the field is an underground art, it is never going to be possible to document the skill of the thirty-one-year-old former collector. Like all good tracers, he has a big bag of personalities and gags. He can summon Cisco's seductive lullaby of empathy or Jerry's Make My Day blast, but he usually operates with a more even friendliness and warmth, the kind of "let's skip work and go on a picnic" sympatico that telegraphs the absurd games corporations and bosses play.

"Hi, Jenny? How're you doing? It's Mark from the Yonkers

office. God, can you *believe* this new system? My screen's been down more than it's been up. How's yours doing?"

His eleven years on the phone have given him the auditory equivalent of a very experienced street detective's ESP. They all get an immediate feel for what the target needs—a joke, words of authorization, a scolding, the right name dropped—and they provide it. But Mark R. seems to take the process further. He can speak to someone and see the hue of an aura.

"I try to close myself out, close myself off from everything around me, and become the person I say I am. I have an answer to every question they're going to ask. Complete confidence. You have to have that in your voice.

"You have to think, 'Well, I'm going into this company to get information.' You've got to think to yourself, 'Well who would need to know this info? Why would they need to know it?' "

The tracers say that the true art of tracing should be learned from a master practitioner, a function served by Mark R. who learned it from a collector named Kenny Cruz more than ten years ago. He had just gotten out of the Navy where his training with microwave technology made the prospects for a secure job with the phone company very promising.

"And I got this call from a friend of mine who said there was this thing called skip tracing and I should try it."

Mark R. did not take to the work right away. There was stammer and hesitation in his voice. He stumbled through the gags, sometimes overwhelmed by what he was expected to ask people.

"I'd say, 'What? I'm supposed to ask them what? And they're supposed to tell me?' "

Then, like Newman taking on Redford in *The Sting,* Cruz took the kid under his tutelage and stuck with him. He let him make the classic mistakes, and gave him encouragement. It worked. Mark R., still in his early twenties, was soon raking in the cash, but not dealing with his success especially well. He bounced from one agency to another, took time off, and eventually settled into the work.

In 1984 Vinny Parco hired Mark R. and a friend of his to merge collecting skills with the more restrained dictates of private investigation, and the room was set up. Parco is a hands-on boss, and always the instructor. He enjoys a good gag himself once in a while, and he understands that sometimes tracers just don't hit. If they need a break from the phones, the tracers can plod through the ever-present tedium of public document hunting, go into the field for an afternoon, or just take a day off, which they sometimes have to do.

The tracers see most of the agency's cases at some point. Their link to the administration of the company is Jo-Ann Kunda, who has the ambivalent job of being their supervisor and keeping the action going. A case almost always comes into the agency through Vinny, who processes it, then hands his notes over to the front office where a retainer contract is sent out, usually for ten hours of work at seventy-five dollars per hour. Parco's philosophy is never to dispatch a field person when a tracer can get the information.

Jo-Ann's decision on who gets the case is a matter of speed. Who can snap it shut fastest? Although the three main tracers have their dominant areas, all can jump on a case and close it. Tracers work on a couple of basics. If you know the language of your target industry—banking, insurance, credit reporting, whatever—information will flow. You only have to present yourself as a person who needs, and has a right to, information, then ask for it with the proper intonation, usually with such practiced casualness that it sounds like the last thing you want is some joker's personal information.

"Oh, before I go, do me a favor. My damn screen is down again. Are you guys still up? Really, what a miracle. No one else is. Can you give me a current [current balance] on 5805-2299 [the target's account number]?"

The second basic of telephone information gathering is one that will never be remedied by legislation and constitutional battles over privacy. Our most intimate secrets are in the hands of clerks. Some are responsible and take their jobs seriously. Many are slow-witted drones who hate their jobs and will give out our health, money, family data, party affiliation, credit ratings, and anything they know if someone is shrewd enough to ask for it in the right way.

If approached correctly, management can be as vulnerable as the clerks. Vinny Parco recalls getting a call from an attorney who wanted the name of a corporation holding title to a bar. The corporate name was probably so far removed from the bar itself that it would have taken hundreds of hours and thousands of dollars to find it in the labyrinth of New York's corporate filings.

However, the attorney did know the name of the insurance company carrying the bar's liability. Parco closed the case with one phone call.

"I called the insurance company as another insurance company. Indignant. Irate. I was pissed off. I said, 'I want the claims manager.' "

And when he came on the line, he got an earful.

"This is Bill Whelan of United Mutual Insurance Companies," Vinny recalls saying. "Hey, I want to tell you guys something. Our company's being sued because of your company. We're coinsurers, and there's this bar on Thirty-fourth and Tenth. Someone falls in the stupid bar, our asses are being sued, and my staff says your staff won't provide the name of the corporation."

Having come on strong and put his target on edge, Parco eased off a degree until two fellow claims managers were talking about staffs and how they can't do anything right these days. They commiserated for a while about the business, the manager convinced that Parco was one of his brothers in the insurance game. How could he help?

"Do me a favor and give me the corporation name on that so I can send you a letter."

The letter the man got was not the one he expected.

Once the tracers tracked a woman who occupied five rent-controlled apartments illegally, and was presumed to live with her boyfriend near Sutton Place. Parco called the managing agent and got "the nastiest woman you've ever heard" on the phone. The lady was so arrogant that the investigator could practically see frost coming out of the phone. Most people would be intimidated to ask such a closed case for information. Parco pressed ahead evenly.

"I said I wanted to verify the tenancy of this lady. She says in the snottiest voice, 'We cannot do that without written authorization.' "

Then he gunned it. "Let me tell you something, lady," he said, breathing more snot and dismissal than any nouveau riche creep in the lady's apartment building. "This is Vito Palermo from Park Avenue Rolls-Royce Limited. Your tenant came in here today, put a twenty five thousand dollar deposit on a new Rolls-Royce. I have to give her seventy-five thousand dollars credit on a car . . . *And you don't want to tell me where she lives? I'm not going to give her the credit!*"

The lady begged him to take the verification, tripping over herself to apologize.

"When I'm doing a gag," says Parco who oversees the training of his tracers and works with them constantly, "I have to size up the situation. What's going to work best. Sometimes I just play the indignant, nasty part and get more information that way. Other people go in very nice, sweet, and innocent and get everything they want. You have to instantly read the person on the other end of the phone and tell that person the exact thing that will make him or her part with the information."

One afternoon an Israeli lawyer followed by two associates burst into Parco's office. He had returned from a business trip only to find that his partner had closed their company's bank accounts and left town, a classic embezzlement scenario. The businessman was out several million dollars.

By the end of the afternoon, the tracers had an answer, but not very good news. Through their telephone company sources, they were able to trace the partner and the money by the calls that were made. He first checked into a New York hotel where he headquartered himself for several days, presumably because he assumed correctly that no one would look for him there. Then he made travel reservations to South America and, at the last minute, arranged for a wire transfer of the money to a bank in Ecuador, a most unfortunate choice since Cisco Villar, who was working the case because of his fluency in Spanish, was born there.

Meanwhile, Jo-Ann and Mark verified the swindler's flight and Parco arranged through the World Association of Detectives to have a local P.I. tail him as soon as his plane landed. Parco, knowing that his client had been a combat officer in the 1967 and 1973 Arab-Israeli wars, did not predict a lifetime of happiness for the swindling partner.

One advantage of phone work is that you don't have to see the face that the horrible news from your investigation sometimes produces. Inga Swenson, once a dazzling model from Denmark, sat in Vincent's office. "He always said he'd take care of me," she said in a Scandinavian accent. "He said we'd be together forever. He said I'd never need anything."

She handed Parco a framed photograph of herself as a bikini-clad bathing beauty on a beach sometime in the fifties, next to a handsome husband with that era's version of a good build.

Through the sobs she tried vainly to stifle during the whole session she said, "I called him, you know, and she answered. That woman he's living with. She said he wasn't there, but I could hear him in the background." She bit her lip. "He was laughing at me. I could hear him laughing in the background."

Parco, who had had the tracers check the husband's finances, said quietly, "Uh, I don't have very good news, Mrs. Swenson. He closed out his account in New Jersey. In New York, it's all gone too, except for a thousand dollars or so.

"For a while, there was money in the Caymans, like you said, but that's gone. Inga, I'm afraid all his money is out of the country. I think he took it to Singapore. I know he has an apartment there. Did you know about that?"

"I know he does a lot of business there. Do you know how old she is, Vincent?"

Parco shook his head. The older he gets, the better he's able to seal himself off from the emotional shock waves of his caseload, that pus of the human spirit that sprays every P.I.

"She's twenty-one. How can he do it?"

To Parco, the woman's real problem was not the one that she now expressed as giving her the most pain, painful as it was. Her real problem was that the man to whom she made a commitment long ago when the picture was taken and she was beautiful enough to have a thousand choices, was now leaving her a spent, destitute, and haggard woman. That was the essence of the betrayal, although the twenty-one-year-old bimbo was no incidental issue.

The stark walls and smoky gloom of their working quarters seem right, for hour after hour, gag after gag, they are ear to ear with evidence of a national morality clubbed so hard in the New Age that it may be brain-dead. A fender bender with minor personal injury routinely turns into a decade of litigation. Creative divorce, that brilliant watchword of 1970s sexual egalitarianism, means that you want to be creative enough to clean out your account and hide it from that conniving bitch and her sleazeball lawyer. If business is bad, burn it down. Everybody else does. If someone gives you a hard time, or if you just don't like him, rip the fucker off. Who's going to do anything about it?

The tracers are very tight. "It's very much a family," Cisco Villar says. "A lot of hugging, kissing, that sort of thing. If someone says something bad about someone in this room, we talk about it and work it out right here."

Except for Jo-Ann, the tracers shy away from the agency's hangouts, parties, and nightlife, although they are not so reclusive that they don't sometimes fraternize with clients or the rest of the agency. But when the nine-to-five world closes out its business day, they usually vanish until morning. When their work traffic is heavy, the tension in their underground lair is as compressed as the gas in an aerosol can. Puncture a wall and the whole place would probably blow up like the *Hindenburg*.

"We have to trust each other," Jo-Ann Kunda says. "If one of us is down, the others try to help out. We know so much about each other because the problems of the work are so esoteric, so tense, something you can't even share with other P.I.'s."

"We know when someone's full of shit," Cisco says. "That keeps us all pretty honest with each other. I can tell from someone's voice if he's telling the truth or bullshitting. We all can. We do this every day, we've been doing it for years, so we know dishonesty. And we don't like it."

Their high sense of integrity is one of the most unsettling paradoxes of the skip trace room. Lying all day seems to create a fierce need for unshaded truth which, to the outsider, is as jarring as finding Cub Scouts in hell. But ethics are integral to the work, for each tracer has a well-defined line he will not cross.

There is no computer hacking going on, no stolen or black market access codes. If, in the process of their gagging, they uncover such information, none would sell it. Anyone who would does not last long in the room. Industrial spook stuff—uncovering corporate plans or blueprints—is also out. The only way the agency goes on that issue is to catch the ones stealing it. They will, however, use subterfuge or field infiltration to sniff out a corporation for a competitor or a prospective business associate.

The room's premier ethical consideration is confidentiality, both to the clients who hire them and, in an odd way, to the targets whose privacy they invade. A tracer at Vincent Parco & Associates is as carefully screened as the subject of an investigation. Before he will hire a tracer, Parco must assure himself that the candidate will not be tempted by the fraud and blackmail possibilities from thousands of credit card numbers, hidden assets, stock fraud, adultery, and other human frailties investigated daily.

The tracers have no problem about the work they do. How would they feel to be so surgically probed?

"Fine," says Cisco Villar. "No problem. I have nothing to hide and it will show when someone checks me out. I should be checked out. What goes on in here is right. We're in business because of so many illegal subtenants, so many people committing fraud against others. When I catch someone fradulently renting a thousand-dollar-a-month apartment for two hundred dollars, it makes me feel good to know they're out. I like that. Who is someone to tell me I can't check someone out."

"We're accused of putting old ladies out on the street," says Parco. "It's more like the opposite. When a landlord comes in here and has an elderly tenant he wants to evict, we say, 'Look, there's nothing you can do if the person's paying the rent on time.' Most of the people we see evicted are greedy frauds who are anything but poor."

Parco, on the basis of hundreds of assets investigations, offers the workings of a financial sniff out.

"Say someone, call him Alan Becker, owes someone else a hundred thousand dollars," he says. "There are definite steps that have to be taken, beginning with a credit check."

The credit check on Becker says he has bad credit in five banks. "Say he has three judgments, including our client's judgment against him. The only previous address we have to go on is one the credit report picked up, but it's five years old."

First, the front office, probably Parco, and certainly Jo-Ann Kunda, analyzes everything they have. The old address is a big starting point. Maybe Becker filed a credit card from there. Maybe there was a car registered from there. They use documents to pinpoint anything coming out of that address five years ago.

A motor vehicle check is next. It turns up a history on the driver's license. The detectives learn that Becker had a car registered to the old address in Amagansett, New York.

The field investigator goes to the county clerk's office in Amagansett and determines that he did, indeed, own the property at the old address, but sold it three years ago. This is good news because the money from the sale can resurface in only a limited number of ways. The county clerk's office also produces documentation of the sale of the property three years ago.

The field investigator's next stop is the county clerk's office where she gets a copy of the new deed. The mortgage, as expected, was given through a bank. The agency has nothing earth-shattering to report to the client, but knowing that the target sold the property is good. He got consideration. Money.

Next is a visit to the tax assessor's office where a tax stamp is on file. The tax stamp gives the value of the property sold. Now Vincent Parco & Associates knows that the property was sold for $325,000, and that it was purchased four years earlier for $150,000. The target, who stiffed the client for $100,000, is now known to have made $175,000, minus expenses, which Parco figures amount to $25,000. Now there's $150,000 floating around somewhere, probably not under a mattress.

The field investigator's paper shows that the new owner has a second mortgage on the house, payable directly to target. The field investigator goes back to the office and hands the case over to a skip tracer.

The tracer first contacts the buyer. Though it is unlikely that a personal relationship exists between buyer and target, it cannot be assumed. The tracer chooses to use subterfuge.

"You make up a name," says Parco. "You're United Mutual Savings and Loan of Wilkes-Barre, Pennsylvania."

The tracer makes the call. "Mr. Becker has just applied for a mortgage with us and he claims that you have a second mortgage with him and that you have been paying it promptly."

Parco is a big believer in asking leading questions designed to elicit a positive response.

"Oh, yeah, sure," the mortgagee says. Now he's friendly, but not ready to talk yet. The tracer's job is to try to enlist him as an ally.

"Mr. Dunham, we understand that the transaction's gone well since the closing."

"Oh, yes."

"And everything's been fine."

"Oh, yes."

The traditional problem with novices or anyone looking for information is that they're greedy or rushed. A pro takes his time.

"No problems?"

"Oh, no."

Now the tracer takes a little break with a series of seemingly irrelevant comments about the weather up there in New York, and have you ever been out here to Pennsylvania? The Dutch Country, the Poconos, the Hershey factory? Really? Come on out, where the quality of life is pretty darned good.

Then, in a yawning way, zero in, like the information is unimportant.

"By the way, when you make the payment, do you send it to his address in Jersey?"

The person may, at this time, want to reaffirm who he's talking to.

"Excuse me. You say you're a bank in Pennsylvania?" The tracer then has to be ready with Mark R.'s dictum of always, *always*, having an answer to any question when you gag.

"Yes, United Mutual Savings and Loan of Wilkes-Barre, Pennsylvania." But you don't stop there. The interim target has raised the ante. He wants information in order to continue the game.

"Yeah, he's buying property in the Poconos. A considerable amount, you should see this spread. God, it's been on the market for two years because no one can afford the sucker. The guy must be some sharp businessman."

The tracer has asked an open-ended question masquerading as a nonquestion. The party on the other end of the line might well say, "Sure is, sure is," and the bait's been cast but not taken. But, as Parco says, the person on the other end of the line might also say, "I don't know, I don't think he's such a great businessman."

That is tracer's gold. Now is the time to elicit more information.

"No?"

"Well, you know, he gave me a second mortgage at nine percent. He could have gotten me all the way up to thirteen, see? Fourteen percent even. If I need a second mortgage to buy the house, he's in the catbird seat. So how come this great businessman didn't know that?"

Oh, boy. In his head, the tracer is now jumping up and down. He's about to reel in his catch.

"Well, you know what they say—do they call you Jim?"

"Yeah, Jim, right."

"Well, Jim, the rich get richer but not necessarily smarter." They both laugh.

"Well, got to get back to the leaves out front," Jim says. "Anything else, I can do for you?"

"Not that I can think of. Oh, wait . . . one more thing. God, my boss will kill me if I forget to ask you this. When you get the check back, do you get it back on time? Does he cash it right away?"

"Let me think. Yes, yes, he does, why?"

"Well, it's on my form, I'm not sure why, Jim, but you know banks. Just one more thing. When you get the check back, do you happen to know what bank is stamped on the back?"

"Beats the hell out of me, but it's right here, I can check in a jif."

"Well, if you don't mind. Not that important, but we're doing this thing, might as well do it right. Hope I'm not putting you out."

"Hell, no. Always glad to help out a bank. Right here on my desk. Just wait one sec . . . yeah, right here. Oh, yeah, now that you mention it, I did notice. He uses the Seventh Federal Savings and Trust of Lodi, New Jersey."

"Now," says Parco, "you know what bank he's doing business with. You know how much property he's sold, and the money he's gotten from the proceeds."

"Hey, thanks a lot," the tracer tells the caller. "Watch out for your back on those leaves. You got one of those vacuums or do you do it with plain old rake and sweat."

"Rake and sweat."

"Well, good luck."

And the tracer, knowing what he does about banks, establishes, in a much more businesslike conversation with the Seventh Federal Savings and Trust of Lodi, New Jersey, that the target has the hundred and fifty thousand and then some in various funds managed by the bank's financial planning department, and in his own name too. Several weeks later, there is a freeze put on those assets pending the outcome of the court fight which will probably go the client's way.

The tracer, having gotten his information, takes a short break before his next probe. He jokes around, complains about the coffee from the deli up the street, argues sports, and gets back to the phones with his next case.

The gentleman from the UK got his father, as Vinny predicted, in minutes. It was done without subterfuge or any magic except

Vinny Parco's insistence that all of his investigators push just a little further than someone else would.

"Goddamn it, where the hell is everyone," Vinny said, scowling when he found the snake pit as empty as it had been when he left for lunch with Ray Melucci. "Do I have to do everything around here myself?"

He first checked a real estate data base and *Cole's* for neighbors in the apartment building. Daniel Reggia had left in 1966. Vinny quickly found out why the other detectives had problems, for the building had undergone extensive renovations. Most of the old tenants were long gone and the spacious apartments that gave the building its charm in 1966 were carved into small units. It was, for all practical purposes, a different building.

But they can't all be gone, he thought to himself. They're never all gone. Life does not work that way. He assumed the building's super had been contacted by the other investigators, so he bypased that route for the moment. To warm up, he called someone in the building, explained why he was calling, and asked if she knew anyone who had been around for more than twenty years. The tenant was happy to cooperate. She gave Parco the name of a woman down the hall. Parco called her, again telling the truth. The woman remembered Daniel Reggia very well. He had moved "somewhere in Florida" sometime around 1980. She wished she could be more help, but Parco assured her that if she remembered that he had gone to Florida around 1980, she had been a very big help.

Joe Rodriguez, one of the newer tracers, came in with Marla Paul.

"Joe," Vinny said, "find me this guy right away." He handed Rodriguez a slip with the man's name on it. "He moved to Florida in 1980. Get him fast, and bring his address and phone number across the street."

Rodriguez nodded and looked at the slip.

"Pick a city in Florida," he said to Marla. "Any city."

"Kissame," she said.

"I'd love to. No, make it another one."

"Tampa."

"Too big."

She named a medium-sized city where Rodriguez called the police, explained the situation, asked if they would help out a fellow investigator by running a quick DMV. The cops, convinced of the legitimacy, were glad to help. Had they not been, Rodriguez could have called any number of Florida P.I.'s who would have gotten the information in a flash.

The two British gentlemen, stunned, shocked, and delighted, changed their flight reservations from London to Miami. They told Parco and Melucci that if they were *ever* in London, they would be pleased to put them up in their private castle.

Private castle? Now I find out they own a private castle, Parco thought. And I charged them only two hundred bucks. Fuck.

19

Joe Howard, Jr., went with his father to the Upper West Side of Manhattan.

"When I broke into the job, back in fifty-seven, only thieves and cops walked this street at night," Howard said as they walked north on Columbus Avenue, the yuppie Left Bank.

The senior Joe had promised Gus Chakas that he would come up to speak with the troublesome peddlers personally. They got to Gus's property, a block of stores and restaurants on the ground floor of an apartment building, and checked them out.

"That one seems to be in charge," Joe Junior said, pointing to the fruit vendor. His father nodded. "The others probably pay him to be here," he said.

The peddlers clustered near the corner beneath a fire escape. The fruit stand owner had the primary spot, right in the middle of pedestrian traffic. He also blocked the door to a jewelry store where the rent, Howard knew, was close to three thousand a month.

A large stand with wool hats and scarves was further down the block, along with a man who took up enormous sidewalk space selling used paperbacks and old magazines. Squished in the remaining space was a young black man who sold audio cassettes, batteries, and very cheap imitations of the Sony Walkman. Absent today, Howard could see, were the peddler of counterfeit Rolex watches, and the kid who showed up to sell umbrellas when it rained.

Any beat cop knows the pecking order of peddlers in New York. Once a vendor grabs hold of a spot on the sidewalk, it's his real estate until a stronger contender comes along. Sometimes it's easier to kill a challenger than to go through the hassle of a daily fight.

Mostly, though6olence is unnecessary. A peddler dominates a corner, a few others pay him to be there, and the rest of the street bugs off. The beat cop may speak to him a few times on behalf of the merchants, issue a summons or two, and life goes on.

But Columbus Avenue and streets near it are expensive phoenixes that rose from the ash heaps of neighborhoods urban sociologists confidently pronounced dead in the 1970s when New York was going broke. Those crazy enough to hang in had to face the creatures Charles Bronson fought in *Death Wish.*

But merchants like Gus Chakas didn't much give a damn what sociologists said about the disappearing urban middle class. They toughed it out to collect big rents from the new rich. The peddlers came with the yuppies.

The Howards walked to the fruit stand where Joe Senior looked over the tomatoes.

"Nice tomatoes. How much are they?"

"Seventy-five cents each."

Howard whistled. "For one?"

The man was older than the other peddlers, in his early forties with a dark complexion that Howard took to be Middle Eastern. He shrugged and said, "How many you want?"

"Actually, I wanted to talk to you."

The man looked away and suddenly found himself very busy, dusting off his plastic containers of dried fruits and nuts. The other peddlers looked up, then away.

"You know, the tenants on this block pay a lot of rent here," Howard said. His tone was neither condescending nor tough. "I guess you know that the owners of this property aren't too happy with your being here. I'm here to ask you nicely to leave."

"You leave, I stay." The fruit stand owner said.

The one selling the scarves came forward and said, "You cops?"

"No. I don't want any trouble any more than you do. But you're going. You're all going."

The scarf peddler spit on the sidewalk, nearly hitting Joe's shoe.

"I'm glad we understand each other, gentlemen. These businessmen don't want you on the sidewalk and it's not legal for you to be here. So, you're leaving. I'll be back."

Exiting to jeers, catcalls, and obscene gestures, the Howards went into Gus Chakas's small candy store.

"Joe, young Joe!" he said. "How're you doing? Come in, come in."

Though the stores and restaurants on the block he owned were a testament to the eighties, with facades that cost more than most people paid for a house, the store Gus Chakas inherited from his father, Pericles Chakas, was a throwback to the 1950s. A Breyers Ice Cream sign announced that this was the home of Acropolis Lunch, and inside was only a slightly updated version of the kind of candy store Ray Melucci knew as a teenager in Brooklyn.

Acropolis Lunch smells of coffee, fresh-squeezed orange juice, and several decades of cigar smoke. Gus Chakas stood behind a grill where he flipped hamburgers, looking like John Belushi on the original "Saturday Night Live."

Chakas has no accent. He is a second-generation, forty-three-year-old Greek-American businessman with a degree in business administration from NYU. Gus works hard. He gets up early in the morning and spends a long day flipping a burger here, moving a pencil there, and always shouting orders over one shoulder to half a dozen employees who really hustle.

Chakas gestured at the two detectives to follow him into his stockroom where, amid piles of neatly stacked boxes, there was a wooden desk. Chakas grabbed a seat behind it and said, "Sit, sit." Joe Junior sat on a chipped wooden chair, while his father leaned against some boxes.

"Thanks for coming up, guys," he said. "I know you're busy. You had a talk with them?"

"Yeah, and if you look out the door, you'll see I really scared them shitless," Howard said.

Chakas smiled, but it was a smile of resignation.

"I'll tell you what my father would say if he were here right now, Joe. He'd say 'Take care of it the old way,' and he wouldn't leave any room for argument there. Christ, in the old days it wouldn't have even been an issue. Everyone around here, whether they were white, black, or purple, they knew you just don't mess with a Greek guy. My uncles would have showed up and they'd either pack up nicely or get their merchandise stuffed up their asses."

"You can't do that now," Howard said. "They all have lawyers."

And there was way too much at stake. When Chakas, Sr., owned the block, there was a bodega, a convenience store catering to Spanish-speaking people, the Acropolis Lunch, a bicycle repair shop, and at least two empty stores at any one time. Now there were million-dollar restaurants run by million-dollar people, a jewelry shop, a leather goods store, and a unisex hair styling salon. The tenements upstairs that went empty half the time in the fifties, when Gus was growing up, were now converted to one-bedroom apartments that rented for three thousand and up.

Chakas shook his head. "Do me a favor if you can. The tenants want to bring in this outfit called—where the hell is it?"

He shuffled through papers on his desk and took out a business card. He handed it to Joe Howard, Jr., who was sitting closer to him.

"Urban Protective Services, you heard of these guys, Dad?" He passed the card to his father.

Howard looked at the card and shook his head. Urban Protective Services billed itself as a security consulting firm with a president named Lawrence I. Benjamin.

"Never heard of them," he said. "That doesn't mean they're no good. What's the deal?"

"The deal is there's a meeting next Tuesday night and these guys are supposed to give some kind of presentation."

"The tenants are going to foot the bill?"

"I'm not, I'll tell you that. They want me to chip in. Screw that. Can you come and listen to what these guys have to say?"

"I'll be here," Joe Junior said.

"Me too, if this slave driver here isn't sending me out of town again."

Howard told Chakas about the Calgary job, had some coffee in the luncheonette and took some notes. The fruit stand guy was named Emile and came from Morocco. Given his age and authoritative demeanor, he probably used his real name and could be checked for outstanding charges, or status as an illegal. Howard made a note to talk informally with police and immigration contacts. The rest would take more legwork because of their age. Even the summonses would probably not produce a real identity.

Meanwhile, Gus Chakas was getting criticism from all of his tenants, especially the jeweler who said that the guy with the clothing, the one who had spit near Joe's shoe, was in the habit of making crude kissing sounds at female customers. The others were taking up sidewalk space and sometimes heckling customers. There were no physical threats or robberies, just overt defiance to shop owners paying big rents.

The tenants all said they were losing big money.

"The cops," Gus Chakas said. "The cops, you know and I know, can only chase them away. That's it. We need a plan fast."

Howard allowed that these people were not especially attentive to summonses, but that he would figure something out. As he left, he went back to the fruit vendor. The clothing guy, the spitter, started to move toward him, but Howard stared and it was enough.

"Hey, Emile," he said, "you've got one very pissed off Greek in that store. You don't want an angry Greek. You're better off leaving."

"Fuck the Greek," the vendor said, "and fuck you too."

"Have a nice day, Emile."

"Your problem, gentlemen," said Larry Benjamin, "is a common one, not only in New York, but everywhere."

Benjamin wore a very expensive dark suit with understated pinstripes and a cut that impressed Joe Howard, who sat at the back of the room with his son and Gus Chakas. The tie alone, Howard figured, could run fifty bucks if you were dumb enough to buy it from one of the Fifth Avenue stores, as this jerk obviously had. Benjamin had not expected another security firm at his presentation and, when Gus Chakas introduced Joe Howard his response was condescending.

Benjamin billed himself as a "new breed security consultant." He had never been a cop, and most of his staff, Howard gathered, had no law enforcement experience, which, for Howard, is not a problem in itself. Those "new breed" claims, however, worried him. "New breed" sounded expensive.

"At Urban Protective Services, we understand the limitations of the police. They're not bad people," he said with a nod toward Howard that dripped a mocking respect, "they're simply overworked."

The meeting was held in the back room of the jewelry store. Folding wooden chairs rented for the occasion were arranged in rows. Besides the two Howards and Gus Chakas, there were about a dozen people present. Benjamin spoke next to an easel which had flip cards, the first of which said "Urban Protective Services—Security For Today's Business World."

"Our plan is three-pronged," he said. "First, we install a complete video monitoring system with screens in each of your stores and an all-weather camera mounted here," he said, pointing to a sketch he had made of the fire escape. The camera would be mounted directly above the peddlers. "And here." He flipped the paper on the easel and showed a camera that would point head on at the peddlers.

"But anyone can do that," Benjamin said. "The reason Urban Protective succeeds where others fail is because we speak the language of our problems." He took a long pause as though he had just given the date and time of the second coming of Christ.

"If you have an Arab peddler, we speak to him in Arabic. If he's Hispanic, we speak to him in Spanish, and if he is black, we have black people on our staff who will relate to him. We will make it clear that whenever they show up we will be there, and they *will* leave."

One of the merchants, a nervous-looking man with gray springy hair said, "Do you use force?"

Benjamin seemed happy to field the question. "We are forceful without using physical force," he said.

Your ass, Joe thought. These bastards aren't going to move unless you come after them with a howitzer.

"So," he said, flipping a new card on the easel:

WATCH
APPROACH
EXECUTE

"First, you do the watching. That saves time, ours and yours. It also saves you money. We don't have to put a man on the screens. You do it from your stores."

Howard figured their video monitoring system would cost fifteen to twenty thousand dollars and after about four days, no one would watch it.

"Next comes the approach. When you see one of those peddlers out there, you call us right away, and we'll send a radio-dispatched security vehicle to the site."

God, they won't live through the fright, Howard thought.

"And that's when we talk to them in *their* language. I guarantee you, when you know someone's language, you can get them out pretty fast. And," he said with that pause again, "that brings us to phase three. Our idea of an execution is not the electric chair, although a lot of you have asked me if I can get one wholesale."

There was nervous laughter among the merchants, more because Benjamin so obviously expected it than because he had said anything funny.

"But in the execution, we work *pretty closely* with the police. When they get a call from Urban Protective, they take it *very seriously*. With our kind of pressure, your peddlers will peddle elsewhere."

There was wild applause. It was obvious to Gus Chakas that his tenants were going to try to get him to pay at least half the twenty thousand for the installation of the video system plus the two thousand a month retainer that Urban Protective wanted for its "three-pronged" approach.

"What'd you think, Joseph?" he asked.

"I think it's a crock of shit, Gus. Let them get all excited about these guys, but don't promise them anything. I think I know what I'm going to do."

20

When Vinny Parco called, Rainer Melucci was at home in Brooklyn brewing a pot of gourmet coffee and talking to Corky, his parakeet. He stuck his face close to the cage and said, "Hello, Corky," and tweeted.

Corky hopped from his swing to the water trough at the edge of the cage, put his face close to Melucci's and tweeted back. Melucci tilted his head to the left, the bird tilted his head to the right.

Melucci tweeted again and the bird returned the call. The phone rang.

"Hi, Ray, Vinny. I've got some fast work for you if you've got the time."

He did. Melucci is a link to the netherworld of electronic countermeasures, bugging and debugging. It is a dark place whose denizens often have no names or faces, past or future, and where good and evil are abstractions best left on the sane side of the looking glass.

Melucci learned the basics of his electronics as a law enforcement officer, on stakeout in the subways. He and his partners found they could cover more surveillance distance and keep out of the cold by the wiring of tollbooths most frequently targeted for robbery. "When I retired," he says "I lost all interest in putting them in."

The former Transit Authority detective will talk about his work. Not many in his field do. There is an adage that a lot of the same people who take bugs out put them in. There are no reliable figures on illegal electronic eavesdropping, but it is widely believed to be running rampant in American business and industry. Tiny listening devices are sold commercially in telephones, calculators, pens, replicas of cigarette packs, lamps, and miniature automobiles. They can be installed anywhere and they work well. Demand is high.

The clients read about bugs and they want the goods. They want a video close-up of every sexual calisthenic, they want to keep employees honest by snooping on them, and they like having something illicit. It gives them a source of braggadocio, a power trip. And because they're willing to pay, they find no shortage of technology and operatives willing to connect the wires.

Bugging can be a felony. A P.I. could go to jail for ten years if successfully prosecuted under the Omnibus Crime Act, the Privacy Act, or hundreds of state and local statutes forbidding the use of these toys. Right now, prosecutions are down. Liberals say it's just another Reagan Era excess, while cops and a lot of P.I.'s say it's a problem of manpower and getting a case that will stand up in court.

Melucci is a soft-spoken, thoughtful man who could be a decade younger than his forty-nine years. The wary, seen-it-all expression of the street cop mops up some of the youthfulness, but his is a countenance that also says, Trust me, I'll get you through this.

Melucci grew up on Flatbush Avenue in Brooklyn. Candy stores, street corner harmony, wise old birds from the old country out on the stoop, street gangs, and fast cars were part of his teenage years in the 1950s.

"That's when I had hair," he jokes.

Melucci was held back from joining the police department by a dim academic record, a military obligation ahead of him, and not being Irish. You could get on the job as an Italian boy, of course, but an Irish friend in the late 1950s talked a lot louder in the department ranks, especially if your grades were such that high school graduation was something akin to a pardon.

After a stint in the Army, during which he married a girl from Massachusetts, Melucci tried again. This time he got a little help from a captain in the Transit Police. Transit, Housing, and Port Authority cops take regular police training, then spend their careers enforcing the law in their chosen areas. Transit cops spend most of their time in the New York City subways, and they have a friendly debate going with Housing cops as to who sees more of God's mistakes. It's probably a toss-up.

Transit cops are a tight, isolated breed who see inhuman levels of violence, if not on a daily basis, often enough so they can't shut it off at the end of a watch. Melucci calls himself a "Wambaugh story" whose job-related stress cost him his first marriage. One day he came home to find his wife and two children had moved to Massachusetts.

His rise to detective came after a well-publicized bust in the early 1970s when he and his partner stayed up more than thirty hours to break a theft ring. Thousands of dollars worth of hot merchandise was recovered before it could be fenced.

Ray considers himself to have been a good cop, but one who didn't always fit in. A good cop isn't about to report his buddies to Internal Affairs if they resort to unusual means in unusual circumstances. If, for example, a gang raped a little girl, then one of the members slit her throat, there are "tactics" to find out which of the group did the actual murder.

Assuming all the gang members have long yellow sheets that attest to the suffering they've caused, one way of getting the answer is to question the members one by one. Ask each of them about his mother, the last time he went to school, and will the Yankees ever see the pennant again. Then put a shotgun in his mouth and ask which of his buddies killed the ten-year-old girl. When the same name keeps surfacing, the puzzle is complete.

Do such tactics occur in the Transit Police on a daily basis? They do not. Are they unheard of? They are not. Ray Melucci had no problems with what might be called the pragmatism of inner city interrogation in extremely violent cases, but he did begin to develop a compassion for the kids who might steal a purse on the way home from school when there isn't a lot to eat. He had a hard time concealing it, especially when he didn't curse loudly at cuffed prisoners, or give them a final whack before locking them up.

Again, he states, he was a good cop. If a fellow officer went a little nuts with the violence, kicking some maggot in the face while he's cuffed, Melucci wrote it off to the ugliness of the work. But as time passed, his compassion began to show.

Part of it was that he was now more educated. Melucci, like Vinny Parco, got a college degree the hard way, by going to school at night until he'd completed enough credits for a bachelor's in psychology. Always a tinkerer, he learned many electronics tricks as a detective and learned a lot more after a job-related injury forced him to retire in 1979.

Basically, Ray Melucci sweeps for two kinds of bugs, room transmitters and phone taps. He has more than thirty thousand dollars worth of equipment that he takes all over metro New York in his burgundy BMW, working for other P.I.'s, Fortune 500 corporations, union officials, and, he'll admit, a few wiseguys who hire him legally when they think the Feds are bugging them.

Technology has perfected their miniaturization so well that a transmitter can fit inside the eraser of a number two pencil. With a relay transmitter, a device this size can transmit a quarter mile or more. More often, they nest inside electrical outlets or telephones, in walls and ceilings. Corporate security debuggers always check wastebaskets where intelligence operatives have a habit of gluing transmitters in paper clip boxes, discarded coffee cups, matchbooks, or other trash.

Room bugs usually send out a radio signal, often on a standard 88 to 108 megahertz FM band that can be picked up elsewhere in the building or outside in a car or van. In the movies, they pick up every nuance of conversation with Tiffany crystal clarity. In life, even expensive bugs can hiss, crackle, and amplify room noise.

But, whether or not the bugs work well, and whether or not they even exist on as massive a scale as debuggers claim, any agency that wants to remain competitive needs to have an electronic countermeasures specialist like Ray Melucci on the premises or on call.

Melucci has seen it all. One of the most common bugs is called the infinity transmitter, so named because it gets an endless supply of power from a room's telephone or electrical current. This quarter-inch monster can be hidden under carpets, in vases, behind curtains, in walls, ceilings, in the always hospitable phone itself, or behind the switch plate of an electrical outlet. It can even be "hard wired" with conductive paint that carries electricity as effectively as copper wires, and can be covered with real paint without sacrificing transmission quality.

The infinity bug is activated by telephone. A caller punches up the target's number and blows a whistle into the receiver as he hears the ring. This shorts out the ring itself and activates the transmitter. The room conversation then becomes a radio show for as long as the intruder chooses to listen. A really proficient operative can plant four or five bugs in strategic locations that will have the same effect as miking several guests on a talk show. Anyone calling in during the snooping would get a busy signal, and if the target picked up the phone, he'd get a dead or hissing line. The spy can check in with his target anytime and from any telephone in the world.

Melucci finds infinity bugs with a suitcase-sized device known as an RF (radio frequency) detector. RF detectors are highly sensitive bloodhounds that track radio waves. As Melucci gets close to his quarry, he listens for a high-pitched tone that coordinates with a visual register on a radarlike screen. When the scope's electronics are dancing, the needles on the machine's meters move sharply to the right, the tone shrieks in his headphones, he finds the bug and removes it with pincers, like a dentist taking out an abscessed tooth.

RF generators can also capture video signals from a hidden camera. Thanks to microtechnology, video bugs will probably become common in the 1990s. For now, the audio technology that has been in place since the 1960s gives a P.I. or unlicensed intelligence operative all the information he needs.

Melucci's first stop that day was a regular client, a contractor who thought he'd lost a couple of important jobs because a competitor had tapped his phone and submitted lower bids. Melucci doubts it, but sweeps regularly, checking electrical outlets, picture frames and hooks (one bug is made specifically to look like a picture hook with the spike serving as an antenna), and, of course, the wastebasket.

"It sounds like a spy movie," Melucci says grimly, "but these things really go on all the time."

He checked the phone bill for evidence of an off-premises extension, a phone installed in another location which can be tapped without detection in a sweep.

Melucci then swept for carrier current bugs which operate within the electrical system of a building. The operative places a bug inside an outlet and, when he wants to tune in his target, he uses a radio in his own office, a stockroom, or basement of some other place where he's not likely to be interrupted. There will be some hiss and crackle, but the conversation will be unmistakable. Carrier current bugs esape RF detectors because they send no waves through the air. Melucci locates them with a device for checking voltage drains in electrical lines.

Mostly, he finds paranoia instead of bugs. "God bless paranoids," he says. "They have a need that builds up, a psychological desperation to have someone purge them of their demons for a while." Like Vinny Parco, Melucci gets calls from psychiatrists and other therapists who actually hire them to sweep the homes of clients agitated to the point of panic over imagined invaders of their privacy.

But the paranoia that keeps Melucci and hundreds in his field working is the less clinical and far more rampant strain found in major corporations whose ideas and patents are being ripped off wholesale. These clients don't imagine bugs and taps. They're there.

Computer data, unless properly shielded, can be tapped as easily as a house phone. Most security effort goes into protecting access codes, but, several years ago, Sean Walker, a reporter for the British Broadcasting Corporation, demonstrated more plebian computer vulnerabilities. He walked through a trade show pushing a cart with a video display terminal, a signal generator, and a CB antenna. As he went from aisle to aisle, he twisted dials and tuned into one computer after another, his screen registering the data as mortified exhibitors stared in shock. The cost of the components for such a rip-off is five hundred dollars. Computer screens can be tapped from a van parked up to two miles away.

An important telex coming in from Europe, a memo from one divisional vice president to the next, or a personal letter typed by a secretary during lunch are all up for grabs if one has the right equipment. Shielding computers to prevent them from emitting buggable electrical impulses adds up to 50 percent to their purchase price.

Microwave intercepts are another easily accomplished form of electronic snooping. Much computer and voice communication is relayed by microwave dishes to communications satellites. Snatching that information as it works its way into space can be as easy as netting a butterfly on a spring day.

Even when Melucci finishes a job, he can't be 100 percent sure he's found everything. For every countermeasure, there seems to be a counter-countermeasure. A shrewd bugger will tune his transmitter to a frequency close to a large commercial broadcast outlet, making it very difficult for most RF detectors to pick up.

New circuitry enables bugs to store information and compress it into the electronic equivalent of freeze-dried coffee. Then, when the operative wants it, he hits a remote-controlled switch and hours of data or conversation are transmitted in a millisecond. To date, only the hit-or-miss task of tuning into the proper frequency during the half second or so of transmission can detect such a bug.

Even electric typewriters can be invaded with a special microphone that translates the taps of a ball on an IBM Selectric into electrical impulses that work their way through a series of relays to a computer screen where the operative reads the correspondence as it is typed. Given the dominance of computers in the office environment, this piece of technology will probably not earn its creator a chateau in Cannes, but it's there for whoever wants it.

Later that day, Melucci visited a union official who thought he was being bugged by the FBI. Melucci came up empty-handed, but covered several windows with foil to shield the room from a laser shotgun, easily the most flamboyant bug of the 1980s, a device Ian Fleming should have lived to see. Once thought to be either make-believe or a toy for the highest levels of the CIA and KGB, this thirty-thousand-dollar wonder is working its way into private and local police use. Because of the precisely focused quality that laser beams have over ordinary light, the gun can be pointed at a window from a rooftop up to fifteen hundred feet away and the operator can pick up conversations that vibrate off glass. The laser is said to be detection proof, at least for the moment.

Reports vary on the laser gun's effectiveness. Some say the bug has bugs, for it does not distinguish between the outside noise vibrations—cars, construction, or a pigeon on the sill—and the targeted conversation inside. An improperly shielded laser bug can also cause severe burns. But, like VCRs and electronic calculators, the quality is expected to go up and the price down.

To uncover body bugs or wired briefcases, legal surveillance techniques used by P.I.'s who do a lot of undercover work, Melucci uses a device called a nonlinear junction detector, a vacuum cleanerlike gadget that can find a tape recorder even if the batteries aren't operating. The nonlinear junction detector "reads" semiconductors, essential components of radios, tape recorders, and other devices concealed by undercover agents.

One of the most important aspects of debugging is the visual search, or "environment sweep," as Melucci calls it. Besides room and phone bugs, Melucci scans for evidence of "thru-wall devices," or "spike mikes," embedded through a tiny hole on the other end of a wall. Spike mikes, which attest to the continuation of the keyhole-peeping image most P.I.'s would like to bury in the past, can hear whispers though concrete.

Melucci also warns clients against discussing sensitive information in a parking lot where conversations can be heard a block or more away. This is accomplished by using shotgun and parabolic microphones whose clarity has long allowed football fans to overhear NFL quarterbacks cursing the refs on national television.

Most P.I.'s are ex-cops who don't exactly clutch their hearts and exclaim, "No!" when they find electronic eavesdropping. As law enforcement people, they usually remember dozens of cases that would never have been closed without evidence collected by court-approved wiretaps and room bugs. And there's no way to calculate the value of the indirect evidence gleaned from a legal bug—conversations with girlfriends, voiceprints that prove thug A is linked to thug B, coded drug and gambling banter that can be cracked by cryptographers. This is the information that fuels hunches, the cops' main weapon against crime. Like them or not, bugs are an essential weapon in the fight against organized crime, drug dynasties, theft rings, and terrorists.

But the same bugs that are available to the police are available to the crooks, the general public, computer hackers, buffs, and plain old voyeurs. The mob has all the latest gadgets. No one likes to talk about it, but bugs are easier to score than an ounce of marijuana. Most of the technology is legal.

Like Molotov cocktails and pipe bombs, electronic surveillance devices are dangerous, devastating weapons made from everday components. Infinity transmitters are available commercially as burglar alarms that protect, say, a mountain cabin from trespass. An electric guitar mike that can be picked up in any music store can be used to listen to conversation on the other side of a wall. So can an electronic stethoscope that a cardiologist uses to save lives.

The government could outlaw the most sensitive miniature microphones ever manufactured, close down the plants, and arrest the cads who make them, but they'd be trashing hearing aid companies and incarcerating the selfless souls whose R&D allows the deaf to hear again.

Hobby shops such as Radio Shack feature aisle after aisle of components that any high school student can fashion into a bug. Wireless intercoms, for example, are legitimately sold as office implements, but if you take them out of their casing and stuff them into a light fixture, they work as well as any superspook toy sold for ten times the price. Even a kid's do-it-yourself disc jockey toy, the one with the mike that sends a voice into an FM radio, is a bug in the rough.

And the fancier bugs are sold legitimately by police supply houses whose "law enforcement only" policies stringently require that all requests for catalogs be on law enforcement letterhead, to mail-order houses that don't look too carefully at who buys the goods.

A laser shotgun can be mail ordered outside the country or assembled in your basement if you order a 35-watt H1A1 industrial laser from General Electric plus a reflecting telescope from Edmund Scientific Company, two reputable outfits whose executives would paint graffiti on the White House before they would enter the bug market.

Kafka would have had a hard time dreaming up the scenario for bug installation that many P.I.'s, cops, and sources who prefer not to say *what* they do report as SOP.

A client who wants to bug someone calls a lawyer who doesn't want to know it. The lawyer calls a P.I. who doesn't want to know it either. Officially, all bugging requests stop right there.

Somehow an intermediary who might even be a convicted felon gets called and puts together a team, usually consisting of an electronics expert and, though the word is not used, a burglar, someone skilled at getting into locked places at night. In true Watergate fashion, the team is not directly connected to the P.I., lawyer, and client. They not only don't know who they're working for, they might not even know the true identity of the intermediary who, in the fancier version of the scenario, does not even go on the job.

Sometimes, a competitor wants information on one of a company's key executives. A reliable way to get that information is to bug him in the privacy of his home. Here, it must be said, is an opportunity even the most jaded industrial espionage operatives, not to mention thousands of licensed P.I.'s, refuse. The Bill of Rights becomes a lot less interpretive once that threshold is crossed. However, where there's money, there are always those willing to take the risk.

A van bearing the logo of the local telephone or utility company pulls up. It parks up the block from the target household and two men get out. They wear hardhats and bear the reassuring crackle of walkie-talkies that hang, along with lots of other equipment, from their tool belts. They climb the utility pole, disconnect an electrical lead, and the power goes out up and down the block. They politely go from house to house showing laminated IDs and reassuring everyone that the lights will be back on momentarily. It is important that their progress is seen by someone, usually the executive's wife, in the target house. Then they knock on the door.

The team usually makes sure the target is at work. They introduce themselves to the wife, flash the badges, and apologize for the problem. If the woman is shrewd enough to verify the employment of her visitors by calling the number on the ID, she'll get a scam line with another operative answering the phone, "Con Ed Security, good morning."

Can they go into the basement?

The wife may notice that one of the guys is really cute. He's the one who will suddenly find her fascinating and stay upstairs to chat while his partner wanders around putting in his room bugs and telephone taps.

In the garage or basement are a series of uninteresting meters and scratchy old gray utility boxes. By the time the partner comes upstairs, there's one more, usually with a very official or threatening looking decal that reads Con Edison, Pacific Telephone, Central Illinois Power and Light, or Danger High Voltage. It's usually locked. Inside is a voice-activated tape recorder that documents every telephone call coming in or going out. If it's a matrimonial case, the inquisitive spouse simply goes to the cellar, removes the cassette, and listens while his once beloved makes cooing noises to her lover.

If it's an industrial espionage case, the information can be checked by a beeper, just like a telephone answering machine.

Late that afternoon, after a day of finding no bugs, Ray Melucci found not one, but two such machines. One was hooked to a private line Louis Gloskin shared with Joel Stein at work, and another was in his garage.

"Bingo," Melucci said, as he pulled the Panasonic voice-activated cassette recorder out of its scratched metal housing. Gloskin looked pale, but Parco and Melucci were thrilled. Louis could now remove the cassette and listen to conversations once Melucci gave him a tape recorder modified to run at the superslow speed that buggers use for taps.

"I have to warn you about that, Louis," Parco said.

"It's not something you necessarily want to hear, your wife talking to her boyfriend."

"I can handle it," he said evenly.

"Good man," Vinny said. "Be sure to use the phone for routine business, no more, no less than you have right along. And I want you to call me in the office tomorrow. Right from the tapped line.

The next morning, Parco received the call on schedule.

"Vincent," Gloskin said. "I have to let you go."

"Let me go, why, Louis?"

"Because you haven't found anything. I feel I should go to my best friend and my wife and ask their forgiveness for my terrible suspicions. I feel so guilty, Vincent."

"Hey, Louis," Vincent said. "I understand, but now we know. You shouldn't feel guilty. It turns out that you suspected your wife and best friend of something they're not doing and we found out for you."

And with any luck, we'll catch those turds the next time they go out, Parco thought.

"Well, I want to thank you."

"May I make one suggestion?" Vinny asked. "Louis, don't confront or confess. Let your suspicions be our secret. Take Sarah out to a nice dinner and forget the whole thing. Hey, mazeltov, it looks like everything worked out."

They discussed billing and hung up.

Parco decided that he'd see this one through himself. The next time Sarah and Joel met, they would have company.

21

"Mary Costa was her name," Barry Silvers told both Girards on the telephone.

"Is that Spanish?" Karen asked.

"Portuguese, I'm told," Barry said. "But you can't get too excited yet. There's still a lot of looking to do. That's not an uncommon name in the Providence area," he said.

He'd flown from Providence to Washington where he changed planes for West Palm Beach. He had an appointment that morning with Amanda Sagamore, the woman who believed she had lost her jewels to the Duke of Audley.

"I have the address," Silvers said, "and I have someone checking it for me, a free-lance P.I. We know the street was in a housing project, but I don't know much more than that yet."

"We sure appreciate it," Jeff said. Silvers was gratified with the young man's response.

"Well, as I said, I wouldn't be too optimistic yet. There are a lot of Costas in that region. I have this one stop to make, then I'll shoot right back up there."

Silvers felt good. He ate breakfast and took a cab to Rolls-Royce country.

"Nice of you to see me, Mrs. Sagamore," Barry Silvers said, as he seated himself on a rattan chair overlooking several acres of shrubbery and crew cut lawn in Palm Beach. A black servant in a white coat brought him a soft drink. "I know you have other things you'd rather be doing."

"Not at all, Mr. Silvers. I'd like to see this son of a bitch exposed," she said. "And I'd like to see my jewels, especially the emerald brooch. It's an extremely sentimental piece," she said, taking out a photograph of a basket-shaped pin studded with emeralds. Flowers coming out of the basket were made of pearls.

"Yes, I've seen this photograph. So lovely. Such a shame. Maybe I can help. I've been following Mr. Hammond on a case of bank fraud. That's all I'm free to discuss, I'm afraid."

"I understand," she said with a smile. "Some of us in Palm Beach still respect confidentiality, not many, but some." She laughed. She wore ivory slacks, a printed silk blouse, and a wide-brimmed straw hat to protect her from the sun. "And what questions might I answer?"

"Well, I'd like to start at the beginning and ask how you first came to meet Hammond."

"The first time I saw him was in Washington, at a party in Georgetown before an opening at the Kennedy Center. My friend, Lance Dillon, introduced me. Now, Lance really is a duke and this young man, Hammond, was keeping company with his son, Jasper, who will take over the family title soon.

"Well, my God, I've known Lance since before the war, and the first time I saw Jasper, the kid was in diapers."

"So, if Lance introduced Hammond as a duke—"

"Then he was a duke, of course. He never said, 'I'm the Duke of Audley.' Real dukes don't. Of course, I never thought to check him out. You don't do that. If you're introduced by someone you know to be his friend, you accept that he's all right."

Silvers nodded.

"Well, it turned out that the so-called Duke of Audley knew a lot of people I knew, or at least I thought he did. That's the thing, Mr. Silvers. He named a lot of my friends who knew him either slightly or not at all, it turns out, but the young man was so convincing."

"So convincing that he believes his own act, I've heard, Mrs. Sagamore," Silvers said.

Mrs. Sagamore took a sip of her iced tea. "That's it precisely. You have the man. When he's conning, he does think he's a duke. He gets himself so worked up, you could give him a lie detector test and he'd pass. You'd never question him, that much I know."

"But I understand you were skeptical just the same," said Silvers. He was getting a little thirsty in the sun. "May I trouble you for a little more of this diet soda?"

"Oh, of course, you poor man, you must be roasting. I'm used to the sun down here."

She ordered some more Diet Coke for Silvers and iced tea for herself and continued.

"Yes, I became skeptical when I started asking him a few questions that he couldn't answer. I asked about the health of a mutual friend. In these circles, Mr. Silvers, you're always poking around, trying to find out if someone knows the real story of a family.

"Do they know that so-and-so's youngest had a tiff with someone? How's poor Uncle Raymond doing after his operation?

"For a man who was supposed to be close to one family, then another, this guy didn't know so much. He was fudging. Part of it was that he was from the north. Audley is a little isolated, but I started watching him more closely and I said to a friend, 'I think this guy's kind of a phony baloney.' "

One night Hammond called and they set a date for dinner. He said he had some business to discuss, an opportunity that she shouldn't miss.

"That's when I got really suspicious. At the last minute, I invited a friend of mine, George Harvey, to dinner. I called up Mr. Hammond and asked if that was all right with him. Well, he tried to talk me out of it, saying that this deal is very hush-hush and involved names that have to be kept in confidence. Was there any way I could have dinner with George another night?

"Richard can be very persuasive. Very, very persuasive, but I've been around a long time, Mr. Silvers, and if I don't wish to be persuaded, I hold my ground."

Barry Silvers had found out about Mrs. Sagamore when, in the course of the fraud investigation, one of his sources had mentioned that the Duke might have been involved in the robbery of a posh hotel in New York. His source was able to tell him only that the robbery occurred in " '82, '83, maybe even '84." From there, it was a matter of painstakingly poring over the text of the *New York Times Index* until he found the robberies that might have matched the profile.

New York's high-roller hotels—the Plaza, Pierre, Sherry-Netherland, and others—usually have resident guests like Mrs. Sagamore whose privacy is one of the security chief's highest priorities. The staffs are not merely reluctant to speak with anyone about robberies, they don't acknowledge their existence, even if the *Times* wrote it up.

"That's where you have to show the security people you're one of the gang, so to speak," Silvers says. "They're mostly ex-cops and when I showed them that I'm an ex-Fed, they talked a little unofficially."

A little unofficially was enough to guide Barry Silvers to a police detective who, though now in another division, wanted very badly to see Richard Peter Hammond put in prison.
This detective called Mrs. Sagamore and asked if he might give her name and phone number to Silvers.

Now, as he sipped his Diet Coke, he asked her about that dinner with the Duke.

"He was nervous all night and very cold to my friend," she said.

"Well, then he wanted to go to all the clubs downtown, Mr. Silvers. My God, have you—I'd say you probably haven't been inside the Palladium very much."

"Mrs. Sagamore, you've got me pegged. I've never been to the Palladium."

She laughed. "Well, I think you can probably guess that the night scene is the good-night scene for me too. You're still a kid compared to me. I think Hammond was trying to ditch poor George and maybe show off a little, because we got into all the celebrity rooms of the clubs, you know, and the Duke of Audley never paid a cent for the Dom Perignon. Celebrities don't. You know, Mr. Silvers, this man is so stylish, so fashionable, that even the *celebrities* in there, this rock star and some kid that's in all those high school movies, I hear . . ." Mrs. Sagamore tried so hard to remember a name that Silvers wouldn't recognize that he felt obliged to help. The only name he could think of was Madonna.

"Not her. It doesn't matter. Afterward, when we got back to the hotel, he insisted that we talk business in my suite. I said I was tired, we could discuss the plan at another time. Then he insisted that he had to see me upstairs. I gave George the eye and right away he picked up on what I wanted and came up too."

When she got to the part about entering the room, Mrs. Sagamore's voice began to tremble. Her hand shook so much she put the iced tea on a table.

"Two men in ski masks came out of the other room of the suite. Obviously, they'd been waiting there all night. They handcuffed all of us—me to the bed, Richard to the other side of the bed, and they took George into the bathroom. My God, I thought, they're going to shoot him, but they threw him to the floor and put handcuffs on him, then fastened him to the plumbing fixtures below the sink. Poor George. I didn't realize that handcuffs could hurt so much. They broke the poor man's wrist."

And walked away with $750,000 worth of Mrs. Sagamore's sapphires, diamonds, rubies, and emeralds. Insurance came to about $400,000. She hadn't kept up with inflation.

Mrs. Sagamore gave Barry the number of the New York P.I. who had helped her with the case. She promised to call him and ask him to share information, and offered Barry Silvers all, or part, of the hundred thousand dollar reward she was paying for the safe return of the jewels, no questions asked, if that was the way it would have to be.

Silvers thanked her and caught a plane north. At some point, he'd have to go to Rio and St. Maarten on this, but the Girards were anxious. First, he'd go to Providence and continue looking for Jeff's biological mother.

22

"I don't care what you heard on the tape, Louis," Vinny Parco said into the telephone. "Joel is not running off to Israel with her."

Louis Gloskin had become edgy and obsessive, unhealthily consumed by the tape and his wife's affair. He called Parco constantly with new suspicions. Now he thought Sarah and Joel were planning to flee to Israel with Gloskin's children. "By the way, Louis, where are you calling from?"

"The Spartacus Diner."

"Fine. Now calm down and listen. There's no movement of funds on his part or hers. You say she has no passport?"

"Not that I know of," Gloskin said, "but can you check that out for me?"

"Louis, that costs. We have no evidence to go chasing around a federal office."

"He said it. What more evidence do you need, Vincent? He said it."

"Tell me what was said exactly."

"She said, 'I'll be glad when we're together all the time.' And Joel said, 'It's coming, darling. All the time. But you know it's going to take some time.' "

Parco blinked. "I don't understand. Did either of them mention Israel?"

"Not in so many words, but I know they'd both like to live there."

"Louis, I'm beginning to wish we hadn't found the tap."

First, he and Melucci had to trot down to police headquarters and fill out affidavits that they'd found the bug, a necessary, but time-consuming activity. Now his client was hearing things.

"Louis, your children would tell you if mom took them to the passport office. And he has kids too."

Parco thought that Joel bugged Louis out of paranoia, to see if Gloskin had a side deal or two going. Business partners do it all the time, especially when they have a friend or a relative who brags about having done it himself. The tap, according to Melucci, was a workmanlike but rudimentary job probably done by an amateur. A pro would have either put in an off-premises extension or run the tap outside where there were a dozen different places to hide the casing. If they had to, they could bury it.

But Joel was not a man ready to pack it in and leave the country. His assets remained in place. Parco didn't rule it out, but he couldn't take such a theory seriously on the basis of what he had right now.

There were two more calls from Gloskin that day. One was to ask if Sarah could apply for a family passport without taking the kids to the office (she could not), and the other came at six o'clock when Sarah went to pick up the kids at the babysitter's and he checked the damn tape again. The lovers were meeting tonight.

They weren't hard to follow this time. Stein picked up Sarah in the Caldor parking lot and they headed toward their destination with Vinny and Marla two cars behind.

"The Cross Island," Marla said. "They're headed for the Cross Island."

"No problem," Vinny said.

Marla kept count on the expressway. When they lost Joel because they had to stop at a Yield sign, Marla found him right away by counting the number of cars that went by while they were stopped.

"Right there in the middle," she said. "I've got them."

Then they got stuck behind an eighteen-wheeler, but Marla again counted the number of cars that passed them on each side, added the number of cars she knew separated them from the target car before the truck got in the way, and found them again.

"He's turning, Vinny," she said, "he's getting off the expressway."

The off-ramp led to a two-lane gasoline alley that had been through a tough couple of decades. Video stores that advertised X-rated movies in movable type on canary yellow signs stood in buildings once occupied by middle-class restaurants and stores.

Parco could see a couple of motels. Don't get greedy, he said to himself. Now you know where they come. Progressive surveillance. Next time, start here. Let them zig and zag up the ying yang, let them commit hari-kari on the freaking boulevard, but when they get to this tawdry little setting for their passion, you'll be waiting.

There was enough traffic to cover them, and Joel was now moving slowly down the road, convinced that he had not been followed. Parco breathed more evenly. He didn't need to see them check in just yet. He pulled over to give his target more time to settle.

Hot sheet motel owners spend ten or twenty grand putting up big fences around their buildings to keep private eyes from jotting down license numbers. Then they hire desk clerks at minimum wage who will give up every bit of information one needs, plus their own sisters, for twenty bucks. Vinny was sure he could get the guest register page with Joel's alias and signature.

Once they were inside, Parco would find the car, log the time, and size up the situation.

"You religious, Marla?"

"I observe. I'm not as religious as I'm supposed to be, I guess."

"You know, it's funny. I've followed priests, ministers, rabbis, you name it. The more extreme they are with the religion, the more repressed, the crazier they get when they let loose. Would you come to one of these shitholes with a man?"

"You kidding?"

"Now, I'm not saying there's anything wrong with religion, Marla. Religion's good. But the ones with the weirdest kinks are the very, very religious people."

Parco started the Riviera and cruised down the avenue, driving by a few motels that would be candidates.

"Down there, Vinny," Marla said.

Parco saw Joel's car parked on the side of a big parking lot next to the Sea Breeze Motel, about as near the sea or breezes as the Mojave Desert. He made a sharp turn and drove quickly toward the car. It was still raining slightly and Vinny could see the neon glow of a sign.

He had intended to pass the Toyota, but Parco had to swerve to avoid a car that suddenly backed out of a parking space at top speed. Parco will never know whether the driver of that car was impaired in his judgment by the high drama of infidelity, or was just your basic idiot who would shove a car into reverse and gun it without looking. Either way, Vinny was forced to slam on the brakes, bringing the Riviera to a stop nose to nose with Joel's car.

"Vinny," Marla said, with near panic in her voice.

"I know," Parco said.

They hadn't known until they were almost on top of the Toyota, until their headlights told them that they had stumbled into one of the big no-no's of surveillance. Joel and Sarah hadn't yet gone into the motel.

There are no unbreakable rules for sane conduct as a detective, but one that comes close is that you don't make contact with your target on a surveillance. Parco had come a few inches from flattening his. He could see them shielding their eyes against his headlights. Sarah was now covering as much of her head as she could with her hands.

Shit, he thought. Shit. Shit. Shit.

23

Vinny Parco took a second to anchor himself. The less confident you feel, the more confident you act. Parco threw open the car door and walked directly to Joel Stein, still dazed from the near miss. He didn't waver. He was heading for his natural habitat, the edge. He tapped on the window and started talking.

"Hey, buddy, you okay? God, I almost mowed you down there."

Parco moved closer to the window. Sarah was under the dashboard, literally on the floor.

"I'm fine, I think," Joel said. Parco could see that Joel was a handsome man in his early thirties. He wore a yarmulke, but unlike Gloskin, his clothes were stylish. Tonight he wore a sweater that had to cost two hundred bucks at Bloomingdale's. Parco kept talking.

"My lawyer—goes to show you how much those clowns know, right?—my smart lawyer says, 'Take the road the same speed you took it the night of the accident,' so like an idiot I take the same road at the same time and almost get into another accident. Glad you're okay."

Then he went back to the car and took out his camera with a special thirty-five-hundred dollar night vision infrared lens.

"Hey, Marla, hon, come on out." Before she even stepped out, Parco had started snapping his pictures. Up, down, around his car.

"Sit right there, babe," he said, patting the Riviera's headlight. Marla climbed to the top of the fender.

"Big smile, honey," he said and snapped a few shots of her.

Joel backed his car into his parking space. Sarah sat up and Parco whirled around and got four shots of them together. "Smile," he said, as the camera whirred.

Joel threw his hands over his face too late.

"Hey, you ducked," Vinny said. "Someone is cheeeeaaattting. Naughty, naughty." Then he studiously photographed a manhole cover that was slightly ajar.

"Look at that sucker," he said to Joel. "That's what did it. I come barrel-assing down that half-assed driveway and that thing was open. That son-of-a-bitch almost took the freaking ball joints right off the car. Now they're trying to close it and say it was never open. Give me a hand, will you buddy? It'll take one second."

"Ah . . ."

"Don't worry," he said, "I'm cheating myself." Joel and Sarah didn't say anything. Parco took a couple of more shots of the manhole cover.

"I'm Vinny and this is Marla. We're where we shouldn't be ourselves."

"Vinny," Marla said, annoyed. "Let's leave these people to their own privacy, okay?"

Parco then became a wellspring of sincerity. "Hey, seriously, I know what this is. I'm really sorry. It's tense enough, as it is."

"I'm Joel," Stein said. "And this is Sarah. You're right. It's tense."

Sarah had gotten out of the car but was standoffish, as Parco expected she would be, but he kept the conversation flowing, and, for the next ten minutes, they exchanged cheating horror stories.

"Yeah, so I said to my wife, 'I just dented the car a little,' and she says, 'Where?' and I say, 'Mostly under the driver's side. It doesn't show much.' But she doesn't let it go at that. She says, 'I mean where were you when you dented it?' 'Oh, over on Queens Boulevard.' "

Parco had moved closer to Sarah to let Joel get a look at Marla. He had paid close attention when Louis Gloskin said he thought Joel Stein was the womanizer his father had been. Though Louis Gloskin was his client, he was not without some sympathy for Sarah's situation. She probably hadn't had much of a youth, and she was probably pretty hooked on Joel. That he could understand because this man was handsome, stylish, and charming, everything her husband was not.

Bad move on her part, he figured, but there it was. Sarah was in love with Joel, but he was in love with himself. That much,

Vinny knew. Yamulke, rosary beads, Buddhist incense, it didn't matter. Vinny Parco knew a guy who valued himself pretty highly as a cocksman. This guy was a walking hard-on. Parco, ever on the edge, decided to gamble.

"Hey, you girls, it's cold, why don't you sit in the car while Joel helps me with this manhole cover." He was hoping that Marla and Sarah would get into one car, but they didn't.

No problem. Maybe it was even better.

"We pretty much come here in the afternoons," Parco said, putting strain on his voice as he pried the manhole cover with a tire iron, "but you can't live on whoopie, much as I'd like to try. I'm self-employed."

"Oh, really," Joel said. "I am too."

"I'm in real estate. What business are you in?"

"Plumbing supply."

"No kidding. Where?"

"Forest Hills."

"You know a contractor named Vito Mancuso?"

Joel didn't, which was a good thing because Vito Mancuso does not exist, not as a contractor in Forest Hills, anyway. Vinny said he could help get Joel some business and they agreed that maybe they'd get together. Then Parco took the chance.

"Hey, Joel. Did you get a look at the broad I was with? A good look?"

The next thing Marla knew, Joel Stein was in Vinny's car and Vinny was talking to Sarah.

Marla sat quietly and gave Joel one of her warmest smiles. She wasn't sure exactly what was going on, but she knows what her smile can do to a man.

"Vinny and I were talking, you know, maybe it's crazy," Joel said. "But I hear the two of you might be looking for another couple to—swap with."

Good old Vinny—You Never Have to Do Anything You Don't Want to Do—Parco. Vinny—Our Policy Is No Sexual Encounters on the Job—Parco had offered her to this total stranger.

She smiled shyly and said, "Well, you're very nice, but I'd have to talk it over with him."

He smiled and looked deeply into her eyes, moving closer and running his hand over the top of the seat. He let his hand touch her shoulder and moved even closer.

"It would be the most incredible time you ever had," he said, then stuck out his tongue and wiggled it.

Sarah had bolted when Vinny got into the car, but she warmed to him after making it plain that swapping, swinging, or whatever it was called, was not something she and Joel were willing to do. Vinny said he understood and respected that decision, but she should maybe talk it over with Joel because he seemed to be seeing it a different way. Sarah said she would talk to Joel, and Vinny had a good idea what she would tell him. Meanwhile, they talked for a few minutes and, as people usually do, Sarah Gloskin opened up to Vinny Parco.

"What do you call those guys who look like Amish? Hasidim, right?"

"That's right," she said.

"Now, between you and me and the car, Sarah, these Hasidim—are they or are they not the horniest men in the world?"

Despite nervousness and a growing agitation with Joel for being in the car with Marla, Sarah Gloskin let herself laugh.

"No, really, the only guys more horny are Born Again Christians. I'm telling you. I've got this Hasidic client and he calls me up, Sarah, I swear this is true. He says to me over the phone, 'Veeny, you know, I am a happily married man. You know that, of course, Veeny.'

" 'Yeah, sure,' I say to the guy. You know what he wants? He wants to go out with my secretary."

A disaster had turned into an opportunity. Parco had been able to read both Joel and Sarah up close. He saw it as a given that Joel had, or would have, other women. His few minutes of talking to Sarah told him that she would probably go down hard with this guy. He saw major pain for her, the kind of acute misery that those with limited experience in relationships feel when they get their first good burn. Sarah would hurt as badly over Joel as her husband had with her.

But it would be worse. In the next car, the man she loved, and for whom she was prepared to give up a marriage, was flicking his tongue obscenely at a twenty-two-year-old woman and jotting down her phone number. And with no malicious feelings, and even a lot of sympathy, the self-effacing, likeable man who shared the front seat of a Toyota with her, who understood why she didn't want to swing, who told her funny stories about horny Hasidim, was there to take away her children.

24

In New York's garment district, the steel pushcart rules the sidewalk. Thousands of pedestrians form a human mass that moves molasseslike down the pavement in a weaving conga line that bobs around the huge metal carts stacked with furs, dresses, coats, wooden crates, cardboard cartons, or empty display racks. The pushcarts claim the pavement before eight and stay out until dusk, pushed, as they were a century ago, by non-English-speaking immigrants.

Jo-Ann Kunda got out of a taxi and took her place in the flow moving west on Thirty-fifth Street toward a sooty building just off Broadway. She was more nervous than usual this fall morning. She had to be Jewish. The cliché about all New Yorkers being Jewish might have its roots in truth, but Kunda, raised Catholic, was concerned that she might get tripped up on the rapid-fire mix of Yiddish and English that is the norm in the district.

The lingo of the trade itself was no mystery. She knew many people in the business and had worked briefly in the field herself. The case was a trademark infringement job where the target, Marty Ross of Manhattan Modern Incorporated, was suspected of copying a blouse, stitch by stitch, button by button, from a pattern registered to Buddy Glick's client, Hollywood Styles International.

Glick was a pro who knew his turf well. He called Ross and talked shop convincingly enough to pave the way for Jo-Ann to pose as a buyer from New Jersey. When Kunda called to set up the appointment, she gave a call back number with a New Jersey area code.

The call back number was a gag line that rang in Glick's

agency. When Ross called to verify Jo-Ann's status as a buyer, he was put through to an operative who identified himself as her boss. The operative said that Modern Ladies was a new retail chain with stores opening up in Bayonne, Camden, Atlantic City, and Newark.

Ross enthusiastically welcomed the business and apologized for the verification, saying, "These days you can't be too careful." The operative agreed.

Kunda took a crowded elevator to the eleventh floor where she introduced herself to a receptionist and was led into the office of Marty Ross.

Kunda, dressed smartly in a two-piece suit, marveled, as she had when she worked in this field, that so many people whose livelihoods depend on handicapping fashion trends dress from another era. Marty Ross was outfitted like a man forever trapped in 1974—salt and pepper curly hair in a modified Afro, a silky red Quiana shirt with a collar that sprawled nearly to the end of his shoulders, and two gold chains.

"I'm a fuck? *I'm* a fuck? You don't deliver the merchandise and it's me that's the fuck. That's very funny, Sy. Tell me another one."

He held the phone out at arm's length, covered the mouthpiece, lowered his voice, and said to Jo-Ann, "Excuse the French. Give me just a minute."

He continued to keep the receiver away from his ear until the voice seemed to run down, like a toy with dying batteries. "Wonderful, Sy. You sue me, I'll sue you, but you get paid when I see the goods." He slammed down the phone.

Jo-Ann opened the briefcase, removed a legal pad, a pen, and some business cards. She closed the case and looked for a place to set it down. Ross tapped the edge of his desk to indicate that she should put it there, which was precisely what she wanted him to do.

In a hidden panel below the legal pads and business cards, a cassette recorder had been activated when Jo-Ann opened the case. There were eight tiny microphones hidden in the handle, the latches, the hinges, and other corners. For Glick's purposes, an audio recording was sufficient. It was more manageable, and more efficient, than a video briefcase with a pinhole lens. Unless Jo-Ann forgot to turn it on, the case, with all its backup electronics, was certain to do its job.

P.I.'s draw their gadgets from a dazzling bazaar of catalog items, forensic labs, mail-order kits, toll-free numbers, and trade shows. Everyday tools like hidden cameras or electronic countermeasures equipment are sold next to exotic items like blow dart guns or goods that blatantly tap the lunatic fringe, such as brass knuckle "paperweights," or step-by-step manuals on the use of explosives. The dealers themselves range from legitimate law enforcement supply houses to Bugs-R-Us fantasy stores that sell overpriced garbage and operate on the principle that a buff and his money are soon parted.

Also in the game are faceless craftsmen who customize their devices to an individual's needs and hint of glory days fighting the cold war in terrain that wouldn't have pleased Congress. If you can't brag to your buddies that you have at least one gadget free-lancer who was a contract worker for the CIA, or did some pretty scary stuff for the Mossad, you're not really into gadgets.

Briefcase audio and video recorders are easy to use and currently legal, although some lawmakers want to curtail their use by making it illegal to tape someone on his own premises. Thus, a surveillance van recording an "injured" insurance claimant playing touch football on his lawn, or a briefcase "left" in someone's office would be an illegal search on a par with bugs and phone taps. To date, hidden cameras and body mikes are legal security devices.

The camouflaged camera, or "CC," has become the standard peephole in industrial security, matrimonial work, and illegal intelligence gathering. Motel managers have been known to stand aside while P.I.'s install a CC in a sunburst clock, picture, fire extinguisher, television set, radio, bookcase, or light fixture. Remote transmitters beam the signal into a van outside or into the next room, eliminating the conspicuous, bulky VCR.

The voice stress analyzer is a handy, if questionable, gadget favored by corporate security people. Once billed as "voice lie detectors," stress analyzers are plugged into a telephone to read the truth or falsehood of the person on the other end of the line. The theory is that lies put subtle stresses on the vocal cords that can be picked up electronically.

Proponents claim that, given the proper training, stress analyzers can be very effective. Enemies say they're flawed bells and whistles favored by those too lazy or dim to learn the polygraph.

They often sell for more than five thousand dollars and are illegal in a number of states including New York.

Polygraphs are a big part of the P.I. and security industries, too big for civil libertarians, not big enough for business owners plagued by skyrocketing employee theft losses and insurance rates.

Polygraphs measure bodily functions—blood pressure, pulse rate, respiration, and sweat. The extent to which these responses can be confidently interpreted as truth or lie is a fifty-year debate. Though the courts have never accepted the results of polygraph tests, their use in industry has tripled in the past five years to as many as two million tests a year in private indutry.

Wilbur D. Jones, a federal judge in Macon, Georgia, says, "No device known to man can read an individual's mind and indicate whether that person is lying." A polygraph test, he says, "is nothing more than the polygraph examiner's personal opinion of the truthful or deceptive manner in which the questioned person responded."

Twenty-two states and the District of Columbia prohibit an employer from requiring an employee to take a polygraph test. In May 1987, a study commissioned by the Congressional Office of Technology Assessment held that polygraphs cannot be said to be valid or invalid at present, because of inadequate scientific research. In the four-thousand subject study, there was no way of knowing whether those who passed the test were telling the truth or fooling the machines.

Central to the problem of polygraphs are a standardized "base rate" of responses to truthful questions, and "countermeasures" that a subject can take to fool the machines. Toe pressing, tongue biting, and mental techniques such as counting backward from large numbers have been known to produce inconclusive results. There is also the problem of liars so good at their mistruths that they convince themselves, and the polygraph operators, of their own honesty.

The polygraphers themselves acknowledge these problems, but maintain that the polygraph would not have survived so long if it never caught liars. An experienced and well-trained operator, they maintain, can successfully interpret a machine's readings to sift truth from fiction.

In March 1988, the U.S. Senate, by a vote of sixty-nine to twenty-seven, approved a bill sharply limiting the use of polygraphs in private industry to screen job applicants or test employees. P.I.'s with heavy polygraph practices aren't selling their machines, however, for the bill permits the use of polygraphs after a theft, provided there is "reasonable suspicion" and the employees tested had access to the stolen property.

Forensic labs that test a potpourri of body parts and fluids have sprung up to accommodate the security and investigative boom. P.I.'s send out samples of fingerprints, blood, urine, hair, skin, and semen stains for testing. From parents who want their teenagers checked for drug use to Fortune 500 companies with lucrative drug and alcohol testing contracts, the white coat may replace the trench coat as today's investigative outerwear.

Supposedly nonlethal weaponry is a big item at equipment conventions. For sixty-three dollars, postpaid, one can send for an electronic voltage wand known as the "stun gun," a device that, in the words of one distributor, will "put fifty thousand volts in the palm of your hand." The stun gun is not supposed to be used in many states, including New York, but there are dozens of "mail forwarding" services in the business of "protecting privacy" by acting as a way station between a consumer and the post office.

The stun gun and its cousin, the electric dart firing Taser, are designed to paralyze a target. New York City cops, who use the wands to calm violent mental patients (and in one well-publicized case to work over a drug dealer) have found out that they don't always work. Occasionally, they make a psychotic more psychotic—and stronger.

Super Pen, is a ballpoint pen and a radio transmitter billed as being able to pick up whispers from twenty-five feet away and broadcast them to an FM radio in another room or in a car outside. The user shouldn't plan on driving too far. Super Pen's range is only fifteen hundred feet. The device retails for $399.95 and really writes.

For that commando feeling, Executive Protection Products, Inc., of Napa, California, sells Clear Out, a tear gas grenade with a continuous discharge valve that displaces twenty-three thousand cubic feet of air in about half a minute. Sixty-six bucks for a six-pack. The company's ad leaves it to the imagination why anyone this side of Beirut would need to displace twenty-three thousand cubic feet of air six times.

Tattle Tale III is a "telephone recorder interface," meaning it will activate a tape recorder any time a call is made to a particular telephone line. When coupled with a cassette recorder, Tattle Tale III works like an answering machine minus the message, the tone, and the little amenity of informing two people that their conversation is being recorded. Under those circumstances, the police might arrest the Tattle Tale's owner. They wouldn't call it an "interface" at all. They would use a word like *felony*. Tattle Tale III retails for $49.95.

Darts seem to be a high-volume item in the catalogs. The MX5 Mega-Dart Pistol retails at $49.95 and, according to its retailers, "drives a wire dart through half-inch plywood." Midwest Sports Distributors, Inc., calls a six-foot, takedown blowgun with a range of two hundred feet an "ideal gift" at $24.98.

An alternative to pistols are dart projectile systems under the category of "immobilization equipment." One, designed originally for zoological use, shoots syringes at high speed. Advertised "for protection of home or business," this beauty comes in pistol or rifle form, shoots from 1 to 15cc of any liquid, and injects it on contact. "The use of a chemical irritant, such as vinegar injected into the intruder will guarantee his nonreturn," says the catalog copy. Just don't miss.

From Armament Systems Products of Atlanta, Georgia, comes the Blowpen. "In tight spots when a standard length blowgun is clumsy, our Blowpen may be just what you need. In a phone booth, elevator, limousine, or across an alley, it gets your point across."

Night vision optics is a complex, high tech field requiring an enormous amount of homework. A P.I. with a serious need for night surveillances can easily spend between five and ten thousand dollars for a single lens. Night vision systems are expensive lights not visible to the naked eye which can turn darkness into daylight, usually up to a hundred yards. When used in conjunction with a telephoto lens, and infrared film, pictures can be taken from two or three miles away.

Reading mail without opening an envelope is accomplished with the purchase of "letter bomb visualizer," a bottle of clear liquid used by law enforcement agencies as an antiterrorist device. Once the visualizer is sprinkled lightly on a letter, the paper making contact with the envelope's outer wall is visible for a minute or two. The fluid then evaporates and disappears without a trace. The cost is about forty-five dollars. The fluid is made from Freon, the gas used in air conditioners and refrigerators.

The First Amendment is often taken to its outer envelope, some would say to the fire-in-a-crowded-theater limit, with such books as *Sneak It Through: Smuggling Made Easier, Hard-core Poaching, Improvised Explosives: How to Make Your Own,* and *How to Kill,* volumes I-VI, available through Paladin Press of Boulder, Colorado.

The Real World of Alternate ID Acquisition by D.P. Rochelle tells readers how to steal the identity of a dead baby, a common practice in the black marketeering of phony IDs to illegal aliens. Paladin's catalog copy reads, "By obtaining the birth certificate of someone who died as an infant, you won't ever cross paths with the true owner of 'your' birth certificate, because that person no longer exists."

Many mail-order books are accurate and darkly useful. Even experienced detectives order them just to see if they're missing anything. Paladin offers a number of responsible missing persons and debugging texts as well as Lee Lapin's *How to Get Anything on Anybody,* a thirty-dollar paperback marketed with an NBC reporter's lament that it is "possibly the most dangerous book ever published."

How to Get Anything on Anybody has a wide audience among P.I.'s, especially those under age forty. Lapin covers most of the industry's standard tricks and functions as both the Siskel and Ebert of subterranean surveillance. The book offers reviews on bugs, eleven devices for listening through walls, guidelines for tricking polygraphs, and a chapter on how to obtain confidential information from the phone company, complete with 101 inside numbers whose publication could not have pleased Ma Bell's security chief when the book was published in 1983.

The Bionic Ear is sold as a home security and hunting device that is not intended for eavesdropping, but somehow, gosh, gets used that way anyway. It is a set of headphones with a microphone and amplifier advertised as being able to hear a whisper at a hundred yards, a trespasser from a mile away, or a hunting dog from two miles away. If there is a loud noise, the sound cuts out, protecting the user's delicate hearing apparatus. The Bionic Ear costs $69.95 and comes with an optional $29.95 dish for further amplification.

The briefcase Jo-Ann Kunda brought on her field assignment to Manhattan Modern Incorporated was one of the better models. It cost Buddy Glick about twelve hundred dollars. His video units are custom-made by a friend from "military intelligence" for about thirty-five hundred apiece. He could get both units cheaper, but Glick is a stickler for broadcast quality recordings, audio and video.

"Great blouse," Kunda said to Marty Ross.

"One of our hottest numbers right now," he said. "We got an extra shift on just trying to keep up with the demand."

"I'm not surprised. Your own design?"

"Better believe it. Everything we sell is our own design. How many you need?"

"I can only take three dozen to start."

"That's fine."

"I can pay you now if you want."

"Well, we usually do take payment in advance, especially the first time out."

"No problem."

She paid Ross, the client company issued a subpoena, and he ended up settling out of court.

25

"*Look* at the bazongies on this one," Vinny Parco said as he flipped through a pornographic magazine. The client would get a bill for about fifty dollars that the agency had spent on sexually explicit publications.

The woman Vincent admired took a quarter page picture ad: "Julie. I like it in the day, I like it in the night. Anytime, anywhere, (212) 234-9224."

"How disgusting," Marla said. "Don't these people know about AIDS?"

"For the money they make, they think it's worth the risk," Parco said.

Vinny was enthusiastic about Julie, but he was in a bad mood. Too many cases were open and he wanted them closed.

To Vinny a crisp, juicy case isn't one with a lot of steamy love scenes or human drama. A great case is one that is over and billed. And one case that he very much wanted over was Dr. Lynette Simons.

Everyone with a free minute was reading the classified and display ads in various swinger publications to see if Dr. Simons advertised as a purveyor of bondage and discipline, or if she billed herself in the more legitimate publications such as *New York Magazine* or the *Village Voice* as a primal scream therapist.

They circled any ad that offered pain, group sex, or any activity that looked like the MO of "Doctor" Simons, then passed it to Marla who ran a quick check in *Cole's* to get a name and address for the listed phone number. If a number was unpublished, she put it aside. The skip tracers would track it as easily as a classical musician runs scales. Suspicious ads were further checked in a data base which provides detailed information on tenancy and property ownership in Manhattan. If someone in the same building or neighborhood offered primal scream therapy or bondage and discipline, there was a strong possibility that the service was either an alias or an associate of Simons.

The task hinted at, but did not typify, the eye-straining numbness of daily detective work. The private investigator has to pore over fine print for hours, days, or weeks at a time to close a case. The mind first asks to be relieved of the task, then begs, insists, or just plain walks off the job. And, as is the case with a surveillance, a single instant of wavering can torpedo hours of painstaking work.

If the phony shrink was running a whorehouse, especially one that sold punishment, there was probably some promotion beyond word of mouth. An ad made sense. Having established that Simons had no formal psychotherapeutic credentials and was not registered with any professional associations, referrals were eliminated as a source of clientele. The landlord said there were people going in and out all the time. Parco knows that plenty of high-volume houses of prostitution don't advertise, but those are usually class acts, like that of the Mayflower Madam. Lynette Simons did not seem to be selling to such a high-ticket clientele. The absence of an ad made Parco wonder if his client might not be exaggerating.

Parco got bored with the pornography after an hour. It would have been nice to find an ad. That way, Marla could just say she read about the good doctor. But, there were other ways.

"Gag your way in, Marla," he finally said. "Tell this quack you met a guy named Mark at NYU when you took a night course. Describe him as a guy with dark hair and a mustache. Tell her you can't remember his last name."

Parco reasoned that everyone in the world knows someone named Mark with dark hair and a mustache. He may be right. Marla called and got an appointment for the next afternoon.

The thirties and forties are alive and well in the prewar buildings of the Upper West Side. The halls wear their original art deco fixtures and mahogany trim under muted light, and smell of a half century of cooking, cleaning, cologne, fur, and, always, children. The doormen and elevator operators still dress like movie ushers in dark uniforms with gold braid, white shirts, and dark ties.

Doormen make good money, and the jobs are often passed, like the apartments themselves, from generation to generation. Doormen are not Vinny Parco's favorite people, but they are a large part of the New York investigative equation: They know what goes on in a building and can often be persuaded, either through guile or cash, to give up the information.

Marla Paul studied the doorman to see if there was a glimmer of extracareful scrutiny, anything that might connnect him to Dr. Simons. If so, she couldn't see it. He called upstairs and verified her appointment.

She took the elevator to the eleventh floor and walked down the hall where a woman in her late sixties with dyed red hair waited for her.

"Come on in," she said without introducing herself. She led Marla into the apartment's living room where she pointed to one of two leather-backed director's chairs facing each other.

"Who did you say gave you my name?" she asked, as she settled in.

"I can't remember his last name. His first name was Mark and he had a mustache."

"Mark, Mark . . . light hair?"

"No, dark hair, with a mustache. Mark, I think his last name was Jewish."

"It doesn't matter," Dr. Simons said. "Tell me about yourself, and why you're here."

"I'm frigid," she said.

Dr. Simons nodded sympathetically. "Is this new or has the problem always been there."

"I think it's always been there, but it's especially important now, because my boyfriend and I are planning to get married."

"That makes this a good time to get going," Dr. Simons said. "Follow me, Marla."

She followed Dr. Simons into another room. This would be a critical issue later when they testified in court. Dr. Simons was allowed to practice psychotherapy, however unorthodox, in New York State. They probably couldn't even get her on using the term *doctor* because she could have some marginally legal certificate or degree. But they could get her if she used more than one room for her therapy.

The large room had probably once been either a master bedroom or a living room. The floor was covered with exercise mats and mattresses from wall to wall.

"Marla, do you know anything about primal scream therapy?"

"No, not much."

"Well, we're going to make you feel a lot better about yourself by the time you leave here. Let's start with your clothes. They're in your way. Take them off."

"I'm not comfortable with it just now, thanks," Marla Paul said to her new therapist. "I can work with my clothes on."

Dr. Simons frowned and led Marla to a padded gym horse.

"Put your hands on it, Marla. Put your hands on it," she said.

Marla put her hands on the gym horse. "Now, I want you to scream with me. Do you trust me, Marla?"

"I trust you," she said, leaning against the gym horse with both hands, "but I don't think I get what you want me to do."

"Bend over, Marla," she said. "Grab the handles and bend over." I don't think I like this at all, Marla thought. She grabbed the handles and bent over.

"Say 'I can't.' "

"I can't."

"Louder. Make it last, like this. *'I caaaaaaannnnnnnn'ttttttttt.'* " Dr. Simons screamed with such a piercing shriek that Marla thought she would fall to the floor.

"I caaaaaaannnnnnnnnnnn'tttttt," Marla screamed.

"*Yes, you cannnnnnnnnnnn,*" Dr. Simons screamed, then softened her voice. "Now say, 'No, I can't,' Marla."

"*No, I cannnnnnnnn'tttttttt.*"

"*Yessssss, you cannnnnnnnnnn.*"

They went on for some time, always with Marla bent over the horse and Dr. Simons behind her. Sometimes Simons instructed her to scream that she could, and sometimes that she couldn't. It was therapeutic in its way, she supposed, but weird.

Not as weird as two days later when Marla showed up for her second appointment. Again, Dr. Simons asked her if she wanted to take her clothes off, and again she declined. This time she had to lie on a mattress on the floor and kick while she alternated screaming that she could, and could not, have an orgasm.

"Now, get up, Marla, and take this," the therapist said, handing her a stick with a padded glove on it.

"Hit the wall with it, good and hard now."

Marla hit the wall.

"Harder!" the doctor said, starting that scream again.

Marla hit the wall.

"Tell the wall to go fuck itself, Marla."

This is too strange, Marla thought.

"*Fuck you, wall!*" Lynette Simons screamed.

This is no way for a sixty-nine-year-old woman to be talking, Marla thought.

"Come on now, Marla, trust me. *Fuck you, wall!*"

Marla hit the wall with the stick and gave it the command.

"What's your boyfriend's name?"

"Vinny."

"*Fuck you, Vinny! Fuck you, Vinny!*"

Marla complied, hitting the wall. Maybe I could get into this after all, she thought, as the doctor urged her to continue beating up the wall and cursing her boss. She wondered what earthly good it would do if she was frigid, but she kept at it for the rest of the session.

"She told you to tell me to go fuck myself?" Vinny asked. "She *said* that?"

"Yes, she did. I don't know what we're in for today."

It was time for Vinny to join Marla in therapy.

"I could go for punching that wall with the glove," he said, "but if she asks me to bend over a gym horse with her behind me, forget it. Never."

Inside, Vinny was introduced as Marla's boyfriend.

"Would the two of you like to take your clothes off?" Dr. Simons asked. "I've been trying to get Marla to disrobe, but she hasn't wanted to."

"Maybe later," Parco said. She asked a number of questions about their relationship that they both answered.

"Would one or both of you like to masturbate?" she asked.

"That sounds like a good idea," Vinny said. Marla glared at him.

"But I can see Marla here isn't quite ready for that. I think if we were in private, we might do it better."

Dr. Simons nodded. "You love Marla don't you, Vinny?"

"Yes, I do."

"Hug Marla."

They hugged.

"Now kiss Marla."

I'm going to kill him, she thought. There is no reason for him to be here, no reason for me to be telling walls to go fuck themselves while hitting them with a glove on a stick, and no reason for me to be kissing my boss. As he bent to kiss her, the absurdity of it all caught up—the gym horse she had to lean over, the exercises on the floor, that ridiculous glove, and now she was kissing her boss. She started to snicker.

He touched her face and moved closer.

She couldn't keep her lips straight. This was like laughing in church.

Vinny kissed her.

She broke into uncontrollable laughter.

He shoved her head into the mattress, and she laughed into it.

The client wanted them to testify that they thought Dr. Simons was a madam, that she ran a whorehouse, and urged them to have sex in her presence.

But all they could say was that Doctor Lynette Simons was not a practitioner of any of the mental health professions and that she occupied more than a single room of her apartment for therapy. That would be enough to get the apartment back for the landlord. But there was no evidence of additional wrongdoing. She was legal. Parco thought her methods might be weird, but, in her way, she was honest. She believed in what she was doing and that alone set her apart from a lot of mental health people he'd seen. She probably did patients reams of good. Instead of that ridiculous kissing escapade, he wished he could have hit that wall and told it to go fuck itself. That would have been fun.

26

Detective agencies are not for the economically disadvantaged. They serve businesses and, lately, the middle class. When poor people need a private detective, they do without or live with the state pittance allocated to back up Legal Aid cases—about enough for a DMV, a couple of calls and, if the client draws a real knight, an afternoon in the field.

P.I.'s don't snub the penniless because they are heartless swine, but because they are business people, information storekeepers, who don't hand out their inventory any quicker than Sears gives away power tools. Sometimes, though, a P.I. will take a case just because he should.

Peter Castillo got a call on a Monday night.

"Hi, Pete, Nick George." George is a businessman in Arlington who had hired Castillo on a matrimonial.

"Nick, what's doing? Everything okay?"

"With me, yeah, but I'm calling for a friend I went to school with who's now a priest, Rick Nieman. And he has someone with a problem. It's bad."

"What happened?"

"Friday night this woman's little girl doesn't come home from school, so she calls Metro, they take her name and tell her they'll get back to her. They don't, so she calls back late that night, and they say they'll get back to her. By now, she's a basket case and she calls Rick."

"How old's the little girl?" Castillo asked.

"Ten. Ten years old, Pete, and she isn't back yet. The cops are telling the mother, don't worry, don't worry, no news is good news, there's nothing they can do."

"Enough said. You want to bring the priest and the mother by?"

"You think there's anything you can do?"

"Who knows, Nick? I'll try. The mother married?"

"No. She must have had this kid when she was a kid herself."

Martha Cruz was about twenty-five and, even though her English was good, Castillo chose to speak to her in Spanish. It was more comforting. To no one's surprise, the woman seemed to be close to clinical shock and was scarcely able to look at Peter or answer his questions.

"It's a good sign that the police haven't called you," he said gently. "If they haven't called you, it means Pilar is probably alive, and if she's alive, there's a good chance I'll find her. But you've got to help me out, Martha. You've got to snap into it."

Outside Castillo's office, Nick George and Father Nieman sat gloomily in two leather chairs. They jumped when he opened the door.

"It's going to be a long night with her, guys," Castillo said. "Head on home. There's nothing you can do here."

He took Martha Cruz out for something to eat after a drive in Fairfax County. He did not try to talk to her about Pilar, but he spoke constantly and tried to reassure her that she was not alone now, that he would work on nothing else until Pilar was found. Father Nieman had taken her to a doctor earlier in the evening and she was pronounced in good physical health, but Castillo wasn't going too far from a hospital just the same. To him, Martha Cruz was in as much danger as her daughter, maybe more.

Though the young mother could not eat, she did get some tea down.

"Very good, very good," Castillo said. "Would you like to try to eat something?"

She shook her head.

"Okay, Martha, that's up to you. Let's start. Pilar went to school Friday morning. What school?"

"Lincoln, over on Nelson Street."

Lincoln was in a Hispanic section in the southeast section of Washington. It was a high crime area and it didn't surprise Castillo that Metro police hadn't done much.

When Martha got pregnant at fifteen, she moved in with her mother's sister and her three children. The family made room for her when the baby was born.

Little Pilar was a beautiful child, with dark curly hair and a "sparkle like she was from heaven," Martha said. To the teenage mother, she was. Martha, who had dropped out of school, took a job in a factory and Pilar became her life, her dream.

"She will be Miss America one day or a movie star. Or a singer. She sings so beautifully," she told Castillo. "If she lives," she said as her voice cracked and she started to sob. That was a good sign.

Castillo couldn't even wait until morning. He had to get every detail, every thing Martha could recall the little girl saying or doing in the days before she disappeared. He had to get Martha to show him the neighborhood, even after midnight, and he would have to note every square inch between the tenement building where Pilar lived and Lincoln Elementary School.

"God bring her back. My God, my God, bring her back to me," she sobbed. Castillo did not rush to the other side of the booth to comfort Martha, nor did he give her any more reassurances. In a couple of minutes, she would cry it out, and then they would go to work.

He waited.

She stopped sobbing, blinked her eyes, and seemed to be looking at him differently now, like she was able to make out his features, the coffee shop, and her tea.

Castillo still said nothing. Then Martha Cruz started to talk.

"I can't pay you very much money, you know."

"I know. Whatever."

"Oh, I'll pay you every penny, don't worry."

"Do I look like I'm worrying?"

"Every penny. What do you need to know?"

They were up until after two and Castillo was at Martha's aunt's house again at seven, Pilar's rising time. Castillo's pace is a slow one, so slow that he sometimes seems not to be moving at all. His strategy, if that's what it could be called, was to do a microscopic trace of the little girl's movements, everything she had done four days ago.

"She had breakfast where?"

"Right there, right in that chair."

"She ate what?"

"Rice Krispies, and a banana."

"Sliced?"

Martha Cruz smiled. "You are asking me if the banana was sliced?"

"That's right."

"I think so. Yes, yes, it was sliced."

"What did she wear? I want every detail of what she wore, I even want the underwear, stockings, colors, everything."

Before leaving to go to the school at a quarter to eight, Castillo looked at snapshots, and selected a few that he could carry with him. He first walked the eight blocks to Lincoln School. He found several fifth graders who knew Pilar, but heard only that Pilar never showed up at school on Friday. Then he began the slow process of going door-to-door.

He would skip no door, no doorway, no bum on the street. Being Spanish-speaking helped. He dodged dogs, heard reluctant grunts, peered through chained doors at men in undershirts and women in robes. Most of the neighborhood knew Pilar was missing and no one had anything to offer him.

One of the neighborhood children said that most of the kids stopped at a small store near the school to browse through fan magazines and buy snacks before going into school.

"I heard," said Paul Gomez, the store's owner, as he looked at Pilar's picture.

"She's missing since Friday," Castillo said.

"She didn't go home after school?"

"She never got to school. Was she in here Friday?"

Gomez strained to recall. "I think so. I can't tell one day from the next," he said. "I'm sorry."

Castillo gave him a card. "Would you just call and leave word if you hear anything at all?"

Gomez took the card, hesitated and said, "Who do you work for again?"

"Her mother. I'm not connected with the police."

Castillo had figured the man was holding back for his own reasons. Stores in such neighborhoods aren't always so quick to welcome police through their doors. They sometimes deal a little backroom dope, sell beer without a license, or take some numbers action.

"The police aren't involved with this at all right now," Castillo continued.

"Okay, fine. Just between you and me?"

"Yeah. If it gets real bad and they come looking, I can't make any promises, but I'm not going to be talking to them about anything we say."

"She wasn't alone when she was in here. There was someone who came in here with her, and I mean a lot. We are talking maybe even every day for the last month. Shit, I should have known something was up, but you know what I'm saying. You don't ask questions around here.

"Shit. I mean, he acted like a big brother, but I thought there was something a little off. You know what I'm saying now, don't you? You see things all the time and you keep it to yourself. If you went and started looking into everything you see—shit."

"What'd he look like?"

"Eighteen, twenty. Nice-looking kid, dark wavy hair, very well dressed. Not like in a suit, but he always had nice dungarees, the fancy kind, and a leather jacket, what do you call that fuzzy leather?"

"Suede."

"Yeah, like brown suede, very stylish. I don't know his name or nothing."

"Did he pay for the little girl's stuff?"

"Not at first, but, yes, eventually he paid for things she got before and after school. Candy, potato chips, the kid ate a lot of that. She liked the peanut butter cups."

"Did he come in just in the morning?"

"Usually, sometimes in the afternoon too." Gomez paused in thought. "Yes, sometimes he did come in in the afternoon. Not with her though, with his friends."

"What time of day?" Castillo asked.

"I'd say about four, five."

"I'll be back. Paul, I want to thank you. I'll be back around three-thirty."

Gomez was not the only person to see the man with the suede jacket.

"There was a man in a light leather coat I used to see, but I never saw him with Pilar," said Theresa Wray, Pilar's teacher. Martha Cruz had called the principal of Lincoln and asked him to see Castillo. The principal, who did not know Pilar by sight, called Miss Wray, a black woman in her twenties, out of class.

"I was coming in a couple of times and I saw the guy looking over at the school, and I thought, 'I don't like the look of him, there's something funny,' but I didn't see him after that. Never thought about it again."

"How long ago, Theresa?"

"Oh, a ways back. At least a month, maybe even two months ago."

"Do you remember anything else?"

"No, nothing. I'll call Martha if I can think of anything. Poor, poor woman. How is she?"

"Not good," Castillo said.

At Paul Gomez's store, there was no one that afternoon who resembled the young man, and no one Gomez could identify as the friends.

"Anyone else you can think of who would know this guy?" Peter asked.

"I'll make some calls," Gomez said.

By Wednesday morning, the word was further out that the little girl was missing which was good news because Castillo had strong feelings that she was long gone. Now he needed the street grapevine, and anything anyone could do to feed it would help him.

"I can't help you, my friend," said a detective at Metro. "You're talking about a twenty-year-old guy and a ten-year-old girl?"

"That's what I'm hearing," Castillo said.

"All I can say is we'll call you if anything turns up. What more can I tell you? It doesn't make sense."

It made no sense to Martha Cruz either.

"She wouldn't go with him willingly," she said. "I know Pilar. She would never go with him. He forced her."

But as to who *he* was, no one seemed to know anything.

Mark Chalas, owner of Mark's Bicycle Sales and Repairs, across from Paul Gomez's store, remembered seeing the man. "He didn't look like a pervert or nothing to me, just a young guy talking to this little kid. Christ, you think he took her?"

"That's what I think, yes. How far back can you remember this going?"

"At least a month, maybe two."

Castillo made a night call at the home of Mr. and Mrs. John Esposito whose daughter Iris was probably closest to Pilar. Castillo had not wanted to speak to the little girl at school, preferring instead to let Theresa Wray act as a go-between with the parents.

"This man is trying to help Pilar's mommy find her, honey," John said. "Please answer his questions."

"All right," the little girl said.

"Iris, do you ever remember seeing a man with Pilar on the way to school or on the way home?" Castillo asked.

The girl nodded.

"Do you know the man's name?"

The girl shook her head.

"Were you with Pilar the first time she talked to him?"

"Yes," she said, but her eyes started to shift around.

"John, could I talk to you a minute?" Castillo said. The two men left the kitchen and Castillo came back in alone.

"Iris, I asked your dad to let me talk to you, just us, and I'd like to have a secret between us. Can we do that?"

"Yes."

"Iris, did you and Pilar ever go somewhere after school that your parents wouldn't like? Did you go to the movies, or McDonald's? You don't have to tell me, but if you do, I'll keep it our secret if you want. You might be helping Pilar."

"Pizza. We went for pizza after school and we weren't supposed to."

"And what about this man?"

"He came over and paid for our pizzas. He was real cute and real nice and he told us to come back and see him tomorrow."

"Did you?"

"Yes. But after a while, I stopped going and she started going to meet him after school," the little girl said. "Every day."

"Very important, Iris. What was the man's name?"

"Raymond. Ramon. Sometimes Pilar called him Raymond, sometimes Ramon."

"Did she ever talk about going anywhere with Ramon?"

"No, never." The little girl started to cry. When Castillo hugged her, she broke into sobs.

"Iris," he said gently. "It's okay. You didn't do anything really bad."

He let her cry a few minutes. God, he thought, this poor kid had been carrying around everything for days, terrified to say anything, terrified that she would be punished. She probably even thought she'd be arrested, held responsible for the disappearance of her friend. He held her shoulders and looked at her. "Now, Iris," he said, "I promised I wouldn't tell your mom and dad anything and I won't, but you do it. You tell your mom and dad and I'll stay right here if you like. You'll feel much better. They won't punish you, I promise. I wouldn't lie to you."

The pizzeria was on a heavily traveled road about three blocks from Lincoln School. Castillo had passed by a couple of times since he started looking for Pilar. It had made sense to him since the beginning that a nineteen-or twenty-year-old boy would be near fast food, but the number of young males from the nearby high school who went there, to Kentucky Fried Chicken, Taco Bell, Burger King, McDonald's, and Wendy's must have been five hundred or a thousand, he figured. There were also a dozen or more convenience stores, delicatessens, diners, bars, and smaller take-out restaurants in the neighborhood. Now he knew which hangout to scout.

"I really have no one to watch my store, Peter," Paul Gomez said.

"I wouldn't ask you to do it if it wasn't important, Paul. This guy went to the pizza place about every day with his friends and he used to take Pilar and her friend there after school. I'm asking you to come out for five minutes, ten at the most, sometime around three, three-fifteen."

"I'll meet you there."

Castillo was toying with a slice of pizza and Gomez didn't want anything to eat. Near the back, a group of teenagers took over two or three tables. Gomez said nothing, but nodded to Castillo.

"Up there," he murmured. "He's not there, but that's them." Gomez went to the men's room, then made his exit through a side door. Castillo's back was to the teenagers, but he could see them in a small wall mirror. He was satisfied that they had not noticed Gomez at all.

They were dressed tough, in denim and leather jackets, the mean kind, not suede. Several wore bandanas and, though he could not see bare arms or chests, Castillo was sure they worked out and had tattoos. They probably knew what had happened to little Pilar Cruz. The problem was to get them to tell him.

27

Barry Silvers sipped a beer in the lobby of Rio's Palais Real Hotel, the finest on Ipanema Beach.

"The name under which he registered, Mr. Silvers," said John Santos, the hotel's manager, "was not Hammond. We knew your friend as Sir Richard Thompson. And to answer your question specifically, he left owing us $22,900.72 American for his twenty days as our guest. I have printed out his invoice if it will be helpful to your client."

"I appreciate that. Anything is a big help."

They sat near a large waterfall which cascaded down one of the lobby's marble walls and into a pool near their table in the cafe. Opposite them, guests sped to their rooms or the hotel's revolving Ipanema Skyway restaurant by means of two spacious glass elevators. Silvers didn't want to embarrass the man, but he needed to know how such a sophisticated establishment could be stung for so much by a con game as old as the visiting royalty scam.

"Fakes don't usually come recommended by Mr. Raphael Salas," he said. "Mr. Salas called and told us to expect a royal guest. This," he said, straining to make his voice heard over the roar of the waterfall, "is like hearing from a Rockefeller in New York."

Raphael Salas, who was scarcely talking to the police and not at all to private detectives, had many businesses in nearby Sao Paulo including mining, manufacturing, coffee plantations, and real estate. He also had a home on St. Maarten where he'd spent time with the Duke before bringing him to Rio on his private jet.

"And if a Rockefeller told you that this guest was a hero of the Falkland Islands War where he flew with Prince Andrew, you would be honored to meet him."

The honor was cemented when the hotel's own bank called to say that they had been instructed to inform Santos that twenty thousand pounds had been wired from the Cayman Islands to cover local expenses. Next came an advance team of two men who called themselves Garnett and Frasier. Garnett would later be identified as Hammond's brother Roger, while Frasier, the more arrogant and vocal of the two, was somewhat of a mystery. Authorities showed no one coming or going from the country under that name.

Santos signaled the waiter to bring him another Johnny Walker Black on the rocks. "Another beer for you, Mr. Silvers?"

"Not just yet, thank you."

"That is Frasier," he said, looking at a glossy photograph Silvers had gotten from one of the local newspapers. Frasier was a young man with blonde hair who looked very much at home in his white dinner jacket and black tie. "He was impossible. He regarded my staff as his personal servants. My concierge especially despised the young man."

After a caustic inspection tour during which he had something negative to say about all of the hotel's furnishings, Frasier had pronounced the Palais Real's nine-room penthouse Presidential Suite "adequate." In New York, the Presidential would have cost more than twenty-five hundred dollars a day. Here it was a bargain eight hundred. There was a rooftop garden and pool, a glassed-in dining room that overlooked the ocean, sauna, Jacuzzi, billiards room, library, gourmet kitchen, and four spacious bedrooms, each with its own balcony. The master bedroom was big enough to play touch football in, Barry thought.

"This Mr. Frasier, he complained most vocally about our flowers," Santos said.

The flower shop staff was especially bitter about the Duke's party. Every day they would arrive in the suite with an arrangement that had taken most of the night, only to have Frasier arrogantly shake his head and send them back for re-arranging. No matter how hard they worked, he seemed to have targeted them for an especially vicious scolding every day.

The food and beverage people were much happier while the Duke was there. Unlike the florists, they often met with the Duke personally and felt the radiance of his charm. He learned the names of those who served his parties and took the time to call the manager with compliments. He was very generous with tips and was especially nice to the young women, lavishing them with gold and silver bracelets. Garnett had the job of handing out cuff links, small pins, and gold chains to the lesser figures who served the party.

The Duke himself handed out Rolex watches to the concierge, the food and beverage manager, the chief bellman, and Santos, who regretfully returned it because the hotel chain prohibits managers from accepting gratuities. The hotel's jeweler was constantly engraving personal thanks to this or that staffer. He was always generously tipped for the extra work and paid in cash.

Every day at cocktail hour, unless Frasier ordered otherwise, the food and beverage manager had a standing order to arrive at the suite with several chilled bottles of Dom Perignon and an exquisite arrangement of canapes centered around a tin of Beluga caviar. The food and beverage manager, wearing a white dinner jacket and a black bow tie, used a small gold opener to pry the lid off the Beluga, after which he bowed slightly and exited behind his two attendants with the flourish of a flamenco dancer. A bartender and two other members of the food and beverage staff remained to serve the guests.

The staff people told Barry that this daily cocktail gathering was attended by politicians, athletes, the press, actors, actresses, and young rich fun-seekers from Sao Paulo who competed fiercely for the Duke's attention.

"Were you paid anything at all?" Silvers asked Santos.

"Yes, we were," he said, flushing with embarrassment.

"This Mr. Frasier told us that, for security purposes, Sir Richard would only pretend to be staying in the suite for the first week. They wanted him in a different single room every night, they said."

"Security purposes?" Silvers asked.

"They said there was always the danger of Irish terrorists when a member of the royal family is abroad. They wanted him to only pretend to be in the suite for the first week."

Frasier paid the hotel about nine hundred fifty dollars to cover the cost of three single rooms for the first week. Santos told them it would be fine for them to use the suite to entertain the first week. The only expenses would be the refreshments and staff.

Somehow the Duke, Frasier, and Garnett forgot this arrangement, for when Hammond arrived, they all took up immediate residence in the Presidential Suite and stayed there for three weeks.

The press was uncharacteristically stung. In the States the Duke quietly represented himself as a businessman with a title if reporters asked, which they usually did not. He was just one in the swarm of well-heeled hangers-on who buzz around celebrities with little or no direct connection to them. In Europe he avoided press contact altogether. But south of the equator, it was obvious that he felt free to include the press as part of his strategy.

Frasier had been in touch with local reporters constantly since his arrival. When the Duke flew in from St. Maarten aboard Raphael Salas's private jet, he was besieged with questions about his friendship with Prince Andrew and the state of the marriage between Charles and Diana. As usual, his gossip was accurate. He was vague about his time in the Royal Navy as a fighter pilot and the combat he allegedly saw in the Falkland Islands War, but since most of his contact was with reporters from the social page, the issue was never pressed.

Once he got advance press and VIP treatment on his arrival, Hammond became Rio's social must. His comings and goings through the lobby of the Palais Real were such an event that the flashing of cameras, the stretch limousines, and local celebrities became a nightly show. Thanks to Raphael Salas, he was constantly shuttling to Sao Paulo to discuss business with Salas's contacts. The local bank, it was reported, frequently transferred funds by wire to the Cayman Islands and Switzerland.

"We naturally checked with the bank as our royal guest's expenses mounted," Santos said. "And they assured us that hundreds of thousands of dollars were always in the account," Santos said. "And our staff was happy with him."

They were, at least, until the night he went out for dinner with his entourage and did not come back. Some of his belongings were believed to have been shipped by Garnett to New York, but much of his fine clothing and Louis Vuitton luggage was left behind. Police told Silvers that a man answering his description flew alone on Aero Mexico to Acapulco that night. He was wearing jeans and carrying only a canvas bag. Most of the remaining money was transferred from the local bank to accounts in Switzerland and the Cayman Islands that afternoon. Garnett and Frasier were believed to have left Rio more than a week later.

Patrice Maire was the the only member of the Rio–Sao Paulo crowd willing to speak with Silvers. She found reports that the Duke had left behind his expensive luggage and clothes amusing. "I must go there and get my share," she said. "I'm sure I am never going to see my husband's fifty thousand dollars again."

Elizabeth Taylor in her best years could envy Patrice Maire. Her lush black curls were darker and glossier, and her eyes that extraordinary blue-violet, but even wider. When she smiled, Silvers felt charmed.

"My friends are not happy that I am seeing you," she said. "They are humiliated. Have you seen our newspapers?"

"Yes, but I don't speak Portuguese."

She nodded. "No need. It is simple. He took their money. He took my money. He tricked us."

"How do you suppose he did that?"

"That is simple too. Rio," she said, "is full of achievers. We do not like to just spend the money we were given at birth, you see. That is not a good way to be seen. There is much talent here, but who knows it in New York? Who knows it in London? Paris? They see us always as a playground, you see, always a place where people come to play."

"And you would say that Hammond understood the pride of these aristocrats and achievers?" Silvers asked.

"He understood it, yes, and he used it against us. And," she smiled darkly, "there is greed. We were greedy. Raphael Salas, he invested in a phony gold mine. A *gold mine.* Mining, Mr. Silvers, is a familiar business to us. It is a heritage. Would you think a man like that would be so stupid as to invest in such a thing?"

Salas had met the Duke at a London party and, like so many others, found him charming and authoritative. They'd run into each other at various parties in New York and Paris. The Duke's penchant for accurate gossip and a contrived indifference to Salas's fortune was enough to make the industrialist very interested when the Duke offered him a chance to invest in a mine that certain individuals known for their shrewdness were trying to keep quiet. Pretty soon, the gold mine rumor became so real that otherwise hardheaded businessmen almost begged to be allowed to invest.

Patrice Maire told Silvers of similar schemes that lured the sharklike young business elite of Sao Paulo. Usually it was "inside information" of one kind or another—takeovers, mergers, and other get-rich-quick plans. The accumulating local bank account, brimming with checks from prominent investors, fueled the frenzy. Everyone knew that the smartest business minds in Rio and Sao Paulo were doing business with the Duke.

Mrs. Maire reached into her desk and took out a small brown envelope. "He was most generous with these," she said, handing him the envelope. He opened it and found a gold Rolex watch with an inscription in Portuguese on the back.

"It reads, To a lifetime of friendship," she said. "We all got them."

Silvers's next stop was Chez Oren, a fancy jewelry shop on the French side of St. Maarten where the Duke had purchased the Rolex watches and the other tokens of his largesse in Rio. He had, of course, purchased them in his usual way.

"I see him in Europe, I kill him," said Oren Deiter, squeezing an imaginary neck so hard that Silvers backed away from the showcase. Deiter was a barrel-chested Corsican who owned jewelry stores in St. Maarten, Aruba, and Curacao. He was known for a sixth sense that enabled him to match a person with just the right ring, watch, earrings, or bracelets. Behind Deiter was a wall full of pictures that showed him in an open neck shirt, dripping with gold chains as he embraced vacationing celebrities.

"You have met this focker?" he asked.

"No, no, I haven't."

"Well, you find him, you call Oren, okay?"

"Yes, but you can't kill him," Silvers said. "Too many of us need him."

Deiter laughed. "No one needs him alive. What may I do for you, Mr. Barry Silvers from New York?"

"I'd like to hear about him."

"Why?"

"I have a client who is trying to put him in jail."

"What's his name, your client?"

"I can't tell you that. I can tell you that Mr. Hammond took a lot more from him than he did from you. Not that it will make you feel any better, but I can tell you that."

Deiter shrugged. "You spoke to Salas?"

"He won't talk to me."

"That makes two of us, Mr. Barry Silvers. He don't talk to me now either. But that night he come in here with that piece of *merde,* he talk plenty. I'm getting ready to close and I see Salas's car out front. Big shot, he is. Big blue Rolls Royce so everyone here can wave and say, 'Hey, Monsieur Salas.' Such bullshit, no?

" 'Hey, Oren,' he say. 'Hey, Oren, how are you? I have someone you be glad to meet.' "

Oren had watched the Duke get out of the car along with a couple of the same young rich people who would travel to Rio aboard Salas's private jet.

"He speak to me in French," Deiter said. "He say he pick out rings and bracelets for his wife. Then he say he need something nicer for his mistress. We laugh about that. But what he really wanted was my watches."

"Rolex?"

Deiter nodded with solemnity, as though Silvers had introduced a religious word. "Rolex. He say he want every Rolex I can sell him. I say, 'You want them now?' And Raphael Salas say he have to have them now because they must leave for Brazil tomorrow. He say he can get me a check from his own bank on Grand Cayman the next day. I say, 'Okay, that sounds good.' "

"And did you give him the jewels that night?"

"No, Barry Silvers. I was stupid, but not that stupid. He come by the next afternoon with the check from his bank. Then he take the jewels."

"It was a certified check?"

Oren Deiter stared at Barry for what seemed like three minutes. "Certified check, yes. You know, I find out that certified checks have their own special ink, like money. A bank can look at a certified check, look at the ink and those little holes they drill, they can look at the paper and know if it is a real certified check. Did you know that?"

"Yes, I used to be a federal investigator."

"So, if they can do that, Barry Silvers, why did my bank not know that this man's check was counterfeit?"

"You brought it to your bank before he left?"

"Of course. I told you. I'm not so stupid I would not do that.

"They said it was a good check. I say to them, 'You are sure?' They say, 'Yes, we are sure. We will telex his bank so you can be sure.' But things like telex, they don't work so good down here all the time, Mr. Barry Silvers."

"It was broken?"

Deiter waved his hand in dismissal. "Yes, they say, 'Don't worry, we telex, but this is good check. Certified.' "

Deiter laughed bitterly. "They telex the bank, but they telex the bank the next day, after this man has left with my good friend, Mister Big Shot Raphael Salas on his jet airplane, Barry Silvers. Then they call me and say, 'So sorry, check fake. Call police.' "

"And by now, Mr. Salas is gone."

"Yes, I try to call him, the police call him, but Mister Salas, he have girlfriends everywhere his wife don't know about. So, nobody can say where he is. They'll take a message. Ha."

"Did you ever reach him?"

"Yes, once I reach him. He say he shocked, there must be something wrong, he straighten everything out. I tell him I do not carry the kind of insurance to pay for twenty-two Rolex watches. He say he get back to me."

"And he has not done that?"

"No, now he terribly busy when I call. Terribly busy, he can't come to the telephone."

"And the police were no help?"

"Oh, yes, big, big help," said Deiter. "They tell me when this man Hammond come back to St. Maarten to be sure and give them a call."

"Well," Barry said. "I'm very sorry for your problems."

"Me too," he said. "How about we go dancing with some nice-looking women when I come to New York? You fix me up with some young girl?"

Silvers laughed. "I think you'll probably fix yourself up a lot better."

"Okay, I fix you up. We go dancing in New York."

"I'm sure my wife will be thrilled. Did your insurance cover anything?"

"Insurance," he said, shrugging. "I have some insurance, but you see that safe," he said, pointing to a wall-sized vault behind him. "That is my insurance. My safe and my gun. This Duke, this big shot, he get by my safe and my gun this time. But maybe I see him in Europe when I go there. Then he not get by so quick."

Tommy Nelson, a big man with a reddish beard, sprawled comfortably behind his desk in the front room of his four-bay

Texaco station in West Palm Beach, Florida. At his feet his Irish setter, Big Red, dozed.

"Don't know's I can help you much, sir," he said to Silvers. "What's done's done, and it sure got done to me."

"I appreciate anything you can tell me about your experience with Hammond," he said. "It might help keep him locked up if the police ever find him."

"Well, if there's anything I can do to keep someone else from getting hit, that's something at least. Not much, but something," he said, laughing so hard that Big Red jumped to his feet in alarm. "It was greed done me in with him. I was just too eager to buy what he was selling."

"Which was low-interest money?"

"Three hundred seventy-five thousand dollars at five percent, ten years to pay, plus an option for another three-seventy-five at seven percent, same terms."

"How did you meet him?"

"One day I look up and he's standing right where you're standing now. He's got this maroon Jag out there that he says needs its brakes checked out. I tell him I don't do Jags, but he acts like he doesn't hear me say that. He sees my 928 out there and we get to talking about it."

"That's your Porsche?" Barry asked looking at his FBI documents.

"Was. So we get to talking and I let it out that I do my own work on it, so now he's really after me to please take a look at his Jag because he doesn't trust dealers."

Silvers, still looking at the FBI wanted poster, said, "That Jaguar was the one reported stolen?"

"Borrowed and not returned from one of his society buddies up north, I think. That explains why he doesn't want to see a dealer. They'd be looking for it."

"So, you did the job?"

"Yeah, brake linings. I can get the parts if I want to, but I just don't like to work on cars like that. I did the work and he started coming here for gas. He'd always set himself right down in that chair and say, 'Ahfternoon Thomas.' That accent 'bout killed me."

One day Nelson told him he had a chance to buy a friend's muffler franchise at a good price, but he was uncomfortable with the bank rates.

"He said he could probably get me this low-interest loan because he had these rich friends who were trying to get their money out of Central America. He said they'd formed this corporation. Bottom line, Barry, is that he wanted twenty-five thousand plus the Porsche for setting up the loan. Now, hell, I loved that Porsche, but money's money. You just don't get terms like that walking through your front door every day."

He chuckled at the irony of it. "Too good to be true," he said, hitting the desk and laughing," waking Big Red out of his slumber.

"So, he shows up with all these papers one day, and it's all official looking, so I turn it over to my lawyer."

"Did he have a lawyer?" Silvers asked.

"Nope, said he had a law degree from Oxford or one of those schools."

"I see. This is the first time I've heard him use that one."

"Now, here's the bitch. He walks into my lawyer's office and my lawyer knows him, right? At first my lawyer doesn't make a connection between the name and the guy. But once he sees him, it turns out that they played golf together at the club, and they're signing papers left and right, and they're going on about this party, and that party, like I'm not even there. So, we sign the papers and I give them back to this guy. Even my lawyer thinks he's a lawyer, and my guy's no dummy."

Silvers shook his head in amazement. That was all he could do. Wherever the man went, wherever he was right now, he never seemed short of an inhuman gall.

"Next thing I know," Nelson was saying, "he calls and says he'll be up on Friday about noon with my certified check for 375,000 smackers. I tell him fine, meet me in my lawyer's office.

"Then he says, 'Oh, Thomas, I'm going to be bringing my brother along. The car has to go in his name because I'm not an American citizen.' I say, 'Hey, no problem.' "

On Thursday Nelson got a call from Roger Hammond asking if he could pick up the Porsche that day, as he had to drive it north to New York. Nelson had his lawyer send over the proper paperwork and, before a dollar was exchanged, the title to the car was turned over and the Porsche was on its way north. Nelson even put on the New York plates himself.

"And you never felt queasy about just signing over the title to a fifty thousand dollar car like that?"

"Oh, hell yeah, but, Barry, when your mind gets caught up in something, it's on that track. All I'm thinking is that I'll have a bigger and better Porsche, or two of the damned things, because I know I can turn this muffler deal into a gold mine. All it needs is someone who knows what he's doing in there running it. So, I felt a little funny when I signed the car over, but I'm counting much bigger money is what I'm doing."

"And Hammond kept his appointment with you at your lawyer's office?"

"Yep."

"And he had the money?"

"Yeah, a certified check drawn on some bank in Chicago. He gives me his, I give him mine for twenty-five thou, we sign some more bullshit papers and it's over.

"Then, he's calling a cab to take him to the airport, so I ask can I drive him? He says, thanks so much, he's got to head on up to Washington for a party at the White House. Man, my lawyer about dropped his drawers on that one. So, now I've got his certified check and he's got mine. And, we get in the car and, like he just remembered something at the last minute, he says, oh, hell, his tax advisers are going to kill him. Listen, he says, could I do him this big favor? Could we stop by my bank and cash this check?

"He says he doesn't mind paying American taxes but those English taxes sure are a bitch, you wouldn't believe how much you have to part with just to be an English citizen. So I say okay, fine. We can do that.

"He should have been an actor for what he did next. He says can we pull over, so he can call an important friend of his to delay the flight a few minutes. He's going to be a little late, but this friend of his at the FAA can hold up the flight, since he's on his way to the White House. Then he says, would I call the bank manager and tell him we're coming so we can expedite this transaction?"

"And you called the bank manager?"

"Sure did. So we go to the bank and I get him the quickest twenty-five thousand he ever made. I don't even deposit my certified check because the Duke has to catch a plane to Washington. You don't keep the White House waiting, right? So, I'm driving my wrecker because the Porsche is gone, and I'm flashing my dome lights and really gunning it. Barry, I hate to tell you this, but I even called the cops on the CB and told them I was bringing a dude to the airport who had to get to the White House."

Silvers just shook his head. "So, you never deposited your own check until Monday?"

"You got that right. It sure hit the fan by Tuesday. The FBI came up to personally break the good news."

"And the Porsche?"

"They got it three days later, sold to someone in Virginia. Remember I told you I put the plates on that car on Friday?"

"Right."

"Well, the ad started running in the Washington papers on Wednesday. It wasn't the White House he was running to, it was to sell my car."

"But you'll get it back, at least."

"Oh, I don't know about that. My lawyer says we'll fight it, but those people up in Virginia are holding title. They're not giving that sucker up. Would you?"

Before catching his plane back to New York, Silvers met Amanda Sagamore for a drink and debriefing.

"Well, Barry darling," she said, poring over the press clippings as she sipped white wine, "I told you from the beginning that our little snookums has no shortage of gall."

"Gall yes, Amanda, but this man is more than gall."

"And less," she said, looking through the newspaper clippings Silvers brought from Rio. "Beyond all that nerve, there's not much is there? The man knows no love, no intimacy, and no real friendship that I know of. Everyone in his life's been there for about forty-five minutes. He respects nothing, so I can only assume he doesn't have any regard for himself."

Then she gasped.

"That little bastard," she said. "That monster."

"What's wrong?" Silvers said warily. He was in a jet lag and so accustomed to people's fury at Hammond that by now he was almost indifferent.

"Remember I told you I met Hammond through Jasper Dillon? His father really is a Duke?"

"Yes, what about him?"

"That's him," she said, pointing to a shot of Frasier. "That's Jasper Dillon." She was so stunned that her voice was failing her.

"That little bastard. Wait until I tell his father. How could he?" Amanda Sagamore was close to tears.

"Barry, he was—is, one of us. How could he?"

It's a strange world, Silvers thought. One man for his own reasons becomes a fake duke to hurt people. Money aside, that's what it was really all about. Hurt and humiliation. And his assistant on this belittling mission was another man who seemed to be using the scam to get away from his own noble heritage. A real duke was helping a fake one.

28

Peter Castillo watched the teenagers eat their pizza. They horsed around, joking in English about girls, sports, wrestling, movies, and television. The leader wasn't hard to spot. He looked stronger, more sure of himself, and claimed a smidgeon of extra space around him. He was softer spoken than the others, but when he said something or just nodded, they paid attention. Castillo looked him over as a possible ally, but his eyes were dead. He wouldn't talk without a little police persuasion, if then.

Two looked like followers who could be squeezed if he got them alone. It was a way to go if he had to.

He watched all of their eyes and faces in the mirror. To them, he was just a blur a couple of tables over, a man eating a pizza, if they noticed him at all, which Castillo felt was not the case. His gaze fell on a thin youth they called Perry, who looked tough but decent. He wore jeans and a white T-shirt underneath a pale denim jacket with a lot of metal studs. His shoes were the thick, steel-toed combat boots that Castillo had worn in the army, and his dark black hair went all the way to his shoulders. The face sold Castillo.

Go, he said to himself. Do it. He got up, threw his napkin away, and walked easily past their table to the door, then turned, like he had just noticed their presence and was trying to place them. "How's it going?" he asked, smiling as he mentally searched. "Ramon," he said, completing his feigned scan. "That's where I know you guys from. How are you doing?" It was a friendly gesture, not an accusing one. Dressed in denim himself, Castillo could have been anyone from the neighborhood. He was no threat and they bought him.

"How're you doing?" the leader asked.

"Okay. Tell Ramon that Pete said hi, and I'll uh, get back to him on that business we discussed. He'll know what you mean."

"Okay, man," the leader said. "We'll tell him if we see him, but he won't be around for a while."

"He took off already?" Castillo asked, looking halfway toward the door, like he was vaguely curious, but had more important things to think about.

"Back to LA, you know him."

Castillo shook his head, like he knew him all right and couldn't figure out why he liked LA so much. "So's he coming back soon?"

"Oh, yeah, you know him."

"I'll probably see him out there," Castillo said, "but if you run into him, tell him Pete says hello."

"I'll tell him," the leader said and went back to his pizza.

Forty-five minutes later, nineteen-year-old Perry Colon got out of his 1973 Chevelle at a fruit warehouse where he worked the second shift loading trucks on a dock. He walked up a short set of steps into a huge open area full of cardboard crates and forklifts, past a few people, and into the washroom to change into an old pair of dungarees and a blue work shirt. He came out of the bathroom and headed for the dock.

"Where's Ramon in LA, Perry?" Castillo asked quietly from behind him.

Colon jumped back, curled his fist, but did not get into striking position. He just looked.

"Where's Ramon? I'm not a cop, I just need to know where he is and I think you know why."

"I don't know nothing, man."

"You got a little sister, Perry?"

"I don't know nothing," he said, not daring to meet Castillo's steady gaze.

"I'm helping her mother, Perry, that's all. I'm not looking to get you into trouble, I just want the girl. You know what I'm talking about, Perry. If she's dead, I can't help any of you. If she's alive, there's no hassle. It's between you and me. You follow me?"

Colon shrugged. "I can't talk here," he said.

"Anywhere," Castillo said. "But do we have time to talk later? Is the girl okay?"

"Far's I know. Get out. I can't talk to you right now, man. Get out of here before somebody comes."

When Perry got off work at eleven, Castillo followed him to a closed gas station on the strip near the fast food places. Perry parked his car, then got into Castillo's Buick.

"Okay, talk to me, Perry," Castillo said. "What's going on?"

"Ray likes young girls, that's what's going on. We call him Raymond the Animal."

"He's done this before?"

"Maybe. I ain't telling you the guy's life history, man. He's got her out there."

Within five minutes, Castillo got the picture, not the whole story, but enough so he knew he had to move fast. Pilar had fallen into the ghoulish landscape that vice and juvenile cops know well. Raymond the Animal was a pederast and a creature almost unique to black, Hispanic, Vietnamese, Cuban, Haitian, and other urban minority neighborhoods where illegal aliens find refuge from the Department of Immigration and Naturalization. He was a jackal who stole young girls from parents who were usually illegal aliens with no legal recourse.

His usual path was to "break them in" in LA, then sell them into slavery in Tijuana where he could get ten or fifteen thousand dollars for a ten-year-old girl on the freak prostitution market. The border towns were especially attractive to seemingly normal middle-class or wealthy businessmen, who crossed over to have sex with young girls and boys.

Castillo traces a lot of missing children. He was well aware of Raymond's world and the devastating variations of the game he plays. Babies are especially easy to steal and there is no shortage of couples willing to pay fifty thousand or more for one. He knows of cases where toddler boys are stolen to order and shipped to South America to be raised as slaves on ranches. Castillo does not know if Raymond the Animal himself did all these things, but he was certain that the man knew his way around these grim roads and that Pilar was soon to go across the border into Mexico where the chances of ever getting her back were next to zero.

If she was going only to Tijuana, Castillo could pick up the trail there and probably get her back. But from a Mexican border town, little Pilar could be shipped anywhere in South or Central America, and possibly overseas.

"Where in Los Angeles, Perry?"

"I don't know, I really don't."

"But you can find out?"

"Not tonight, I can't, man."

"But you know the kid is in LA."

"She's there."

"Perry," Castillo said, "I want the address. Tonight."

"No way, man."

"Tomorrow morning."

"Afternoon, earliest, fuck man, I can't go getting the address just like that after you go up to Chico and start asking questions in the pizza place. You nuts?"

"Who else knows where he is besides Chico?"

"I don't know. I don't. Like, I want to get the kid back to her mother just like you do. I do a little shit, you know, but what Raymond does is too strange. You're not going to bring the police in on Chico are you? I'll get killed if you do that."

"Get me the address. Does he have family here?"

"Somewhere. He's got an aunt or something, but I don't even know the name."

"Find me the address, Perry. Please. Do it your own way, but do it." Then he thought of another question. "Hey Perry, would he kill Pilar if he found out we were looking?"

"I can't say. I think he would, but I can't say."

Castillo didn't want to share his theories with Martha Cruz, but he didn't want to lie to her either. She had put her faith in him, so much so that it weighed on him as a burden. He is a hunter, a stalker by nature. When he is on vacation in North Carolina, he hunts and fishes. Stalking and closing in is Castillo's gift, God-given and honed over a lifetime of practice. However, the quarry gets away a lot of the time. He doesn't always bring them back, dead, alive, or at all. Raymond the Animal was also a hunter. He had patiently cultivated Pilar over a month. He'd have his fun with her if he wanted, but he'd also get his money soon. Maybe she was gone already.

"My God," Martha Cruz said in a whisper. "What can we do, Peter? Please, what can we do?"

"We go to the police now and we go to California," Castillo said.

At Metro they drew a detective who was receptive to their nightmare, but either unwilling or unable to move on their behalf. To Castillo, he was unwilling.

"If you used to be a cop, Castillo, you know what we can and can't do," he said.

"You come in here, you tell us some guy name Raymond or Ramon took a ten-year-old girl. Nineteen-, twenty-year-old guy, ten-year-old girl. One name and no proof. You don't have an address. I can't go to the LAPD with that."

"I'll get an address," Castillo said. "But when I get it, I want you to send a telex to LA. If it comes from you, they'll do something."

"And even if you get an address, where are you getting it from? You're telling me a source. That's all you're telling me, a source." He said the word *source* with an arrogant dismissal.

"Goddamn it," Castillo shouted. "I've got good information on this. That guy's got the kid out there."

"All right, all right, calm down, calm down. Get the address and we'll send out the telex. We want to help, Castillo, but you've got to give us something to do it with."

It was now Friday afternoon, four days since Castillo had heard from Nick George and a week since Pilar had disappeared.

"May I use your phone?"

"Yeah, there's one right there."

He called his answering machine, as he'd been doing all morning, waiting for Perry's message. It was there.

"Yeah, I got that thing we talked about," he said without identifying himself. "It's 2305 San Marino, East LA."

The detective took the address and reluctantly, Castillo felt, typed out a message on the teletype. Castillo helped him with the wording. The police detective continued to insist that the information was too sketchy and wanted to wait until Metro conducted its own investigation which, on the basis of what Castillo and Martha Cruz had said, was now warranted.

"There isn't the time," Castillo said. "Please. Send the telex."

Castillo waited while he transmitted the telex to the LAPD, suggesting that one Raymond Quinones was holding a young girl at 2305 San Marino, in East LA. Assistance requested.

Outside, Castillo said to Martha Cruz, "I don't like it. It's coming up to the weekend, that thing could get lost. Let's go to my office."

There had been odd moments in the last five days when Martha Cruz looked hopeful, but most of the time her demeanor was steely and glazed. Father Nieman had stopped by her house at least once a day and kept in touch with Castillo by phone. Castillo himself was numb and anxious to get back to his other business.

Phrases like, "Hang in," "We'll find her," and "Everything will be okay," were about all he could say to Martha Cruz, and that was starting to get on his nerves. It all sounded so hollow, so inept. Hang in. He wished he could find someone to say it to him.

In his office, he called the LAPD himself and talked to a Lieutenant Bob Cott in the Juvenile Division.

"I'll look for the telex," he said, "but I really need someone out here to identify the child before we can even go in. She's ten?"

"Ten, yes," Castillo said.

"Yeah, well, I can't do diddly without the mother out here. I can't go banging down a door looking for Pilar Cruz when I don't have anyone back at headquarters to make an ID."

"Okay," Castillo said. "I'll send her out. Can your men meet her at LAX?"

"No problem. Sorry, but she's got to be here."

Castillo hung up the phone and looked at Martha Cruz who was absently staring at the pages of a magazine.

"Martha," he said, "you have to go to California, and it might be for nothing." He explained what Lieutenant Cott had told him.

"Just me? You're not coming?"

"I can't, Martha," he said. "I don't dare leave here. I have to keep in touch with people here in case anything changes, in case he comes back, or maybe he never was in LA at all. I can't risk going out there with you."

She shuddered. She had never been farther away than New York. Now she had to fly to California on the chance that Pilar was there.

"If that's what I have to do, Peter, then I'll do it. Do I have time to go home and change?"

Two hours later, Castillo drove her to National Airport where he put her on a Continental Airlines plane for LAX. Then he went back to his office to wait it out. The phone finally rang.

"It's Bob Cott in LA, Pete. My man tells me that this apartment building where this guy Quinones is supposed to be, it's huge. You've got over three hundred fifty units there and you've got three people named Quinones in it. There's no Raymond either. You know these guys. His name might not even be Quinones.

"Bottom line, Pete. I've got to know the apartment number

or I might as well just turn the mother around when she gets here."

Castillo, exhausted, unable to focus, and almost blank could only say, "Okay, Bob. I'll have to call you back."

Perry Colon was in a line of workers who passed wooden crates of lettuce from one to another into the warehouse. When he saw Castillo at the end of the dock, he waited until there was a break in the momentum, then met him on the side.

"What now?" he asked quietly. "What are you doing here?"

"I'm sorry to do this to you, Perry, and I really appreciate your help, but I have to ask you to get me the apartment number. I need it right now. Pilar's mother is on her way out there and we have to move. He could cross her over to Mexico this weekend."

He looked resigned. "You're just like the cops, you don't leave well enough alone. I told you where he is. What more do you want from me? I want to help the kid, man, but you're pushing it."

"If it's too risky, don't do it. All I'm telling you is that we're close and the cops can't help me without the apartment number. It's life or death."

"Yeah, her life and my death," Colon said.

"Listen to me, Perry. I know what you've risked, and I feel very bad asking you to do it again. But I'm asking you to leave here right now and get me that apartment number. We're close now."

Perry Colon did it. The circumstances under which he got the address in the first place and the apartment number later are sketchy. He didn't volunteer the information and Castillo didn't ask.

"Eleven-A," he said.

"Thanks, Perry. Remember now. You get into any trouble at all, any kind of trouble, whether it's with Chico or the cops, you call me and I'll be there."

"Okay, man," he said. "Come tell me if you get the kid."

"I will."

"That's all I need," said Bob Cott. "We'll pick up Martha and bring her on down here. Then our guys will go up. I'm leaving now and Lieutenant Dave Hindman is here if you need anything. He's going to call you."

Hindman called two hours later.

"I'm sorry to tell you this, Mr. Castillo, but it's a big zero," he said. "We sent a radio car up to the apartment but there's no Quinones in there. There's an old couple named, let's see, Collins. They don't know any Raymond Quinones."

Castillo squeezed his fist and exhaled.

"Lieutenant," he said. "This is very good information. I think the guy's there."

"I appreciate that," the lieutenant said icily, "But he isn't there."

"The address is 2305 San Marino, right?"

"Let me see here. Yes, that's right, 2305 San Marino, 11-B."

"You said 11-B? Is that where you went, 11-B?"

"Yeah, right. Eleven-B's what we've got here, why?"

"It's not 11-B, it's 11-A, Lieutenant. You've got to go back. That's very good information. I'm sure the little girl's either been there or is there. Please. Please, you've got to go back."

"You said 11-A?"

"Yes, Lieutenant, that's what I said."

"Maybe that's where we did go. Let me check. I'll get back to you."

Castillo waited the longest fifteen minutes of his life as Lieutenant Hindman checked with the men he dispatched to East LA. If Perry Colon was right about Raymond killing Pilar, if he thought the police were closing in, their visit to the apartment next door could have been a death sentence. He wouldn't let himself think about it.

"Okay, Mr. Castillo," Hindman said warily. "We did go to 11-B. If you said 11-A, you said 11-A, but we took it as 11-B. We'll swing back."

They found Pilar Cruz, unharmed and alone in 11-A. When the cops knocked on the Collins's door at 11-B, Raymond the Animal went out a back entrance, leaving the little girl alone in the apartment. Castillo did not find out, or care to find out, what liberties Quinones had taken with Pilar, but she seemed all right. She was not beaten, slashed, or mutilated, and that had to be enough.

Pilar Cruz had not been taken by force; in some ways, Castillo thought, it was almost worse. Raymond had worked on the child's emotions until she was infatuated, as her friend Iris had described. She had gone with him for a child's loving reasons.

Raymond told her that he was a movie producer and, once in Los Angeles, she would be in films and would soon be rich and famous. Once he got Pilar into the movies, Raymond said, he would call Martha Cruz with the wonderful surprise. This was the way to show her mother how right she was that Pilar was special. Why wait until you grow up to be Miss America, he had asked her, when you can be rich and famous now? There would be a big house in Hollywood, a swimming pool, their own limousine, and Martha would never have to work in a factory again.

Raymond introduced the subject a little bit at a time, piece by piece, and he never told Pilar anything specific about when they would be leaving. He warned her that none of this could happen if she did anything to tip off her mother, her friend Iris, or her teachers. If anyone found out, he would leave her forever.

She was told to go through her days exactly the same as she always did. It would, he said, be the first test of her acting ability. If she could pass that test, she would please him and he would take her to Hollywood.

Every day he met her before school with exciting news of his progress in getting her work. By now, he knew Pilar's favorite television and movie stars and he tantalized her with the possibilities of meeting and working with these people. If Pilar mentioned the name of a movie star such as Judd Nelson, Raymond would say that he talked to Judd's agent yesterday and that there was a role in his new movie. Eventually, he got the little girl to the point where she couldn't wait for the day he would take her away in an airplane to Los Angeles.

When they brought her to police headquarters and an almost hysterical Martha Cruz, Pilar was shocked to see her there, believing that her presence ruined the surprise. To the child, the rescue did not mean a joyous salvation from torture and degradation, but the snatching of the star-studded life that Raymond was about to give her.

Father Nieman and Nick George arranged for counseling, and Castillo is confident that eventually the emotional scar tissue will be minimal, at least where the confusion and anger over the loss of Raymond is concerned.

Perry Colon never got into trouble. Castillo kept in touch with him for a few weeks to make sure he was safe and unaffected by the events in Los Angeles. Raymond did not come back to Washington, D.C., as far as Castillo knows.

Castillo's hunch about the telex from Metro to the LAPD was right. Though he saw the message transmitted, it either never arrived or got lost in the police bureaucracy. Lieutenant Cott never saw it.

Raymond the Animal did not have an arrest record for sexual offenses, though he had been charged with criminal trespass when he once followed a young girl into her apartment building. He claimed he was looking after her safety. Martha Cruz moved away with Pilar and is unlikely to pursue any case against Quinones even if the Metro police did pick him up. Castillo is sure he is still stealing children.

29

Whether they're in Harlem or Providence, housing projects are a forbidding testament to something that went wrong in the land of opportunity. The Rock Hill Gardens development had been built after World War II to accommodate returning veterans. The buildings probably never won any architectural awards when they were new. Now, one of the nicest things that could happen to them would be an earthquake.

The place had the feel of an Army camp that the Army forgot. The "town house" apartment buildings looked like barracks despite a sad effort to humanize them with green, dark red, pale yellow, and brown paint. It was a place where people got used to the idea that what breaks stays broken until someone comes from somewhere to fix it.

Paul Danzig, a free-lance Long Island investigator joined Barry Silvers in the search for Mary Costa. The soft-spoken, bearded thirty-six-year-old Vietnam vet can pick up the big middle of a case and work it, like the Sorcerer's Apprentice, with unwavering focus until he's told to stop. Nothing rattles Danzig, not the scary path to truck hijackers, the ennui of catching shoplifters, or the unlikely possibility of finding a woman named Mary Costa who had delivered a baby at Providence's Mercy Hospital thirty-one years ago.

Costa is a common name of Portuguese origin, so common that Barry Silvers was beginning to have serious doubts about solving the case. In 1956 there were seventy-eight families in Providence named Costa and that didn't take in surrounding towns like Warwick, Warren, Tiverton, Seekonk, all with their own substantial Costa populations. Every third Costa seemed to be named Mary.

Barry had promised the Girards that he would try to hold the first phase of the case to two thousand dollars. So far, so good. He'd found Mary Costa's name for just under a thousand, but now the costs were going way up. Anything over five thousand dollars, he'd eat, but Barry Silvers was going to take this case all the way.

Randall Blaine in the health department, for reasons known only to himself, had taken one final risk for them. He gave them Mary Costa's address as "97 Treadway Street." There was no Treadway Street in Providence or any surrounding town, but there was a Treadway Lane at Rock Hill. On a thirty-one-year old trail, assumptions are a given, and the two detectives considered it a safe hunch that a clerk had typed in "Street" instead of "Lane." Such screwups are so routine in the real investigative world that detectives become suspicious if they aren't there.

One of Barry's most exciting finds in Providence had been the physician who delivered Jeff, Dr. William Bernard, who had given up obstetrics but still practiced as a gynecologist. Silvers had requested and was granted an interview, only to have the doctor call back and cancel it. Now he wouldn't take calls from anyone in the agency.

Mercy Hospital was out as a source for obvious reasons, but there were still several unexplored trails, and very good ones, from the notes Barry took when Mr. Talbot, the hospital administrator, left him alone with the log. Besides the baby's weight and time of birth, which matched the time Randall Blaine had given him, he had also noted Mary Costa's admission number and the name of the scrub nurse. As the birth was described as "common" meaning noncesarean, and there were no notations of abnormality, the chances of a scrub nurse remembering anything about the mother were slim enough to rule her out as a feasible trace. But the two investigators kept the possibility open.

He had also taken down the names and admissions numbers of the two other mothers who had given birth to boys at Mercy that day. He also had noted from the log the birth weights of the babies, which would facilitate tracing the mothers if he wanted to undertake that task. In the fifties, new mothers stayed in the hospital five or even seven days, plenty of time for a woman to know quite a lot about her ward mates.

Silvers and Danzig were not elated to be at Rock Hill. The narrow streets were filled with little children with no apparent supervision or fear of automobiles. Silvers tooted the horn in as nonmenacing a way as he could, and kept his foot on the brake as he inched up Treadway Lane to Mary's old address at number 97.

Ted Davis, a local P.I. whom Silvers had contacted through the World Association of Detectives, had arranged for them to meet the project's manager, a bright woman in her midthirties named Anne Fleming.

Ms. Fleming was not willing to give them carte blanche on 1956 records, but she did allow them to compare their information with hers. Using old phone books, the city directory, and voting records, they had come up with a pretty accurate view of adults living on Treadway Lane in August 1956.

It was not anywhere near a perfect match, however. Low-income housing developments, where rent is determined by household income, are full of phantom tenants and falsified records. Women who live with their husbands report themselves as separated to keep the rent down. Tenants have been known to borrow children, or merely add names to records, just to get an extra bedroom.

Neither the official documents the two investigators had gotten from the Hall of Records, nor Ms. Fleming's tenancy rolls from 1956 showed a Mary Costa at 97 Treadway Lane. But both sets of records indicated that a Mary Costa had lived up the street, at 128 Treadway Lane.

This information was received as a breakthrough, but it proved to be a grueling blind alley.The Mary Costa of 128 Treadway Lane was fifty-five-years old in 1956, hardly a candidate for childbearing. They knew only that she moved out of the project in April 1959.

Norman and Lucille Doucette, occupations listed as fireman, Providence FD, and housewife, lived at 97 Treadway Lane between June 1955 and September 1957. They were listed as having three children, ages seven, nine, and 10. Doucette could probably be tracked through the fire department.

Silvers and Danzig went for coffee and made a list of options that two P.I.'s working at the end of their budget and out of state could follow up. They would certainly need to investigate the obstetrician, Dr. Bernard, who still wasn't returning calls. They were pleased with Ted Davis's work in paving the way for them to interview Rock Hill's manager, so they decided he should check out Dr. Bernard for them.

One problem that might kill the case was the very human tendency of unwed mothers, frightened young girls adrift in the very staunch moral codes of the 1950s, to give hospitals false names. It was done all the time. They believed their lives would be ruined, so they changed their names.

"But they also gave the names of supportive aunts, or just people who looked after them," Danzig reminded Silvers. That led to weeks of fruitless investigation, mainly on the phone from New York, but there were at least three field days in Providence trying to track the Mary Costa of 128 Treadway Lane. She had died a single woman in 1972 and her relatives were not receptive to any possibility that she had befriended a young woman with a problem, or was connected in any way with an out-of-wedlock birth. If Mary Costa had such a secret, it died with her and wasn't open to resurrection.

They were able to find one of the mothers who delivered a boy on the day that Jeff Girard was born at Mercy. She was very nice, but she remembered only that she was very sick and had a delivery that she'd just as soon forget. There was a young girl on the ward, but she wouldn't even recognize the name if she heard it. They gave it to her, and she didn't know it.

That left a final return to the Rock Hill project, where they had stopped searching once they became convinced that the real clue to Jeff Girard's mother lay with the Mary Costa who lived at 128 Treadway. They still had to check out Norman Doucette, the firefighter who had occupied the address that the young mother had given. He would now be sixty-eight. And they had to walk Treadway Lane looking for any scrap of information the street might still hold.

Any project has old-timers who have been there since opening day. There were three people now on Treadway Lane who were there in 1956. Helen Lewey was about ninety. She looked to Paul Danzig like the shrunken corpse in *Psycho* as she sat wearing some kind of bonnet on her living room couch talking to the two investigators who faced her across the coffee table. They discussed food, the old days, the way the kids used to play in the playground nicely, not like today when they dealt drugs there and you could hear them shouting and making a racket all night.

They talked about the neighborhood and how it changed. Did she remember the Doucettes or Mary Costa? Vaguely, but that was about it. Did she have any recollection of a young woman who might have been expecting a child in the summer of 1956? No, she did not.

Andre Potts was full of war stories, and rightly proud of his time in the European Theater. He could remember, it seems, every particle of his life before and after 1956, but during the summer Jeff was born, he couldn't remember anything.

Bob and Adele Varney were a couple in their sixties with remarkable memories. They remembered the Doucettes very well, and remembered Mary Costa as a nice woman who used to get up early every morning to go to church. She had been in her fifties or maybe sixties. She lived alone. The Varneys remembered no relatives visiting her, but they did recall that she liked hats with fake fruit on them.

They went to a senior citizen's activity group in the project, but no one remembered Mary Costa or the Doucettes.

"You were in that shithole?" Norman Doucette asked Barry Silvers. "And you're still here to talk to me about it?"

They'd found him, as expected, through the fire department. Doucette was one of those perennially boyish men who, even now at close to seventy, had the gleam of a classroom prankster. He had no double chin or pot belly. Much of his short hair was still stubbornly black and he wore chinos and a button-down collar shirt as stylishly as a 1962 Ivy Leaguer. His wife, Lucille, had died a few years back, and he talked a lot about her.

"Lucille was what you'd call a busybody," he said. "The town crier of Treadway Lane. Knew everybody's business. You say this is a medical investigation of some kind?"

"Medical, yes," Barry said. "But to be honest with you, it's equally to help a young man find his biological mother. As I say, we have the name Mary Costa and this address."

Doucette shrugged. "Beats the hell out of me, I'll tell you. There might have been a young girl here or there, but I just don't remember."

Then Doucette shook his head and whistled. "Rock Hill Gardens. Good God. And you're sure it was Mary Costa at my address?"

"Well, we're sure that a woman gave her name as Mary Costa and listed your address as hers in 1956," Silvers said.

"I remember Mary all right, but she wasn't ever preggers," and he laughed, like he'd just stumbled on the funniest thing that ever happened in the world. If Silvers and Danzig had found Doucette before they'd spent most of their budget chasing that Mary Costa, they might have shared the laugh more.

"You say your wife was kind of a gossip?" Danzig asked.

"*Kind* of a gossip? That's like saying Stalin was kind of a Russian."

"Is there anyone still around that she liked to gossip with?"

Doucette snapped his fingers and looked at Barry. "I know who'd know," he said. "Peggy Keegan. Peggy Keegan, yeah . . . This is a lady who knew everything on the block. She was as bad as my wife. Peggy Keegan. If she's still alive."

She was. But she didn't remember any young girl. It went that way for weeks.

Back in New York, Silvers nearly gave the case up. Paul Danzig went on to other things. Doctor Bernard, who might have shed some light on the case, was the next target of the investigation, but he continued to not take, or return, any calls. Ted Davis checked him out.

"This guy Bernard," he said on the telephone, "did a lot of adoption work with a law firm called Nepperhan, Wolfe, and Burns. And now that we know that, you can make book on never talking to this guy."

Nepperhan, Wolfe, and Burns had merged in 1966 with a bigger firm. For all practical purposes, it didn't exist anymore. N,W, & B had been known to speed up the adoption process, some would say crossing the rather delicate line that separates the practice of law from baby brokering. Nonprofit groups that help adopted children find their biological parents often found that the trail went dead at Nepperhan's door, never to reappear again. Records had a way of being "lost" or "misfiled." The partners who built the adoption practice were either dead or long retired. In the 1960s when the firm merged with another, the adoption business, no longer lucrative, was retired with the senior partners. As Nepperhan was never accused of misconduct during the half century of its tenure, and there were no real grounds to make accusations now, certain things, Davis said, were probably better left unprobed. Silvers came away from the conversation convinced that Jeff's adoption had been more like a purchase, but he couldn't prove it and wouldn't try.

That about ended it. The Girard case was finished, a painful near miss as so many real detective stories are. There was no budget left and no reason to encourage the Girards to spend any more of their money. If Jeff Girard wanted to start tracking all the Mary Costas in Rhode Island, northern Connecticut, and southeastern Massachusetts, then the rest of the country, he could do it, but he'd need about twenty-five thousand just to get underway. Maybe he'd luck out, but Barry Silvers could not encourage such an investigation. Trails disappear after thirty-one years. Secrets die with people.

But Barry Silvers had caught Norman Doucette at a time in his life when he needed something to think about. In the old days, Doucette was always building something, a doghouse, a picnic table that he couldn't get out of the basement, a duck hunting boat that always leaked. These days, his back bothered him. His energy flagged when he tried to do anything with his tools.

Still, there was only so much hanging around at the firehouse a guy was going to do. He missed his wife, the big mouth, desperately. He decided to kill some time helping the guys from New York. One afternoon, he called up an old fire department friend named Andy Baroody, known as Fat in those halcyon days of less than sensitive nicknames. Fat Baroody had lived on O'Hara Street, which ran behind Treadway Lane at Rock Hill Gardens. On a windy December afternoon, because they were both bored, Fat Baroody and Norman Doucette had a very wet lunch at Connelly's Bar & Grill, then went back to their old neighborhood.

Both men had been there many times since leaving, but as fire fighters who never gave much thought to the deteriorating slum where they'd once lived. That afternoon they drove up O'Hara Street to Fat's old house. Then they snaked Doucette's car through the children playing after school to Treadway Lane, to the place where Norman had lived with his family so many years ago. They parked out front and watched the kids playing on what used to be a lawn and was now blacktop.

The men looked around and remembered. What a shithole, they agreed. In their day, there was hope in the old place. You knew you wouldn't be there forever. Goddamn it, in the old days, you knew you'd get it together to buy your own house. Hell, it wasn't even such a big deal being in a project then. Just somewhere to stay until you got your own place which didn't take all that much moolah . . .

That's when Fat Baroody remembered a little chunk of information.

Silvers got a collect call at Introspect.

"Barry, you're going to drop a load in your pants when you hear this," Norman Doucette said. "I know why you can't find that girl. I just remembered something that's going to knock your socks off."

While Barry was always glad to hear from Doucette, he had become not a nuisance exactly, but an eater of time and toll charges. He'd remember something about "that shithole project," or run into someone who remembered a young girl here or there, and he'd call. Barry was always patient, and grateful for the help, but by this time he didn't think that Norman, who tended to get off on a tangent of reminiscences, could be of much help on the case. No one could.

"I'm listening, Norman," he said, tilting the phone slightly to one side so he could shuffle his papers while Doucette talked.

"You sitting down?"

"I'm sitting down."

"After the project was built, they put in this subdivision up in the north end, and it had this street that was going to be called Treadway Street."

Silvers stopped shuffling his papers. "What?"

"You heard me right. Treadway Street. Not Treadway Lane, Treadway Street. See what I'm getting at?"

"Really? There really was such a street?"

"Well, there was going to be. You could say it was like an almost. The plans went through the city and everything, before someone notices there's already a Treadway Lane in the project."

"So they had to change the name?" Silvers asked. He had had one too many trips to Providence, one too many amazing revelations. He wouldn't call Karen and Jeff on this, but a hunch started getting the better of him. In spite of his resolve not to get excited after he'd been through so many disappointments on the case, he was allowing himself to get charged.

"Well, that's what I'm getting at. No, they didn't have to change the name, and they probably wouldn't have, but they started screwing up the mail for a few of us. We'd get someone else's mail, and they'd get our mail.

"But the thing that made me remember is that I went out to Rock Hill with this buddy of mine, Fat Baroody, who used to live over on O'Hara. Crazy son of a bitch that Fat, real crazy bastard in the old days. He'd do anything. Brave old fart though. Lot of heart, lot of guts."

"So, you and Mr. Baroody went to the project yourselves?" Silvers asked.

"Goddamn right we did. We needed a couple of shots a piece before we did it, but we went there all right. Went right out to the old shithole, the two of us did. Thought I was going to pee in my pants, Barry, it's really the shithole of the western world now, isn't it?"

Silvers grunted agreement, knowing that he would have to sit quietly while Norman, who, from the sound of his voice and the background noise, had returned to Connelly's for more fortification, rambled on.

"Real shithole that place, Barry. Anyway Fat, the crazy bastard, is out there with me and he reminds me that one of the guys who got really pissed off about this was our chief at the time. He really hated it when two streets sounded alike. When your job is to put out fires, Barry, the last thing you want is to go to the wrong street in the wrong part of town."

"I'll say," Silvers said, "I hate to rush you, but I have another call, Norman. Tell me as quickly as you can what you're getting at."

"So, I'm up with Fat and it hits me. Bing. It hits me. Our old chief. Treadway Lane and Treadway Street, see? He raised holy hell about it. So they changed the name, Barry. They changed the name from Treadway Street to some other street. I'll find out for you what it is."

Silvers did not run for the airport this time. He did make a couple of calls to see if he could verify this story about the two Treadways. That's when he started to get excited.

One lunch hour, Mrs. Burgo, the librarian, did some checking for him. She sent him a small item from the Providence *Journal-Bulletin.* It was just as Norman Doucette remembered:

CHIEF MEDEIROS OPPOSES STREET NAME BEFORE COUNCIL

Treadway Street was never on the books long enough to be printed on a city map, but, after much digging, Norman Doucette and Fat Baroody found an old subdivision tract map with a dotted road labeled Treadway Street. The developer petitioned to rename it Springwood Lane in the fall of 1956. But between June of that year, when the first two houses were sold, and October, when the road was finally renamed and paved for the first time, Treadway Street was, indeed, its official name. And Norman Doucette's mail was delayed because someone in the post office insisted on sending it to 97 Treadway Street, a trim white Cape Cod house with an unfinished dormer and red shutters that had been sold new for $11,500 in the spring of 1956. The house was deeded to Mr. and Mrs. Arthur Cabral, and city records showed that they had a daughter named Mary, born May 8, 1938.

Mrs. Cabral's maiden name was Costa.

30

For a couple of weeks, Joel Stein called Marla Paul to ask her out. Marla told him she was flattered, but really could no longer abide the emotional buffeting of a relationship with a married man. He said he understood, but if she ever wanted to get together, she should not hesitate to call. Since Marla was not about to date Joel, and Vinny considered the sinning couple ruse too risky to try again, Davey Pagano caught the Gloskin case.

Sarah and Joel had continued to go to the Sea Breeze two or three times a week. Pagano videotaped them going in and out twice. That took care of the opportunity and inclination for adultery. Next came the assets investigation.

Louis Gloskin remained convinced that Joel Stein was going to rob him, a reasonable enough fear for anyone who had found his best friend involved with his wife and an illegal bug in his basement. The skip tracers, however, could not find any evidence of financial misconduct. They did not locate any corporations in Joel's name, no business ventures on his own, and no large purchases from company funds that Louis didn't know about. Apart from sleeping with Sarah, Joel's conduct was pretty routine and even ethical.

Louis could not accept that assessment. He clung to his belief that his partner was getting ready to go to Israel with Sarah.

Vinny had his own hunch about the bug. He read Joel as being adventurous and competitive in a boyish way. He was obviously a man of taste, yet he chose one of the seediest fornicating strips in greater New York as his trysting place. He was outgoing, friendly, and not above throwing down a few bucks on a football game. Somewhere, Parco figured, he came across a competent, but uninspired, electronics operative who filled his head with intrigue and didn't have to sell too hard to talk Joel into the bug. Parco couldn't prove it, but he felt the bug was a whim.

Joel, in his view, was a man out to get laid. Sarah was probably little more than a convenient outlet for misdirected sexual tension. While the agency had not focused any investigation directly on Joel, the consensus of everyone who had worked the case was that he had no serious inclination to get out of his own marriage. He might dream of a life in Israel, but it seemed to be just a dream.

Once Parco asked Gloskin if he would like to reconcile with Sarah. If so, they could probably find other women in Joel's life, based on his manic persistence in chasing Marla.

"No, Vinny, I have to go through with the divorce now," he said. "Do you understand that I have to do it?"

Parco said he did, but he wasn't sure how he felt. Was vengeance taking hold here? Not that it mattered one way or the other. The staff could ill afford the emotional expenditure of heavy involvement in a single matrimonial, but they all liked Louis and wished him well.

No one at the agency was terribly sympathetic to Joel, but, like professional soldiers anticipating the shock waves of their soon-to-be-fired artillery, they could shudder a little at the impact of their anticipated ambush. Joel assumed his friendship with Louis was intact. He carried on with the same jokes, the same teasing about never getting out to lunch and once in a while maybe meeting the contractors, and the ancient one, had he ever actually been in the same room with a gentile? He seemed to compartmentalize the affair with Sarah as a separate, possibly even not terribly important issue that did not impede the life he planned for himself. He seemed to want to do it the way his father had done it, grow old with his business and his best friend, then pass it all on to the kids.

Joel might even be the most surprised of anyone in the drama. He would probably spend the next several years in bitter legal conflict over the assets of the business. His marriage would undergo a shocking, if not irreparable jolt, when he was named as a corespondent in the divorce that, despite pleas, and threats, would be pursued on the grounds of adultery.

Louis guessed that Joel would be slow to seek proper legal counsel, believing as his father had, that any kind of trouble can be smoothed over with talk.

The business, after all that fighting, would probably end with a settlement of assets. One partner would buy the other out. Joel had the advantage of being a natural salesman, but Louis had the loyalty of the company's valuable employees. Gloskin wasn't Mr. Personality, but he asked about their families, respected their Christmas holidays with the appropriate time off and bonuses, and looked after them. Joel saw employees as parts in a machine. He had no interest in them as people.

Louis wasn't crazy about spending more time outside the office, but he would do it, and he believed the word would get around. The Gloskin-Stein spirit was with Gloskin. If you wanted the parts now, if you needed two hundred elbow joints by Tuesday and expected to get them on Tuesday, you'd go with Gloskin, not Stein. Louis felt clearheaded and confident. He could do it. He had a plan.

But a plan was not enough, his lawyer told him. There was no way that he would get custody of his children on the basis of his wife's affair with his best friend. The courts would probably give the children to their mother, with joint custody as the best Louis could hope for. He wanted to make legal hay out of the bug. Louis needed to prove Sarah was listening to his conversations.

As usual, Vinny Parco had an idea.

"It's going to cost you some money, Louis, but we'll prove Sarah checks that bug every day."

Louis Gloskin was not happy about the thousand dollar rental cost, but Ray Melucci and Davey Pagano came to the house and installed a hidden box of their own, a video countermeasure that looked like a fire extinguisher but was a long-playing VCR set up across the room from the alarm box. The nozzle concealed the lens.

Gloskin got his money's worth. The camera not only recorded Sarah checking calls, but, for the first time in the investigation, caught Joel on the premises. The fire extinguisher was in place for two weeks and recorded eleven instances when Sarah could clearly be seen opening the alarm box, and listening to Louis calling the weather phone, the office, his broker, and the service station about his car's muffler. As it violates eavesdropping laws to record conversations, there was no audio.

But the VCR really paid for itself when it showed Joel in the basement. No one had known that he came to the house. On one occasion, the camera caught Sarah and Joel listening to Louis while Joel made goofy lover's faces and mouthed teasing coos as he kissed Sarah, bit her ear, and reached from behind to fondle her breasts.

"Louis," said Vinny, "we won."

31

Mary Cabral Cogan, Jeff Girard's biological mother, hadn't gone very far. She now lived five miles down I-95 in Cranston, Rhode Island, in a yellow raised ranch house with white shutters. Her husband, Michael, was the service manager of a large Lincoln-Mercury dealership, and she was the office manager for one of the branches of the Ocean State National Bank. Fat Baroody made it easy once he remembered Treadway Street. Ted Davis, the local P.I., found her in a single afternoon. The problem was what to do next.

"It's obvious," Karen Girard said to Barry Silvers. "You or Mr. Davis go see her and ask if you can have a word with her alone. You tell her that you're a private investigator who represents the son she gave up at birth."

"I don't know, Karen—"

"Just hear me out. If she wants to see us, fine. If not, fine. She'll at least probably answer our medical questions, and you can ask her who the father is."

Silvers tried to choose his words carefully.

"You're my client and I'll do what you wish," he said. "But I think we have to know more about her. I don't think we have the right to open an old wound."

"I agree," Jeff said.

Karen shook her head quickly. "That's my problem with the two of you. You're men. You don't understand, you really don't. You're not opening up an old wound, you're *healing* one. Jeff, you understand that, you said you understood."

"I understand, and I don't understand," he said. "Who the hell knows? The woman's got her right to peace, doesn't she? I say we let this guy Davis do some more digging, so we can at least have a better idea of the lady."

They agreed and Davis went to work. A week later, a thick file arrived in Barry's office by Federal Express. In his report, Davis described Mary Cabral as the "other kind" of young woman who got pregnant in the 1950s, a middle-class Catholic girl who probably spent the second and third trimesters of her pregnancy in a home for unwed mothers. The usual cover story was a trip out of state to stay with a sick grandmother or to help out a relative.

Davis's report was standard P.I. fare, a rambling, single-spaced transcription from dictation with few paragraph breaks and not much punctuation. But to the Girards, who attacked the pile of papers with the fervor of famine victims at a banquet, it was Dickens.

"Mary Cabral, b. 5/8/38, St. Luke's Hospital, Providence. Father, John Cabral, bricklayer, b. 2/28/17, d. 10/19/80, lung cancer. Mother, Theresa Costa, housewife, b. 11/11/21, now residing Regent Grove Apartments, N. Providence. Family lived at 327 Central Street, Providence, until 1942 when father joined Army, mother lived with sister, Anne, 42 Melville Avenue, Newport, during war. Subj. has one sister, Antonia, b. 9/12/43, no other known siblings. Attended Our Lady of Fatima School, Providence, grad. 1951, St. Agnes High School, Providence, all girls Catholic school, now St. Bernards, yearbook photostats enc., grad. 1955 . . ."

At St. Agnes, Mary Cabral was in the Booster Club, the Future Secretaries of America, something called the Maypole Assembly, and the technical crew for the senior play. They couldn't tell much from the Photostats of the yearbook picture, but Karen, Jeff, and Barry agreed that Mary Cabral and Jeff Girard had the same smile.

"Goddamn," Jeff said, beaming as he read the report. "Goddamn, this really is her."

After high school, she went to work as a secretary in a factory that made watchbands. That would have been the year she got pregnant with Jeff, and the year her parents moved into the new house. If Jeff wished to pursue the search for his biological father, he would have to start at this point, which, to date, was a black hole.

Miss Cabral next surfaced in 1959 when she got married at St.

Francis Church to Michael Cogan of Fall River, Massachusetts, listed in the *Providence Journal-Bulletin* as an employee of Prendergast's Calso station in Pawtucket. Davis had sent a grainy Photostat of her wedding picture from microfilm. She was alone in the shot and wore a white bridal gown. Jeff would have been three years old by then.

Davis had been told to accumulate as much information as possible, but not to interview Mary's friends or relatives at this time. An asterisk and bold type in the report flagged Cogan as an obvious target for further investigation.

"Assessment that Ms. Cabral did not know Mr. Cogan in 1955, when she became pregnant. Will clarify once cleared to interview old friends/rels."

Though he was far more curious about his lost mother, Jeff sometimes thought about his biological father. He could have been anyone. Providence hosted hoardes of servicemen in the fifties, especially sailors and marines stationed at Newport's huge Navy base. There were also Coast Guard cadets, submariners ashore from New London, and students. Brown and Providence College were men's colleges in those days.

People in middle age do not talk about the sexual practices of long-ago friends. Unless Mary Cabral told her friends or relatives, Jeff's biological father would remain a question mark.

"That's why I say we contact her and ask her," Karen said. She had not given up on her belief that giving Jeff up at birth was a major hole in Mary's life and that it was their moral duty to discreetly offer her the chance to meet her son. At the very least, she would know that he had grown up well.

Neither Jeff nor Barry was in total disagreement with Karen's view, but they remained uncomfortable. Jeff knew he wanted to meet his mother, or at least get a close look. Somehow they had to find a way for him to do that. He also had to admit that he was disappointed that she had, if not a rich life, an abundant one.

From the start, Barry had warned them that she would probably be economically disadvantaged and when the trail led to that project, Jeff was sure he'd find a haggard lady, old before her time.

He had vowed to himself all that time that if he found her, he'd find a way to get her some money. That she didn't need money, or him, was a downer. Karen told him that he was angry over not being put up for adoption because his mother wanted to spare him a life of poverty. Karen had a way of spieling psychology which sometimes frustrated Jeff, but this time it made sense. He'd always thought that whoever she was, she did it for him. But she did it for herself, and that hurt.

There were other moments when he thought of Mary Cabral not as a mother, but a young, frightened kid. That's all she was, a kid. When he thought of her that way, he didn't blame her for anything. He didn't know much more about the 1950s than what he had seen in *Grease* or "Happy Days," but he'd heard enough to know that a young girl who went too far for whatever reason and got pregnant had to carry a lot more than a baby.

She really had only three choices. You got married to the guy, you had an abortion, or you gave the kid up for adoption. No one raised her child as a single mother. Getting married at seventeen was not one of the world's greatest moves, though it was done often enough. Abortions were illegal and dangerous for anyone, unthinkable for most Catholics. When he thought of Mary as just a kid, he felt like the parent.

"Jeff, I'd like to know what you think," Barry Silvers said to him. "What would you like to see happen?"

"I want to see her at close range," he said.

"See her or meet her?"

"See her, I guess. I don't want to bother the lady."

"But if you could see her and meet her without her knowing who you are, how would that be?"

"How are we going to do that, lie?"

Exactly. Ted Davis set up the ruse by calling Mary Cogan's mother, Theresa Cabral, who was living in a retirement community. He identified himself as part of a confidential, interstate medical investigation team doing a survey on hereditary diseases. Did she have a half hour or so to answer a few questions in an interview about her health? He figured that a seventy-seven-year-old widow would be very talkative on the subject. He was right.

Through that interview, Davis got much of the medical information Karen's physician had requested. He also learned that Mary had met her husband on a blind date in 1958, two years after Jeff was born. He then told Theresa that he would like to continue this investigation by speaking to her children, if that was at all possible.

"Well, my daughter Mary is over in Cranston, and my daughter Toni lives up in Attleboro. Do you want to speak to both of them?"

Davis appeared to think this over and said that since Mary was nearby, maybe they'd start with her. Mrs. Cabral called her daughter and put Davis on the phone to explain the "survey." Mary was happy to cooperate with any medical investigation. Davis assured her that it would not take much time. Would Saturday at eleven be all right, and, if so, would she mind if he brought along several of his colleagues from the New York research team?

Promptly at eleven that morning Ted Davis parked his Nissan Maxima on a graded driveway that led to a two-car garage with a big eagle over the doors. Barry Silvers was in the front passenger seat, Karen and Jeff Girard sat in back. No one had said much that morning. No one wanted to eat, talk, or do anything but this.

The couple shyly followed the detectives up two steps to a brick stoop flanked by two milk cans that had been painted black. On the lawn were two wrought iron figures, a man and a woman holding a black sign with white lettering that read Cogan. When Davis rang the bell, they heard a dog bark, a small dog, Jeff figured, one of those ugly little bastards that people dress in sweaters.

The door first opened a crack, then a little more. They saw the flash of a woman's face which disappeared as she drew back to calm the dog, now barking in a steady rasp.

"Douglas," she said, "get back, Douglas. You be a good boy."

She opened the door more and said "Good morning," with a musical firmness. "Mr. Davis, is it?"

"Yes, ma'am," he said as she opened the door to let them inside. "These are my associates from New York; Barry Silvers."

"Hi," he said, reaching out to shake her hand.

"And this is Karen and Jeff Girard, our field researchers."

Karen, dressed in a trim gray suit, extended her hand and smiled warmly, so much so that Jeff thought she'd blow it by hugging Mrs. Cogan. A minute ago, she said she felt like Jell-O, but now she was composed.

Jeff, dressed in his only suit, gave her a quick smile, took her hand, and looked away much too fast, he would think later, for fear she would catch him staring at her.

"Nice to meet you," he said.

"And this is Douglas," she said, pointing to a small English pug that was now sniffing Jeff's ankles. "He thinks he owns the place."

More to get a sidelong look at his biological mother than to please Douglas, Jeff reached down and scratched behind the dog's oversized, rippled head. The little pug wagged his whole body in appreciation.

Mary Cabral Cogan was about five feet two, with dark brown hair flecked with gray. Brown shadow emphasized her soft eyes, and her wine-colored sweater and skirt showed a comfortable figure, not skinny, not dumpy. To Jeff, she was the perennial other kids' mom, the kind of cheerful lady who kept her temper when you slept over and were still telling horror stories at three in the morning.

"Better watch out," she said to Jeff, "or he'll never let you leave. You must be a dog lover," she said.

"I am, yes," Jeff said stiffly. "I'm trying to talk my wife into getting one."

Karen stifled a laugh. She wanted a dog and Jeff didn't.

"He blames everything on me," she said.

Ted Davis started by presenting her with his P.I. license which looked very official with its state seal.

"As I said to you on the phone, Mrs. Cogan, this is a completely confidential survey to gather data on genetically transmitted diseases. Your name will never be used, and, of course, you may feel free not to answer any question we ask."

"Anything I can do to help," she said.

For fifteen minutes, Barry and Ted ran through a carefully prepared list of questions that Karen had gotten from her doctors. They covered genetically transmitted diseases from Tay-Sachs to muscular dystrophy. Karen asked questions and took notes on her legal pad, but Jeff just pretended to take notes. He could not think of anything to say.

Above the fireplace were various family pictures of her husband, not present because he worked on Saturdays, and her two children, a boy of twenty, and a daughter who was twenty-five. Aside from noticing that there was a resemblance, especially around the eyes, Jeff had no feeling of bonding, no sense of them as half-brother and half-sister. They were just a genetic coincidence. He was glad they weren't there today.

There was no subliminal biological connection with Mary either. He liked her. She was a nice lady, a nice mom, but not his mother, not at this minute anyway. His mother and father were Richard and Pamela Girard of Manhasset, Long Island, New

York, the folks who seemed to have paid some law firm real money to make him theirs. As they asked Mary questions, and she answered them, he pictured Christmas in this house, with polite jokes, and Cogan as the ideal dad cutting the meat. What a difference, he thought, from the holiday shit fights in Manhasset.

He wished he could say something to this woman now that the detectives had given him the chance. For a time, he thought, instead, about the woman who adopted him. All his life, she probably worried about this woman he now watched answer questions, worried that she was going to show up and take Jeff back. God, what a thing to have hanging over you. Since Silvers had reported the adoption as possibly irregular, maybe his adoptive mother had lived in fear of the cops coming to the door to arrest her.

Davis got to the part of the interview they had thought through most carefully.

"Now," he said, sounding bored. "To have a complete survey, we have to ask you some questions that you may or may not want to answer."

"All right," Mary said, hands folded.

"Have you ever had a hysterectomy?"

"No, thank heaven."

"Have you ever had a mastectomy or been treated for breast cancer?"

She shook her head.

"Have you ever had an abortion?"

"No."

"Do you have children by any other marriage, common-law-marriage, or liaison out of wedlock?"

"No."

"Did you smoke or take any prescription drugs during any of your pregnancies?"

"I smoked during both my pregnancies and my children are healthy. I don't smoke anymore though."

"Good move," said Davis breaking the ice, and they all talked about smoking for a few minutes.

There were a few more questions, then Davis wrapped it up, thanking Mrs. Cogan for her time. Karen had a few more medical questions, and Jeff added a remark here and there, but did most of his communication with his biological mother through comments about the little dog.

For Karen and Jeff, there was a sense that something momentous should now happen, some kind of psychological breakthrough that would result in all of them tearfully embracing. Davis had left that possibility open when he asked her if she'd had a child out of wedlock, but he never believed she'd disclose a thirty-one-year-old secret to strangers. Her husband might not even know about it.

For the detectives, who had carefully set up the ruse as a look-but-don't-touch event, it was a good piece of work. They had brought a client together with his biological mother. If he wanted to take it further, he could. If he didn't, so be it.

Jeff Girard felt numb more than anything else, like he had watched the whole interview take place from inside a bottle. Much later that night, when he was alone and thinking about her, he wished Mary Cogan well. He would think of her often, at odd times, and, depending on his mood, he would see either the young girl in the faded yearbook Photostat, or the woman he talked to today. The young girl, sketchy as the image was, was his mother, and the middle-aged woman in that living room was someone else's mom, a stranger.

For that kid who got knocked up and went to some home where her friends couldn't know she was going to have a baby he felt so much love that he had to fight tears. He kept thinking about that shy smile in the yearbook picture and he could feel the loneliness and fright of the unwanted pregnancy that came only months after high school graduation. God, what it must have been like to tell her folks that, guess what, your baby's going to have a baby.

For months, and possibly forever, there would be a yearning in Jeff Girard to run back to Providence. It wasn't Mary Cogan he wanted to see, but Mary Cabral. He wanted to go back to Providence and find her again and tell her that he was okay, that *it* was okay.

Karen, with her psychology turned on full blast, would tell him that maybe it wasn't even Mary Cabral he was looking for, but Mary Costa, the terrified kid in the delivery room who couldn't even tell her roommates her real name. He hated to admit it, but sometimes that psychology shit was right on.

For the nice woman in the living room, Mary Cogan, he felt distanced by an irretrievable span of time. She was okay too, and he was glad she was comfortable in her life, but this was a lady who had made peace with herself about his adoption. Sure, there had to be some thinking about it, but Jeff could see that she had learned to live with giving him up. She had left behind that frightened, pregnant kid from 1956. She had other children and he had other parents. The nicest thing Jeff Girard figured he could do for her was to leave her alone.

Karen wasn't so sure, but if Jeff wanted it that way, she wouldn't push it. It was his mother. She had wished that Mary Cogan was one of these instant rapport types who reaches right out and embraces every stranger in her life, insisting that they stay in touch and drop by for cookies. Then, there might have been more of a basis for follow-up.

In the front seat, the two detectives were talking shop. They mentioned triumphs, long shots that paid off, and near misses. They were saying how many times they had known they were close, but had to give the case up because one of the pieces had just disappeared. Karen watched her husband, who was staring out the window as usual. Small wonder that Mary Cogan was reserved. It sure ran in the family.

The investigation had cost, but it was worth it. Barry Silvers had found Jeff's biological mother. They now had a medical history on half of Jeff's natural heritage and that was something. The baby was doing well, and the relationship had thawed. Despite her husband's steadfast belief to the contrary, Karen Girard knew when to leave well enough alone. Mary Cabral Cogan was already drifting into the past.

"Too quiet back there," Ted Davis said, looking halfway over his shoulder as he weaved through the traffic on I-95. "You guys okay?"

"I'm fine," Jeff said.

"How about you, Karen? You fine too?"

"Yes, I am, thank you, Ted."

"I promised a couple of old firemen I'd bring you by before you went back, but if you're not up for it, I think they'll understand."

Norman Doucette and Fat Baroody had told the story of going to Rock Hill and remembering Treadway Street to every fire fighter and at least half the cops in Providence. They were waiting at Connelly's to meet the Girards.

Jeff didn't wait for Barry or Karen's vote on the issue. He didn't care if they missed the next plane, the one after that, or had to hitchhike home.

"Let's go," he said. "I'm buying."

32

Louis Gloskin sat on one side of the conference room with Joel Stein across from him. Both men wore yarmulkes, as did their attorneys and accountants. The attorney from the bank, though Jewish, did not wear a prayer cap.

Joel's lawyer spoke first.

"My client and I are extremely distressed at the turn of events that has brought this meeting about, as I'm sure everyone here is. We had hoped to avoid this meeting, to find a way to keep a profitable family business intact . . ."

Joel didn't like it, but the plumbing supply business that Eddie Stein had started with Meyer Gloskin in 1951 was history. He got the papers the same day Sarah got hers. The dissolution of the company, though long and cumbersome, reflected the easy way the two men had always done business. They decided to move quickly, but not in an abrupt, vitriolic manner that would send the clients elsewhere.

Both men wanted the plant, both men wanted the key accounts. Eventually Louis decided to let Joel buy him out of his share of the building at a good price, provided Joel would not interfere with Gloskin's taking over several key accounts. Louis, in turn, would not try to dissuade several key employees whom Joel needed for his new operation.

With Sarah, it was much nastier. Both wanted the house, both wanted the children. Each asked the other to leave, but, to avoid upsetting the children further, lived an uneasy coexistence under the same roof until they met with their lawyers.

The meeting was a study in contrasts. Sarah's attorney was a short, pudgy scrapper of the genre known in matrimonial circles as a bomber. Louis was represented by Abe Lincoln in a yamulke, a scholarly man who seemed oblivious to his diminutive opponent's rant that Sarah had been maligned, her privacy invaded, and if Louis didn't settle big and fast, he'd be lucky if he got visitation. Custody, to the bomber, was laughable.

Adultery came up. Sarah, her lawyer said, was in love with another man, one other man who shares her religious beliefs and whom she will probably marry. This may be a harlot in the male-dominated traditions of our faith, he fumed, in a sarcastic jab at Louis's orthodoxy, but in family court she would be a woman in love, and at the mercy of a vicious, vindictive husband who went so far as to hire armed goons to hunt the couple like animals.

It went downhill from there. Louis's lawyer listened politely as Sarah's counsel became fiercer and more dismissive. When he paused for breath, Louis's lawyer calmly presented counsel with two videotapes. One, he explained so quietly that everyone had to lean forward to hear him, was a standard, legal surveillance, which proved that the "hunted" couple went in and out of the Sea Breeze Motel of their own volition. This tape, he said, after asking the bomber to please stop shouting and hear him out since they'd spent the past hour listening to his angry outbursts, this tape establishes opportunity and inclination for adultery.

Opposing counsel then ranted some more, after which Louis's lawyer continued. The second tape, he said, should probably be viewed first as it showed Mrs. Gloskin being fondled by her husband's business partner, as well as clearly monitoring an illegal listening device which would be produced in court along with a police report filed by the "armed goons" who found it. Mrs. Gloskin's fingerprints were clearly on the tape, by the way. In other words, Louis's lawyer said before excusing himself and his client, we present to you a videotape of Mrs. Gloskin committing a felony.

Louis was granted temporary custody of his two children and remained in the house. Sarah moved in with her sister for the time being. The details of his settlement with Sarah are still being worked out, but it looks as if it will be settled to his definition of fairness, and out of court. Gloskin will not keep his wife from her children, or close himself to joint custody later. He has no intention of punishing her so severely as to leave her with nothing. For now, he wants the children and the house, and, for now, he will keep them.

33

Felix Mantilla had enough of the man. All week, he'd sat in the cafe as if he, and not Felix, owned the place, speaking in Spanish with an affected British accent, and belittling the staff.

Does the pig think I know no English? he thought, listening once again as his patron told yet another party of spoiled rich sons and daughters of European wealth that the food at Cafe de la Mer was "swill" and the wine "only slightly better than muscatel." He somehow found the generosity to say that the view of the Mediterranean was magnificent.

Merchants are used to arrogance in Palma de Majorca. It's go-go days as a jet-set playground on the Cannes and St. Tropez circuit may be gone, but Palma remains a clean and scenic Mediterranean port that continues to attract young, well-heeled Europeans on holiday.

The man, who had introduced himself as Peter, was very cordial at first. He'd come in alone for lunch, asked for the owner, complimented him on the excellent cuisine and wine, and talked. He said he was in the commodities business in London, here to enjoy the fresh air and surf spray after the stresses of a divorce. He wanted to meet people and was he in the right place to do it? Mantilla told him that if he wanted to meet not just people, but his kind of people, he should go no further than the Cafe de la Mer, and that he should come back that night.

That was Monday. By Tuesday night, he seemed to know half the wealthy Europeans in port this week. He enthusiastically ordered champagne and insisted on picking up the check. He left at the end of the evening with a beautiful blonde who became his companion for the rest of his stay.

By Wednesday, he held court at his own table, and Mantilla

noticed a shift. Peter continued to order champagne and everything on the menu for everyone, but, from Wednesday on, others, especially the blonde woman, paid with their platinum and gold American Express cards.

He showed up for lunch, cocktails, and dinner, always with an expanding crowd of attractive young people. One morning, he waved at Mantilla jauntily from the fantail of a moored yacht. Later that day, Mantilla saw him driving a burgundy BMW with the blonde in the front passenger seat.

Peter had several times cornered him and said that, since they were good friends and that all of these people obviously came there because of him, he should have a limited percentage of their business. It was also time to set up an account for him, a running tab which would enable him to bring in even more of the people he was meeting during the day. These valuable customers would certainly continue to patronize the cafe once the business he had with them was concluded.

Mantilla coldly declined, saying that he managed to attract business before he met Peter, and would continue to do so without him. Peter sniffed and said, "Your ingratitude is forcing me to take my business and my friends elsewhere."

"Do that," Mantilla had said, and turned away.

But the man didn't leave. He continued to patronize the Cafe de la Mer, but with increasing, insufferable arrogance. He rejected steaks, fish, wine, and dessert. He badgered the bartender to make esoteric drinks which, once made to his specification, were pronounced diluted and sent back.

By Friday, the staff complained that this awful man from London was embarrassing other customers. He complained loudly when they gave "his" table to a dignified French couple who had been regulars for more than twenty years.

The breaking point was probably when, at the height of the Friday night traffic, Peter ordered the most expensive red wine in the house, a 1979 La Tache from Domain de la Romanee Conti, 187 ounces of heaven in an imperial bottle, worth more than a thousand American dollars. Mantilla, himself, who took great pride in his wine cellar, fetched and opened it for Peter against his better judgment. He sniffed the cork, swirled, made a face like he was being poisoned, lurched to one side, and spat it to the floor.

"Felix, poor Felix," he said clutching his throat. "Whatever thief sold you this wine should be shot."

This wine, he said, was a rancid imitation of a La Tache that they could not consider paying for. What else did he have for a discriminating table?

Mantilla, so shaken that he could not even speak, took the wine into the kitchen and sampled it. Even in his buffeted emotional state, he recognized the wine as such a robust, heavenly concoction that tasting it was close to an out-of-body experience.

When he saw the two constables come in, Peter stood up and dressed them down like military recruits. How dare they interrupt his dinner, how dare this crooked cafe owner who tried to pass off "rat urine" as La Tache, call them? When they insisted he come with them, he arrogantly agreed to pay for dinner and even that atrocity he had just sampled just to put the incident behind him. If they would accompany him back to his hotel, he would gladly get the cash. Several gold and platinum American Express cards appeared to take care of the check, wine and all.

Mantilla conferred with the two officers, who advised him that he could charge this obnoxious man with creating a public nuisance and attempted theft for his refusal to pay for the wine. It would be enough to put him in jail for the night and, in the morning, the magistrate would release the pig. He might even give him a fine.

Mantilla accepted a credit card from an embarrassed blonde man in his late twenties who added a tip, even though Peter, halfway out the door with the constables shouted, "No gratuity, Marcel."

If Peter had been more polite to his jailers, they might not have taken his prints and run a check. But they did, and Mantilla had the most eventful five days of his life. The next six months weren't too shabby either. Before morning's first light, he had a call from Interpol. They visited him at breakfast. Two FBI agents flew in from Barcelona that morning. They were the first of many grateful agents of the U.S. government who were to promise to show the cafe owner everything from North Carolina barbecue to an evening of jazz at Jackson Square in New Orleans if he ever got to the States.

Inspectors from France and Scotland Yard came too. For

weeks, Mantilla heard from police departments all over Europe, South America, and the States—from Rio de Janeiro, West Palm Beach, Florida, Las Vegas, Nevada. In the next year, he would be visited by more than a dozen private investigators, and his walls would be adorned with framed newspaper clippings about the cafe owner who did what hundreds of law enforcement professionals could not do. Felix Mantilla put the Duke of Audley in jail.

34

Crooks don't scare Barry Silvers, especially not crooks already in jail. But as he filled out his pass form at Florida's Eglin Air Force Base and tried to concentrate on the sentry's direction to the minimum security prison housed there, he felt as queasy as he did the day Jimmy Hoffa's goons told him he might have an accident. He was meeting the Duke of Audley.

Silvers is sketchy about his participation in the Duke's life at this point in the case. He will say that an interview took place, but not how he got through the snake dance of other P.I.'s, angry sting victims, and attorneys who also wanted a little head-to-head with Hammond and his legal counsel. The Duke is widely believed to have charged for his time.

Eglin is one of the so-called "Club Fed" prisons that drew bales of barbed press during Watergate. Aside from the regular entry points to the base, there are no walls or bars. The prison could be any set of regulation buildings, and the khaki-clad staff members gulp when a visitor asks about the swimming pool, tennis courts, and miniature golf courses. The ubiquitous white *USA TODAY* box is available to the prison's well-scrubbed inmates. So is Haagen-Dazs ice cream. If the Duke of Audley was finally going to do time, it just figured he'd land here.

Felix Mantilla and the Majorcan authorities took a more abundant piece of his hide than law enforcement authorities on three continents would have liked. He served six months for creating a public nuisance and attempted grand larceny of the wine.

The French got him next, but Eugene Belliveau was persuaded by the Justice Department that, given a much stronger case in the States and their promise of a speedy trial, his best recourse was to drop charges in France and press them here.

When he finished his time in Majorca, he was taken to New York by two FBI agents, was cleared through customs, and detained in a hotel and several minimum security facilities before the government decided on Eglin as his pretrial home. As a detainee, he could wear his own clothes and be free of the menial chores that awaited him on conviction.

By all reports, Hammond was a cooperative prisoner who played a mean game of poker and had already teamed up with four or five of the more affluent insider traders and other white-collar convicts.

Silvers's queasiness built as one of the correction officers made pleasant conversation en route to the visitor's lounge, which was empty when he got there. The room looked more like the loading area of an airline than the visiting room of a federal prison. There were plastic molded seats in alternating red and blue rows, with pastel walls and several wall-mounted television monitors. Along the walls were vending machines, video games, and a neat box of puzzles, games, and children's toys.

"You can sit right here, sir," the guard said, gesturing to a large table that faced the rows of chairs. "I'll get Hammond for you."

He left through a glass door and Silvers tried to review his list of questions. They had forty-five minutes, most of which would be taken up with various questions about who in his client's organization had given Hammond the inside information he needed to rip him off.

He heard a noise and jumped up with such a start that he almost tipped over the table.

"How're you doing?" asked a short man in a trim dark suit. "I scared you, right? Phil Lipshits," he said holding out his hand.

"Oh, yes, I was startled," Silvers said.

They shook hands and Lipshits, a Daytona Beach lawyer hired by the New York firm handling the Duke, said, "We spoke on the phone." He carefully removed his suit jacket and placed it over the back of a chair. He was a pleasant man in his late twenties with curly hair and tortoiseshell glasses. His job was to see that Hammond didn't get himself into any more trouble during his interviews.

"Quite a place," Silvers said.

"Yeah, I'm here so much, I know everybody. Attica it ain't.

Heaven it ain't either. These guys can't leave. You see that blue line out front?"

"No, I didn't."

"When you go out look at it. That's their wall. They cross it once and they're in at least medium security. And you can't come back here. One trip to the country club per person per lifetime. Get caught again, you do your time with friends you don't need chasing your buns."

"This Mr. Hammond must keep you busy."

Lipshits looked to his side toward the glass door and stood up. "He's about to keep me busy again," he said, walking quickly across to the door where Hammond came in next to the same guard that had escorted Barry.

"Richard," Lipshits said. "You haven't changed since yesterday. How are you doing Mr. Carter?" he asked the guard.

The black and white newspaper glossies and FBI shots had undersold the Duke of Audley. He had sandy hair and deeply set blue eyes that today conveyed an exasperated amusement, like a man who went out to buy a newspaper and mistakenly got himself kidnapped and taken to Russia for questioning by funny Cossacks. He wore a pink jacket with the sleeves pushed halfway up his arms over a blue pinstriped button-down collar shirt that tucked smoothly into a pair of pleated beige corduroy pants with a razor crease. The sea green socks that flowed into soft leather loafers seemed to match nothing, but on him looked like they matched everything.

When Lipshits introduced them, he took Barry's hand in a firm, businesslike grip and Silvers immediately knew why so many women had described his eyes as hypnotic. They were Paul Newman's, only more so.

"Barry Silvers," he said. He enunciated the syllables carefully, nodding as he said the name as if he wanted to be sure to remember it forever. "I'm sorry we can't meet in better surroundings, Barry, but we'll make the best of it, won't we? I trust Mr. Lipshits has not incriminated me?"

"I think you're safe."

"I try to get Philip to lighten up. You would think *he* was facing thirty years in prison, but I'm sure you know these lawyers," he said.

Given his mission, Silvers had been told to expect the Duke's trademark dismissive arrogance. Hammond treated cops and adversarial attorneys with an icy attitude that said, essentially, that anything you accuse me of is absurd because you are a diminished human being. Instead, he was feeling the charm which warmed even an ex-Fed with a heavy con artist workload in his private practice.

"So, what business have we, Barry? Who do you know that I know?"

Silvers laughed. "I'd have to say that I've met a number of your acquaintances."

"Who are not very happy with me right now, yes, I have so many things to straighten out when these," he looked toward Lipshits, "*allegations* are resolved."

"Allegations," Lipshits said smiling from inside an attentive but bored facial cast that he had probably developed to cope with the ennui of shepherding the Duke through his daily visits.

From his first question, it was apparent that the Duke was not going to be helpful. Most of the issues were sidestepped through a deft use of mimicry, wicked gossip, and jokes, and when he wanted to get by a question, Hammond left few holes in his monologue for interruption.

"John Santos," he said, throwing his face and posture upright in a devastatingly accurate impression of the Palais Real's manager. " 'I cannot accept this gracious gift, your highness,' " he said.

"He called me 'your highness.' I said, 'John, take the blasted watch or I'll have to sneak it back through customs.' "

The chess game went into high gear early. Any time Silvers mentioned a name or a place, Hammond had a story that was followed by a series of rapid-fire questions designed to elicit information.

"I'm not saying I did or didn't do anything, Barry, but surely the hotel won't pursue the matter. What did Santos say to you about that?"

Silvers marveled at the intensity with which Hammond turned known truth into fiction. He seemed able to do a number on himself, to believe a lie when he was telling it. To Silvers, the tension was akin to play-off sports. Everything the Duke said was calculated. He knew no other way. So far, it was a stalemate, but the Duke pressed on, admitting nothing, and wanting everything. Silvers, whose job was to do the same thing, was amused, but unrelenting.

When the conversation got to Patrice Maire, Hammond's voice

became a low, conspiratorial whisper that was such a direct communication with Silvers that it seemed to be saying that Phil Lipshits was too young, too unworldly, to understand a secret that only two seasoned explorers of human nature could know.

"Patrice Maire," he said inhaling the name and smelling it like a rose. "Patrice Maire. My God, Barry. Have you ever, ever seen such a woman? I mean, can you believe there is a man in the world who goes to bed with that perfect creature every night?" He held out his hands.

"Cuff me up, dear boy. I confess. I tried to seduce Patrice Maire. And didn't succeed, I might add. I said to her, I really did, I said 'Patrice, you are the only woman in the world who could make me monogamous.' Do you *know* what Patrice Maire said to me? I'm surprised I ever even left Rio."

He leaned forward, crooking his finger for Barry to move closer. Phil Lipshits, bored and obviously used to all variations of the Duke's performance, looked blank. "She said, 'And you are enough to turn a monogamous woman into a sinner.' Now that's all she said, she promised nothing, but it drove me mad, absolutely mad. I must write Patrice. Phil, make a note on that pad. Patrice Maire. *M-a-i-r-e.*"

As Hammond continued to talk, blending accurate gossip with his devastating impersonations, Silvers knew that he was the target of a good detective trick. Hammond was Method acting to an audience of one, providing precisely what his listener wants, or needs, to see and hear. He was the quintessential civilized host, warmly asking Silvers about his family, sharing favorite restaurants in the New York area, and, when Silvers said he was a Yankee fan, he got a glimpse of Hammond's celebrity ploy.

"I was having dinner with George Steinbrenner last year when I had business in Tampa," he said and proceeded to give a blow-by-blow account of a dinner that Silvers knew never took place. But Hammond described the restaurant, the limo, the waiter, the private dining room, not only as vividly as an event that actually occurred, but as if he could see make-believe evolving to three-dimensional reality.

Childlike, Silvers thought. A child makes up a story and sees it happen. This man had the unworldly capacity to defy nature and take the child's vision with him to adult life. Meanwhile, he was also sure that the treacherous adult probably had a photo of himself with Steinbrenner tucked away somewhere.

"We talked about the press and how unfair it is," he said, "I'll probably be tried in the media."

You wish, Silvers thought. The Duke had called several journalists he knew with hints of a hot story, but so far only a couple of investigative reporters with a strong bead on his financial chicanery were eager to speak with him. Neither wrote pieces that were likely to turn him into a folk hero.

"So I ask you, Barry. Do I look like a thief to you?"

Phil Lipshits shifted around in his seat. Silvers didn't need to think about his answer.

"I've seen a lot of evidence that you have done many illegal things."

Hammond shrugged. "Evidence is a deceptive thing. It is evidence only of one's own creation, wouldn't you say? I will tell you something right now. And I want you to hear me out before you dismiss what I have to say."

Silvers stared at him, not wanting to disturb his mood, even with so many obvious lies. The investigator well knew that a master con artist buries his falsehood among truth and slips it in when he knows that truth has bought him some credibility. He was sifting through the scraps to see what truth the Duke dropped for him.

"We are in the same business," Hammond said. "You will not believe me and that is fine, but you will not see me in prison long for those allegedly illegal things. Do you know why, Barry?"

"Why?"

He looked serious now, somber. "Because I did what I did in the service of not only my government, but yours. That is all I can say. Someday I will tell you the answers to the questions you ask, but for now, I cannot. I am terribly, terribly sorry. I have not even told Phil my story. There are too many lives at stake."

Silvers was transfixed. Lies or no, his performance was breathtaking. The Duke continued.

"Drugs," he said quietly, taking a pause. "The scourge of the twentieth century. That is all I can tell you. I was helping our governments with their drug problem in a way they could not do for themselves. Some day I will tell you, and only you because you are a man I can trust with my story."

Silvers wondered how the man's self-sacrifice for the greater good of two nations accounted for walking off with Oren Deiter's Rolex watches or Amanda Sagamore's jewels. Tommy Nelson, possibly deprived of his Porsche forever while the insurance company found reasons not to deal with his problem, would be fascinated to hear that he had given up his fifty-thousand-dollar machine for a secret mission.

"And another thing I want to say to you, believe me or don't believe me. Have you ever heard of me, the evil Duke of Audley, *allegedly* taking money from some poor creature scrubbing floors or some dreadfully middle-class insurance claims representative working extra nights because his children are at a university? You have not heard such things and you shall not. The Duke of Audley's government activities sometimes made it necessary to part scoundrels from their money, scoundrels who stole it in the first place, but there were no penniless or innocent victims, were there?"

"Amanda Sagamore thinks she might be one."

"Amanda," he said, clapping his hands together like a kid at Sea World. "For God's sake, why didn't you tell me you know Amanda? How is she?"

"To tell you the truth, not happy with you right now."

"Me? How can that be?" He paused and frowned. "Barry, you must make me a promise. Promise me you will tell her I have done everything humanly possible to help her with her loss."

"I'll tell her," Silvers said, "but she thinks you're involved."

The Duke went into dramatic contortions. "Oh, God. Barry, please. You obviously are one of the few investigators who took the time to know me. You know I didn't do that. You have to know."

Silvers said nothing.

"Barry, you've tracked this evil Duke of Audley. Is the man's style ski masks and guns? I mean, good God, man, I've been accused of all kinds of outrageous things, asinine things, improper acts. I can live with such lies. But Amanda, my dear friend Amanda, thinks I was involved in—a ski mask robbery." He spat the words out like he'd just sipped gasoline.

Phil Lipshits started to laugh at either the histrionics or the idea of the Duke in a ski mask, but caught himself.

"Phil," the Duke said. "Phil, you must call this woman. She has to know my innocence. She is a personal friend."

Barry Silvers cleared his throat and felt a current of anxiety run through him as he prepared for a distasteful moment.

"Mr. Hammond. Mr. Lipshits. I am here with a proposal from Mrs. Sagamore."

"A proposal? What kind of proposal?" the Duke asked, all ears and eyes.

"It's for both of you in a way. Mr. Hammond, you say you're broke, and that you can't pay your legal expenses."

Hammond said, "I said that I have no money, yes. I'll somehow find a way to pay these wonderful gentlemen who are not only going to clear my name, but seek appropriate recourse for all the disinformation certain enemies of mine have put out."

"I see," Barry said. The Duke had stiffed every lawyer who ever represented him. Mrs. Sagamore had learned that his present firm was already planning to dump him because the publicity he promised in lieu of a retainer had not materialized. Her idea, which Silvers believed to be a sound one, was to appeal to a lawyer's favorite body part—the pocket.

"Mrs. Sagamore is offering a hundred thousand dollars, no questions asked, for the return of her jewelry," Silvers said evenly. "It can be paid through your attorneys to help defray the heavy legal expenses that surely surround your charges."

Hammond's blue eyes now became lagoons of compassion and sincerity. He sighed. "I, of course, know nothing of the theft," he said. "As you may know, I sustained much injury myself from those handcuffs. They should be harder for criminals to obtain."

"Well, think about it," Barry said. "You have many contacts that would enable you to tap into a channel of communication I would not know about."

The Duke thought carefully, as if he were solving the problem of world hunger. He nodded. "It is possible that I *could* do that. There is a reward, you say?"

"Of one hundred thousand dollars," Silvers said. "No questions asked."

"Not that I would accept it, Amanda is a friend, but I do have these legal expenses. But, you see, Barry, there is a problem."

Phil Lipshits cleared his throat.

"You see, uh, there is the possibility of incrimination of another party, a man whose family would be devastated."

Silvers was not about to tell him that he knew that Amanda Sagamore and Lance Dillon had taken young Jasper to the royal woodshed to get him to talk about the theft. He seemed terrified to say anything.

"But I will see what I can do, of course."

They shook hands all around as Mr. Carter, the corrections

officer, looked toward them expectantly from his station at the door.

"Barry, let me ask you a hypothetical question," the Duke said.

"Go ahead."

"I don't know, of course, but there are certain places where stolen jewels go, places that are extralegal, but I do have contacts that could pry open that cesspool world for Amanda."

Silvers nodded.

"But I do know from what friends tell me that it gets—expensive—to recover jewels of such high visibility. Ask Amanda, and I am not saying it is even possible to think about this, but ask Amanda, if we had to, could she bring the reward up fifty thousand? I could probably get her more cooperation. I would not use any more of her money than I had to, but a hundred fifty thousand would be more leverage."

Silvers thanked the Duke for his time and his leverage, shook hands with Lipshits, and drove to the airport where he caught a short flight to Atlanta, changed planes and headed back to New York. As he reclined in his seat and munched Beer Nuts, he thought about the Duke. He had not expected to come away from the interview with much information, and he'd been right. The Duke had certainly lived up to his billing, but Silvers felt a sense of loss for the forever wayward, forever twisted path of a man with such intelligence, looks, and style. He could have been anything, but now he was only going to be a prisoner.

Mrs. Sagamore minced no words about where she would like to see the Duke put that extra fifty thousand dollars, but she said if the bastard could get the jewels back, she'd pay him and be done with it.

The Duke never did produce any leads to the gems either because of some heretofore unseen honor to protect his accomplices or, as Barry and Mrs. Sagamore really believe, because he just couldn't pull it off. He hinted, through his attorneys, that "the incriminated other party" had a taste for cocaine at the time of the robbery and, though he did not say it, the jewels probably ended up fenced way too cheaply into a drug pipeline rather than in the more conventional hot rocks marketplace. If so, they could be anywhere and are probably the prized possessions of a dealer's girlfriend. Mrs. Sagamore's own P.I., a specialist in gems, continues to search without much optimism.

Silvers smiles when he thinks about the case. For most of the chase, he had been the good G-man, tracking a criminal, tracing his path through North and South America, through Europe, resulting in the cop's ultimate reward of seeing the criminal in jail where he belongs—a satisfying, storybook ending.

Then, with full consent of his client, who held no objection to Silvers earning a piece of the reward himself as a finder's fee, the detective had offered his target six figures, no questions asked, to use for the attorneys to help get him out of the same jail. And Hammond, a criminal behind bars with no bargaining power, bargained for, and got, another fifty thousand dollars to locate the jewels he undoubtedly stole in the first place.

35

Gus Chakas didn't ask questions. Joe Howard said to meet him at six in the morning in front of the store, so there he was freezing his buns off in the winds of early December. It was almost as cold as the reception he'd gotten from his tenants when the rent came in. They were in a panic now over the peddlers, and furious at him because he would not consider signing, and paying his share, of the retainer contract from Urban Protectve Services that they had placed on his desk.

Now they were talking lawyers, withholding rent, refusing to pay the escalation increases that were due to take effect on January 1 when the taxes went up.

"Don't worry, Gus," Howard had said. "We'll take care of it."

"Will it cost less than fifteen thousand dollars?" Chakas asked.

"About fourteen thousand, nine hundred, fifty dollars less," Howard said. "We'll meet you."

Chakas, an early riser all his life, got to his store at 5:45, brought in the newspapers from the curb, fired up the grill, and busied himself with the little chores of opening shop that had not changed since his grandfather's time.

Just after 6, a yellow cab pulled up and three men wearing windbreakers and knit hats got out with the driver who opened the trunk.

"Hey, Gus," Joe Junior said.

"Morning, Gus," said Joe Senior as he lifted a large plastic bag out of the trunk and hefted it to his shoulder. "Jesus Christ, how much do these fucking things weigh?"

"Fifty pounds," Bob Katchen said, picking up his own.

"May I ask a dumb question?" Gus asked.

"Grab those pans and you can ask all the dumb questions you want," Howard said.

As the cab driver handed Chakas a small stack of foil pie plates, he asked the men what they were carrying, as it was still too dark to read the product marking on the plastic sacks.

"Peddler repellent," Bob Katchen said.

"It was Bob's idea," Howard said, "so if it doesn't work, blame him."

Chakas moved closer and read the package. They were carrying three fifty-pound bags of birdseed.

"What time do those assholes get here?" Howard asked.

"The one with the fruit . . ."

"Emile," Howard said.

"Whatever his name is, he gets here at about eight."

"That should work out just about right."

"So, can I ask my dumb question now?"

"A smart Greek with a college degree can't figure it out?" Joe Senior said as he walked to the area where the peddlers would soon set up their stands.

"The peddlers can't get up on the fire escape because you own it, right? You own the windows and the windowsills, right? You own those little ledges up there, right?"

"Yeah, right. And you're going to put birdseed up there."

"Brilliant, Gus. We're going to put birdseed up there. The pigeons are going to love your building. Your fire escapes, your windowsills, and your ledges are going to be pigeon heaven. They're going to eat, sleep, and *shit* here, Gus."

"I'll be goddamned," Gus Chakas said.

The peddlers themselves were as cynical as the tenants. At first they were anyway. Emile, the corner lord with the fruit and nut stand extended a middle finger salute at Joe Howard when he arrived to find his turf seeded. He swept the seeds into the gutter and spat, set up for the day, and learned one of the starkest truths of New York. Pigeons are the toughest creatures on the street, more aggressive than rats, less daunted than cockroaches, and more resilient than peddlers. They are muggers with wings.

By nine, the pigeons who had breakfast at six had a complete digestive passage directly on Emile and his fruits and nuts. The scarf and glover was the first to see the futility of trying to sell dry goods that weren't dry. He left for the other side of the street by 9:40. The umbrella salesman was next. He smiled and raised an umbrella against the droppings before moving across the street.

The peddler with the fake Rolex and Seiko watches had his own seasonal inventory to move, having added counterfeit Chanel No. 5 and Christian Dior cologne to his stock. He left next. Emile was the last to go, shaking his fist and cursing as he moved across the street.

It took a few days before they were gone for good. Emile was back the next day with an umbrella over his wagon, but he found that customers would not risk getting their clothes soiled. One man with a blue cashmere overcoat had no sense of humor at all about the whole thing. He came back with two cops.

Gus continued to keep the "peddler repellent" on the sidewalk and fire escape for the rest of the holiday season, but after the first of the year, he cleaned up and put the birdseed away for good. For a while, the tenants still complained that they would need more sophisticated security safeguards to prevent Emile and his subtenants from returning. But they didn't return. No peddlers came to roost under the fire escape again. Once in a while someone tried, but the word was out on Gus Chakas. He now protected his block the old way.

36

A bulb-nosed Santa rang a bell in Louis Gloskin's face as he headed down Thirty-fifth Street to Vinny Parco's Christmas party. He threw a quarter into a black kettle and kept walking. He could sympathize with someone else's bad year, having lost half a business, a best friend, and a wife in 1986.

He does not care for Christmas or Christmas parties, but he was grateful to the detectives and, he had to admit, disappointed that his time with them was ending.

"We'll have whiskey sour mix and maybe even a nice Jewish girl or two," Vinny had said on the phone and immediately thought of at least three of his clients who were must-meets for Gloskin. Louis smiled. Everyone he knew had women for him to meet lately. He had never thought of himself as a "hot property," as Vinny called him, but times had changed. He was a single man who made a decent living. In the eighties, that, he supposed, was a hot property.

Christmas made Louis think of Joel, a loss he was lately beginning to acknowledge and mourn. The lifelong friends had always kept each other propped up during the Christmas season, when the gentile kids in the neighborhood flaunted lavish gifts that dwarfed the more modest offerings of their Chanukah. The less the family had, if you could even call what some of them had family life, the fancier the sleds, bikes, cowboy outfits, trucks, and toy airplanes they showed off all through the school vacation.

Even though he hated Joel, and even wished him dead sometimes, small reminiscences, capsules of a lifetime together, invaded his thinking. At odd moments, the little things would come back, like the way Joel handled school yard bullies. The Steins had close ties to their Israeli relatives, and Joel took it to heart that Jews had to be physically tough. He played football like a gladiator and berated himself fiercely for every strikeout or missed pop-up in Little League. Louis considered even touch football a form of death on earth, but Joel was tough enough for both of them.

That afternoon he had remembered the school yard around Christmas and Easter when the Irish and Italian boys got mean about their visions of history and blamed Jews for killing Christ. Every year they stood mute or ran inside until seventh grade when Tony Bellefuccio and Kevin Walsh started coming for them, cursing and telling them they were going to get it for killing Jesus.

The last Bellefuccio heard before he went down was Joel saying, "Pontius Pilate was a wop, asshole." Then he turned on Walsh, who called it quits when Joel shoved him up against the wall and called him a stupid fucking mick.

They joked about it every Christmas season. Sometimes, just saying "Tony Bellefuccio" or "Kevin Walsh" sent them into contortions, even as adults.

It had been a long year. The pain of losing his wife dominated, but the anguish of betrayal by a lifelong friend was even worse sometimes. And, in the end, the friend and the wife had lost each other too. Louis had relented on adultery and changed the grounds to "irreconcilable differences," but it was inevitable that Joel's wife, Debby, would find out about the affair. When she did, she got her own lawyer and put her own claims on the business while Joel swore to her that he and Sarah were only friends and that he would never stray. And Eddie Stein called from Florida with guilt trips, tears, and threats every other day. It was a mess, a big mess, all of it, but Louis was feeling better than he'd felt in months.

He shocked himself when he made a few client calls and liked it. The detectives, who always made him feel welcome in the agency, brought some of it out of him, and some of it was probably always there.

His role in the Gloskin-Stein Plumbing Supply Company had been presumed since birth. His father was the inside man, Louis would be the inside man, Eddie was the outside man, Joel was the outside man. It always made sense, but, as Louis made plans to set up his own shop, he realized that the business itself had become the demanding ghosts of possessive parents, always telling Joel and Louis what to do, how and when to do it, because that's how things had always been done. With the breakup, he felt free of his father's silent whine.

He could hear the party from a block away. Rock music, singing, and laughter got louder as he approached the town house. Before he went in, Louis scanned the brass plaque that read "Vincent Parco & Associates, Confidential Investigations," and remembered how reassuring that solid, welcoming piece of metal had been to him when he first came here. He wondered if anyone else, with a story to tell Vincent at a low point in his life, got the nerve from that plaque to go inside, to go through with the fight.

He let himself into the office and was swallowed up by lights, noise, and color.

"Louis, hey, welcome," shouted Vinny Parco from the dance floor where he seemed to be dancing with at least three women, and maybe as many men. Parco was a holiday card for his profession with a Santa cap on his head and a shoulder holster over his white shirt. Louis noticed that half the people crowded on the makeshift dance floor wore holstered pistols that bobbed up and down to the music.

Gloskin was hugged from behind by Davey Pagano of Maximum Security. He couldn't hear what the detective was saying, something about a good stiff drink, and what did he want. When Gloskin told him a whiskey sour, Pagano disappeared and came back with a drink that he described as a Pagano Sour, which was a special, top secret concoction, that was more whiskey than sour and guaranteed to put anyone, even a person of the Jewish faith, into the Christmas spirit.

From the middle of the dance floor, Vinny Parco looked around his agency. He felt good, for it had been a productive year in the business, and all these people were connected, in one way or another, to him. He hadn't been in such a festive mood that afternoon when he looked at the accounts receivable and unclosed cases that represented money that should have been in-house a month ago. He also tried to figure out who deserved what Christmas bonuses. Friggin' employees always talk about those things to each other, then bitch and moan like kids. That they would also expect raises come the first of January had turned him into Scrooge for the rest of the afternoon.

Carol Parco was having a good time tonight. Despite short fits of melancholia about the amount of money Christmas costs, Vinny was contagious fun on holidays.

The marriage was smooth these last few weeks. They had gone away together on vacation, then he had taken her to a convention in Colorado where she saw him speak for the first time. She'd been alarmed for him that he hadn't prepared anything; terrified for him when she realized he was not going to prepare anything; and dazzled, even after fourteen years, that an unrehearsed, unwritten talk on financial assets kept the audience transfixed for forty-five minutes. It didn't hurt his image that a syndicated interview he'd done weeks ago with Geraldo Rivera was shown on a local station.

Ray Melucci was off to one side sipping coffee from a hot and cold cup with a reindeer peeping through a wreath. For him, it had been a long year, a transitional one during which he broke away from his business partner and now needed to sort out his next move. Did he want to take on the hassle of a guard business again, or should he concentrate 100 percent on debugging?

"I don't know," he told Davey Pagano. "The problem is that no one knows a good debugger from a bad one. These Fortune 500 companies do business with the such half-assed people, but they're half-assed people they know. With guards, everybody needs them, you don't have to explain what a bonded guard is. He's standing right there. They can see him."

"Louis," Jo-Ann Kunda said, throwing her arm around Gloskin for a kiss. "Having a good time?"

"Very nice, thank you, Marla," Louis said.

"I'm Jo-Ann, Louis, that's Marla over there," she said. Gloskin nodded, but he wasn't seeing very well, although he had to admit he was feeling just fine. He asked Davey Pagano for a second Pagano Sour and was immediately accommodated.

"You're not driving, I hope?" Davey asked, handing it to him.

"I drove here," Louis said.

"You can't drive home now, my friend," Pagano said. "I'll get you home, but your car stays. Where is it, in the garage?"

"Yes, it is."

"Good, you can pick it up tomorrow. You still driving that Toyota?"

"Yes, Davey," he said. "Don't start with the Porsche. I don't want a Porsche."

"We'll work on it, Louis. Excuse me a minute," he said as he went to shake hands with one of his clients.

The bar downstairs was kind of a drop-in center for anyone seeking the hypnotic rush of cops and their war stories. There were a couple of FBI agents, assistant district attorneys, NYPD detectives, health investigators, and other law enforcement types. Though the jokes and irreverent humor roared through the room, and the liquor poured like tap water, it was kind of a holy place, a chapel of spiritual renewal that bespoke membership in the investigative fraternity. Everyone did a little time there.

The skip tracers were moodier and more intense this Christmas, at odds with the agency over a new incentive system that Parco said rewarded them for productivity, and that they claimed turned their room into a factory on piecework. They came out of their lair and into the noise with the squinting shakiness of moles in noonday sun, but, as usual, adjusted to the din and mingled freely. Jo-Ann, in her usual role as diplomat to the upstairs, introduced them to the appreciative clients who were the beneficiaries of their art.

Someone suggested that the tracers call Moscow to gag Gorbachev into world peace, but no one could agree on the proper ruse. Jerry L. was willing to give it a try.

Louis Gloskin was feeling talkative by the time he finished his second drink. The room was a bit blurry and he heard himself saying something about Pontius Pilate not being Jewish.

"But, Louis," Davey Pagano said, "Pontius Pilate had to cover his ass, just like Oliver North. Never mind that. Are you getting any action?"

"Maybe Oliver North killed Jesus," Louis said, starting to giggle, "but I didn't."

"You didn't answer my question, Louis."

"What question?"

"Are you getting laid?"

"No, thank you, I've had enough from women for a while."

"For a while, Louis, for a while. But you know that eventually, a while ends. No one escapes it. How are the kids? Good?"

Vinny offered Jo-Ann a taste of a refreshment he was very excited about. "Here, try some of this, it's really good."

"What is it?"

"It's pear brandy. A hundred proof. Try some."

"I'd better not. I've been drinking scotch." Then, seeing Vinny's disappointment, she took a taste and began to cough convulsively. She moved as fast and as gracefully as she could to the small sink in the kitchen where she grabbed for water.

"God, Vincent, it tastes like kerosene. What the hell is it, again?"

"Pear brandy. It's wonderful. You don't know a good drink when you taste it, Jo-Ann. You know the conventional."

She shook her head, half to marvel at the potency of the drink, half to rid herself of residual fumes. "I don't believe you. The ginger ale king of Mumbles and he's drinking firewater. Watch out for that stuff, really, Vincent."

The worry was genuine. Parco is not just a light drinker. He is a bad drinker. He will pour things into his system that should not be in the crankcase of a junked truck.

Jo-Ann went back to where Marla was talking to Mark R.

"How's it going with what's his name?" Jo-Ann asked.

"Who's what's his name?"

"You know, what's his name? The Yankee fan."

"Oh, him. Long gone, and he was a Mets fan. It didn't work out."

"No wonder it didn't work out," Mark said. "If the guy was a Yankees fan, it would have worked out."

"Sure. I'm glad it ended, though, the guy was really jealous. One day, I got his name wrong and he went really crazy."

"You called him by another guy's name?" Mark said. "You can't understand why he'd have a teeny tiny problem with that?"

"Not really," Marla said, then recognized a false impression. "No, no. You've got the wrong idea. It wasn't that kind of calling him by another guy's name. I just came in and said, 'Hi, Tony.' "

"Tony's the guy from ABC?"

"No, Tony's the movie producer."

"The movies," said Cisco, who circulated over from another group, "I didn't know about that. He's a director?"

"No, a producer."

"What's he produced?"

"Nothing that I know of, but he's a movie producer anyway."

"So, are you still going with him?"

"No. It didn't work out."

In the corner, Davey Pagano and Rocco Leone were singing "Silent Night" while Louis Gloskin looked bravely on. Gloskin, now on his third whiskey sour, was trying to focus on a single thought, any thought, but giddy impulses kept getting in his way. Everything everyone said was very funny and he felt like talking. He had told Vinny at length about his surprising enjoyment of selling, and Vinny offered to set him up with several of his contractor and real estate contacts.

Pagano and Leone finished "Silent Night" and segued into "It Came upon a Midnight Clear." As buzzed as Gloskin was—for the first time in his life—he would never be so far gone as to sing a Christmas carol, though Pagano offered to sing a Jewish song if Gloskin would harmonize with them.

"I got it, I got it," he said, stopping when, as usual, he forgot the words after the first verse. " 'Rudolph the Red-nosed Reindeer." Come on, Louis, that says nothing about Christ. Hey, Santa's not religious."

"But it's a Christmas song, Davey. I can't sing Christmas songs," but Pagano was already halfway through the song. He vowed he'd get Gloskin to sing one seasonal song before the night was over.

The dancing, the talk, the singing, and frolic had dwindled by eleven, but Louis Gloskin wasn't ready to leave. The detectives had given up on his singing a Christmas carol, and he dreamily listened to war stories, feeling warm and unusually philosophical. Somewhere beyond the walls of Vincent Parco & Associates there were problems like the major rebuilding of a business and personal life. But tonight, right now, those problems were far away. The kids were with his mother, so there was no time he had to be home. Even that problem was solved. Maybe Joel was right about most problems automatically working themselves out. He felt a tug on his shoulder.

"Louis, a few of us are going to the Lost and Found for a nightcap," Jo-Ann Kunda said. "Would you like to come along? We'll help find you a cab afterward."

"That would be very nice," he slurred. "A nightcap is one final drink?"

"One final drink, yes," Jo-Ann said. "Or two."

The Lost and Found, like Mumbles, is a neighborhood bar that depends on its staff being on a first-name basis with the locals and knowing their drinking preferences. The bartender asked Vinny if he'd like his usual seven and seven or, given the lateness of the hour, just a diet ginger ale.

"I would like," said Vinny framing his words carefully, too carefully, the bartender thought, "I would like a pear brandy." The bartender looked puzzled.

"Never heard of it, Vincent. How about apricot brandy?"

"Why not, it's Christmas?"

Carol had an early morning appointment and left in her own car. They agreed that Vinny would either share a cab home or crash in the office since he wanted to clear away some work before knocking off for the Christmas holiday.

Jo-Ann ordered her second scotch of the night. She'd had too many late nights this week, and she just wasn't feeling very festive. The men thing was bugging her, as usual, but she'd also been thinking about her career, where she was going, where the agency was going, stuff she knew was for other times, but that seemed to demand her attention tonight. She was talking to Ted Phillips of Executive Security about it when she spotted a man at the end of the bar.

"Ted," she said. "It's him."

"That's probably why you got everybody over here," Phillips, said, telegraphing his usual wry wisdom. Though Executive Security and Vincent Parco & Associates are competitors, Phillips and his associate Robert Hawes hosted Parco staffers at their Christmas party, and the favor was being returned.

The object of Jo-Ann's attention was a Wall Street securities analyst whom she'd met once or twice before, but both times they'd been going with other people. On a previous night she'd stopped by for a nightcap, and he'd been there. They'd had a nice talk, and she'd found out that he had broken up with his girlfriend. She'd kind of hoped he'd call.

"Hey, Ted, what the hell. I'm going to invite him to dinner."

"Go ahead," Phillips said. "All he can say is no, right?"

"Right."

She walked across the room to where Evan Hughes stood sipping a Campari and soda, talking to a couple of friends. "Jo-Ann," he said enthusiastically. "How about a drink?"

She was so nervous she almost lost her voice and her nerve. "Evan, may I see you a moment?" she said. They walked to the corner of the bar. "Evan, I'm wondering if you would consider having dinner with me?" she asked.

He started to laugh, then checked himself, realizing that it might be taken as a laugh of rejection. "I can't believe it," he said. "You asked me out. I wanted to ask you to dinner the other night, but I lost my nerve. I'd love to have dinner with you."

"All right, Louis, you *can't* turn this one down," Davey Pagano said as Louis Gloskin nursed whiskey sour number four. " 'Winter Wonderland,' " he said. "It's a winter song, not a Christmas song. There's nothing in it about the birth of Christ or Santa Claus. Let's go, Louis, no more bullshit." He held an imaginary mike to his mouth and started the song.

"Sleigh bells ring, are you listening . . ."

Louis thought it almost as bad to sing a song he considered stupid as one that violated his religious beliefs, but maybe if he sang he could be free of the silly obligation.

"Come on, Louis," Davey said, now extending the imaginary mike to him, " 'In the lane, snow is glistening' . . . sing it!"

" 'In the lane, snow is glistening' . . . are you happy now?"

Everyone, including strangers at the bar, applauded.

Vinny Parco was beginning to wish he'd listened to Jo-Ann about the pear brandy. Not that he was drunk, but he knew his system would make him pay. It wasn't mixing so well with that apricot stuff from the bar. Had he given everyone the day off the next day? It seemed to him that he had. Why did he do that? It would only be the twenty-third. He walked to the end of the bar, introduced himself to Evan, and asked Jo-Ann if he'd given everyone the day off.

"You didn't. I did. Remember you told me the office staff could take a long weekend."

"Right," he said. "I'm such a nice guy. Shit."

He sang a few more Christmas carols, thought about taking a cab home and decided to have one more apricot brandy before walking back to the office to sack out on his couch for a short, dreamless night.

37

Joe Howard had been taking Fridays off and spending weekends at his home in upstate New York. After a heart attack in the summer of 1986, the doctors told him to cut down on his work and, for a change, he'd listened. He figured he'd won too many to be lucky forever, besides, upstate is a hell of a lot prettier on Fridays than Manhattan. Sometimes he took Thursdays off too. Screw it. Let the kid run the business.

He called to check in with his son.

"Hi, Dad," Joe Junior said, putting the phone to his shoulder while he juggled the guard schedule.

"Everything nice and quiet, I hope?" Howard asked. "No problems?"

"No, pretty quiet. Pablo's out sick, but Stanley's taking his place tonight."

"Where's that, Nationwide?"

"Right, and I've still got that hole at Bensonhurst for tomorrow night."

"Anything else?"

"Oh, yeah, Gus Chakas called. Everything's fine. He gave our name to the store owners across from him on Columbus. Emile's over there now. He said you'd be thrilled."

"I think we'll take a pass on that opportunity, unless you want to do it."

"No, thanks. Dad, hang on, someone wants to talk to you."

He handed the phone to Mike Hickey, Howard's old partner on the Upper West Side. Hickey does an occasional job for the agency. "Hi, Joe. Mike. How's it going?" he said.

"What's a bandit like you doing in an honest place of business?"

"Some captain you are, Jeremiah," Hickey said. "Some captain. You don't even know what's going on in your own shop."

"I don't have to. Joe does the work and I get paid, what's better than that?"

"Well, I'm glad your son still has judgment. It just so happens that I'm spending the weekend in our nation's capital with a Swedish model."

"No shit."

"No shit. You ever watch 'WKRP in Cincinnati,' or was it on past your bedtime?"

"I've seen it, what about it?"

"You know the blonde on that show? Loni Anderson? That's who she looks like, Loni Anderson, right, Joe?"

Joe Howard heard his son agree.

"Oh," said Howard, forcing recollection into his tone. "I get it now. Clara Trow. You're going to Washington with Clara Trow. You know, she does look like Loni Anderson. Joe hired *you* to go with her?"

"That's right. You think she's ready for a man of the world, with a lot of experience?"

"I think so, Michael. Some Irishmen," he said reaching for a Camel, "have all the luck. Have a nice trip."

Even if the Duke of Audley escaped and put up neon signs to Mrs. Sagamore's jewels, Barry Silvers was not going to leave his office this week or next. Holidays are a time to be home. His family needs him and so do his big retail clients who must fend off an annual locustlike invasion of shoplifters. Besides the pros and lowlifes who are at it all year, the season turns housewives, professors, executives, doctors, and lawyers into once-a-year thieves. Silvers hires extra help between Thanksgiving and Christmas to accommodate the crunch.

Diane Kowalski buzzed him. "Barry, Jeff Girard's here," she said. "He wants to see you for a minute."

Silvers went to his front office. Jeff Girard stood alone at the desk shifting from one foot to another.

"Hi, Jeff," he said.

"Barry. Hope I'm not interrupting anything."

"Not at all. Come on in."

When he was settled, Silvers asked him if everything was okay.

It was not Jeff's style to come without Karen. As he noted the anxiety on Jeff's face, he was alarmed and it probably showed.

"Yeah, fine. Karen's working. I just wanted to ask you something sort of between the two of us."

"You mean, not including Karen."

"You've got it."

Silvers thought about it. Karen had been his client on the case and, assuming this was about the same issue, he wasn't sure and said so.

Jeff shifted uneasily. "Well, I've got something I want to do. I guess I'll tell Karen about it if I have to."

"I just think it's best in general," Barry said. "What do you want to do?"

"I want you to keep tabs on her every once in awhile, you know, let me know if she needs anything, or has troubles ever."

"You mean Mrs. Cogan?"

"Yeah. She probably won't, but, uh, hell, I just want a report every once in a while that she's okay. How much you think it'd cost if you did that for me?"

"Not much, but I have a better idea."

"What?"

"You call her every once in a while. She already thinks it's part of a long-term survey anyway. You could tell her, if it's okay, you'd like to check in once or twice a year. How would that be?"

Jeff thought about it, but shook his head. "Nah. Not my thing. Not my style. I'm glad we did what we did, you know, and I wouldn't want to do it any other way. But, I can't explain it, but . . . Jeff looked away.

"But you can't lie to your mother."

Jeff laughed. "You got that right."

Silvers looked at him. "I understand," he said. "Let me think this through. You don't have the need to see her again, at least that's the way you feel right now. Is that about it?"

"That's about it."

"But you might want to see her down the line, or do you think you won't?"

"I really don't think so. I think it's best if I don't."

"But if she gets sick or into any financial trouble, you want to know about it."

"Yeah. That's what I want to do."

Silvers was sure Jeff Girard would not contact his biological mother again, or attempt to establish even as peripheral a relationship as the medical survey. That was fine too, because ruses of any kind, especially this one, are not healthy long-term remedies. But he now understood that the young man needed to keep the void filled, that he needed to be a vigilant, dutiful son even if he didn't see Mary Cogan again.

"I'll tell you what," he said. "I'll talk to Ted Davis and we'll find a way to check on her every year, see if everything's okay, and we'll give you a report on how things are going. It shouldn't cost more than a few hundred. And if you ever do want or need to talk to her, we have that door open too."

"I'd like that a lot," Jeff said smiling. "I really don't see me getting in touch, but to know she's all right would make me feel a whole lot better."

They shook hands on it.

Peter Castillo had been stalking a bank robber in Montana. He hadn't nailed him yet, but he had learned enough about the man's habits to know he'd get him after the first of the year in either Montana or Wyoming. He opened a Christmas card and found a check in it. Inside, the tiny and meticulous handwriting of one who doesn't write much covered both sides of the card.

> Dear Peter,
>
> I hope things are good with you this Christmas season. Pilar is doing better in her new school and has a very nice teacher, I think. She still does not talk much about what happened, but the psychiatrist says that is normal, and that she will probably be able to forget. I pray she will, but when she grows older, I hope I can talk to her about it all and when I do I will tell her about you. You should never be forgotten. Here is a check for fifty dollars. I know it's not much, but I want to keep paying you until you get all the money you have coming. God bless you and I hope 1987 is full of good fortune.
>
> Sincerely,
> Martha

Vinny Parco had been up for an hour when the phone rang. The pear brandy had gutted every organ, every system, in his body, and, even though his is a modern phone with a muted ring, it could have been Con Ed in the office with a jackhammer.

"Vincent Parco & Associates."

"Hello there. Is this the detective agency?"

"Yes, it is. How may I help you?"

"Tell you. Maybe you can, maybe you can't help me. I'm trying to find my ex-wife."

"Right. Well, sir, could you call back on Monday? We're closed for the holidays."

There was silence on the other end of the line for a minute and the man said, "Well, the thing is, see, I wasn't so good to her and I just want to wish her a Merry Christmas. It will be a little late for that by Monday."

"Better late than never. I'm sorry I can't help you," Parco said. But the disappointment in the man's voice took hold. Freaking holidays bring out the craziness in people. What the hell.

"All right," he sighed. "Tell me her name and where you last saw her."

He jotted down the information and put his Indy 500 thinking to work for an unseen stranger. The woman was a fabric cutter, the man said. Vinny asked him about the type of fabrics she cut. He thumbed through the yellow pages until he found a factory in lower Manhattan that probably employed fabric cutters. They did and he asked a secretary the name of the fabric cutter's union and learned that it was the North American Brotherhood of Textile Employees. Then he called the union itself, which seemed to be functioning with only one piston pumping, but functioning just the same on December 23.

"Hi, this is Vincent Perkins of Tidewater Mutual Insurance out in Marion, Ohio. How you doing?" He worked his way, small gag by small gag, through various office fiefdoms to the highest ranking union representative at work on that day. He started his insurance rap from the top.

"Listen," he said, "I've got a benefit check for one of your members and I think she'd like to know it's here before Christmas. She was really worried about it. But this dumb bimbo, this girl I fired, throws away your member's address. Can you believe that?

"Anyway, if I give you the name, can you put me in touch?

Well, see, the problem is I've got to talk to her myself. There's a couple of minor problems that I won't go into, but I want to straighten it out because I'm going away until after the first of the year, see? Here's the thing. If I don't get her today, she probably won't get paid before March by the time these idiots in our claims department get the check through."

Five minutes later he called his unseen client back.

"Damn, you don't mess around, do you?"

"I work fast. Okay, you got a pencil? Good, write this down. Your ex-wife is working until noon at the Syosset plant of Gerhardt Textile Manufacturing Company, area code 516-693-3822. Till noon, right. After that, she won't be back till Monday. What you've got to do is call her now and ask for the cutting room, extension 301. Got that? Now, the thing is, you can't call her directly. You have to get her through her foreman. The guy's name is Walter Tate. T-a-t-e. Walter Tate, extension 301. How's that for fast work?"

"Hooee," the man said. "I don't even know what to say." Then there was a long pause on the line.

"Something wrong?" Vinny asked.

"Well, uh, hell, I hate to ask you this right now, after you done what you done, but how much do I owe you? I don't have lots of bucks, if you catch my drift."

Parco's head was throbbing and he wanted to go home. "Tell you what, my friend," he said, "forget it. Merry Christmas."

Afterword and Acknowledgments

The truth means more to a good P.I. than almost anything. P.I.'s have an unsettling Orwellian pragmatism about honesty that makes sense to them and possibly to no one else. They lie to get to the truth. Then they cross a threshold where the lies stop and they go sanctimonious, holding their newfound truth on a pedestal when they report to their clients. The good ones are repulsed by a report with even slight misstatement.

I struggle to understand this mindset even after two years with P.I.'s, but it looks to me like role playing. They're actors in the field and on the phone, and civilians when they shut down. The handful of P.I.'s I got to know well struck me as not liking even white lies after work.

I don't pretend to speak for the one hundred fifty or more P.I.'s who shared their views with me, or the more than fifty thousand licensed private detectives in this country, but what I think is that P.I.'s lie all the time to get to truths they value. So did I.

Don't look for Louis Gloskin in Whitestone or the Girards on the Long Island Expressway. Don't look for a caring bureaucrat named Randall Blaine in Providence or a dazzling, stung beauty named Patrice Maire in Rio. But look for them somewhere near you, because all the stories in this book are true. I saw most of them happen.

I didn't see everything, and I made substantial changes to accommodate the detectives' condition that the identity of their clients be protected, but most of the cases in this book unfolded between February 1986 and April 1988 when I was in regular touch with the detectives and their staffs. There is no typical day in a detective agency, but, as you sip your coffee in the morning, you know that you won't have to wait very long before you see something bizarre.

During my first three weeks in the field, I saw three seven-figure embezzlement cases at three different agencies. Not one made the newspapers or seemed very surprising to the staffs. When I first met Barry Silvers in August of 1986, the Duke of Audley was still at large. I was fascinated, but not prepared to write about it. I didn't want war stories. Even though Barry made the documentation of the case available to me, I dismissed it as a movie plot that was way too sensational for this book.

Months later, I realized that the Duke was no war story. Every P.I. I interviewed had some version of the tale, less flamboyant in most cases, but not always. One day at lunch, Vinny Parco made a wistful complaint about this "freaking pirate" he'd been chasing for years. The man sunk his own ships for the insurance money, possibly killed his crews, and got away with it repeatedly in the Sargasso Sea of ship registry and maritime law. Parco was not his buoyant self as he told me about this case. He was angry that he'd been after this latter-day Blackbeard for years and couldn't get him.

I asked a number of present and former vice detectives if it surprised them that Ramon the Animal would steal Pilar Cruz and sell her across the border into prostitution. Peter Castillo himself could only offer an educated guess that this was going to happen to Pilar, but the vice people were prepared to make book on it. Their surprise was that the little girl survived at all. When I called Castillo to double-check a couple of facts on Pilar's story, it took a while to reach him because he'd been out of state on a similar case. That time, he told me he'd found the child imprisoned in a doghouse, chained to a steel pole. Did I want to hear the story? I'll tell you the truth: I did not.

I like to think my imagination is vivid, but it's not colorful enough to dream up Marla Paul bent over a padded gym horse shouting obscenities under the direction of a sixty-seven-year-old woman, or a man walking in off the street with a pair of his wife's panties in a plastic bag and his semen in a jar, looking for forensic proof of infidelity. These were routine events at Vincent Parco & Associates. Routine. And their two main bars *were* Mumbles and the Lost and Found.

I saw all investigative techniques in the book firsthand. It would have been fun to use some of the swashbuckling stories I heard—long-distance computer hacking, terrorist chases, and hints of missions for the FBI or CIA. I even found a few people willing to tell such stories under assumed names, but they weren't about to let me watch, or show me documentation of the cases. I can't say I'm surprised.

Many P.I.'s were not thrilled to have me around. Conversations sometimes had a way of coming to a quick halt when I joined a circle at the SPI. Nevertheless, there were a lot of P.I.'s who didn't want their names mentioned, but wanted to set the record straight on what they do and how they do it. I thank them. I also thank those P.I.'s who welcomed me into a field they love and talked to me about the work: Jo-Ann Kunda, Ray Melucci, Marla Paul, Mark R., Cisco Villar, Jimi Russo, Gabe Laura, Jerry L., Joe Rodriguez, Alden Moore, Don Kasten, Joe Mullen, Bob Volpe, Joe Howard Junior, Bob Katchen, Dave Cohen, Joe Chapman, Mike Hickey, Marty Meehan, Lou D'Ambrosia, Phil Tambasco, and Tony Carter.

Thanks, too, to P.I. wives Carol Parco, Mary Ann Melucci, and Susan Howard; authors Leonard M. Fuld, M. Allen Henderson, and George Hayduke; Drs. Gershon Yelin and Ari DeLevie; Karen Weiss and Steve Shapiro of the American Civil Liberties Union; Sue Spritzer of the FBI press office; the officers and members of the Society of the Professional Investigators; Attorneys Richard Emery, Andrew Carlin, Charles Eric Gordon, and Philip Cowan; and Chip Gibson, Andrew Martin, Karen Strauss, Keith Foxe, Jennifer Schwartz, Fred Goss, Ken Sansone, Peter Davis, Leonard Henderson, and J. Wilson Henley of Crown.

Lisa Healy, my editor, friend, bursar, director, and ad hoc shrink went with me into this world and occasionally had to fish me out to remind me that the, ahem, book was just a trifle overdue and could we maybe pull ourselves away from the detectives and Mumbles long enough to do some writing? I thank her for two years of enthusiasm and guidance.

My final, and deepest thanks go to the four agency heads—Vincent Parco, Joe Howard, Barry Silvers, and Peter Castillo. With all the reservations I have about the amount of private information up for grabs, and some of the ways people grab it, I rest easier knowing that investigators of their caliber are around if, God forbid, I get into the kind of trouble they see every day.

Bibliography

Adler, Rick. "House Detective." *Los Angeles Magazine,* September 1986.

Bennett, Georgette. *Crime Warps: The Future of Crime in America.* Garden City, New York: Anchor Press, Doubleday, 1987.

Berger, Warren. "What's New in the Private Eye Business." *New York Times,* August 9, 1987.

Blye, Irwin, and Andy Friedberg. *Secrets of a Private Eye.* New York: Henry Holt and Company, 1987.

Brandt, Anthony. "The Case of the Missing Raphaels." *Gentlemen's Quarterly,* January 1985.

Clark, Cathy, ed. *The Paper Trip I: For a New You through New Id.* Fountain Valley, California: Eden Press, 1971.

———. *The Paper Trip II: For a New You through New Id.* Fountain Valley, California: Eden Press, 1977.

Clark, Kenneth. "Gumshoe." *Philip Morris Magazine,* Winter 1988.

Cochran, Tracy. "Mullen, P.I." *New York,* October 13, 1986.

"Computers and Privacy." *Whole Earth Review,* January 1985.

"Diguise Your Data." *80 Micro,* August 1986.

Ferraro, Eugene. *You Can Find Anyone!* Santa Ana, California, 1986.

"Five City Detectives Suspended in Bribe." *New York Times,* April 3, 1973.

Free, John, Naomi Freundlick, and G. P. Gilmore. "Bugging." *Popular Science,* vol. 231, #2, August 1987.

Fuld, Leonard. *Competitor Intelligence: How to Get It, How to Use It.* New York: John Wiley & Sons, 1987.

Gaines, Leigh. "Steps to Cut Employee Theft." *Security,* vol. 25, #4, April 1988.

Hayduke, George. *Get Even: The Complete Book of Dirty Tricks.* Boulder, Colorado: Paladin Press, 1980.

———. *Make 'Em Pay: Ultimate Revenge Techniques from the Master Trickster.* Boulder, Colorado: Paladin Press, 1986.

Henderson, M. Allen. *Flim Flam Man: How Con Games Work.* Boulder, Colorado: Paladin Press, 1985.

———. *Money for Nothing: Rip-Offs, Cons and Swindles.* Boulder, Colorado: Paladin Press, 1986.

Henican, Ellis. "Getting the Bugs Out Pays Off." *Newsday,* April 5, 1987.

"How Business Battles Computer Crime." *Security,* vol. 23, #10, October 1986.

"How Your Privacy Is Being Stripped Away." *U.S. News & World Report,* April 30, 1984.

"Italy's Supersleuth for Stolen Art." *Art News,* February 1983.

Jahnke, Art. "Banking on Terror." *Boston,* December 1986.

Johnson, Kirk. "Landlord Can Evict Absentee Tenant from Apartment, Court Says." *New York Times,* October 27, 1987.

Lapin, Lee. "How to Get Anything on Anybody." Foster City, California: Crocker-Edwards Publishing Company, Inc., 1983.

"Lie Detectors by Private Firms." *U.S. News & World Report,* February 3, 1986.

Lindorff, David. "Exposing Corporate Negligence." *Maclean's,* June 30, 1986.

Lyndon, Kerry. "New Perspectives in Loss Prevention." *Security,* vol. 24, #7, July 1987.

———. "What Chief Executives Should Know about Security." *Security,* vol. 25, #6, June 1988.

Lyons, Richard D. "Getting the Goods on Those 'Nonprimary' Renters." *New York Times,* June 22, 1986.

McCullough, David Willis. "The Detective, Updated." *Signature,* May 1987.

McMorris, Frances. "Batmen Bag $6M Art." *New York Daily News,* Feburary 10, 1988.

Nix, Melinda. "Manhattan's High Stakes Gamble." *Investing,* Fall 1986.

Paladin Press Catalogue, vol. 18, #5. Boulder, Colorado: Paladin Enterprises, Inc.

Pileggi, Nicholas. *Blye, Private Eye.* New York: Pocket Books, 1976.

———. "Daylighting: Going Undercover with Gillian Farrell and the New Private Eyes." *New York,* April 20, 1987.

"Security Snoops Set Up Computer Network." *New Statesman,* vol. 107, March 2, 1984.

Senzel, Howard. "Snoop." *Esquire,* January 1984.

Shortell, Ann. "The New Crime Sleuths." *Maclean's,* June 30, 1986.

Stewart, Doug. "Spy Tech." *Discover,* March 1988.

Straw, Deborah. "Vermont Detectives Are Living on the Edge." *Country Courier,* January 23, 1987.

Taylor, Stuart, Jr. "Police May Search Person's Trash without a Warrant, Court Rules." *New York Times,* May 17, 1988.

"The Tempted Workplace." *Security,* vol. 23, #3, March 1986.

Thomas, Ralph D. *How to Find Anyone Anywhere: Secret Sources.* Austin, Texas: Thomas Publications,

Thomas, Shirley. "Snoops for the Plaintiffs." *Insight,* December 8, 1986.

Toole, David, and Ann Shortell. "Why the Boss Steals." *Maclean's,* June 30, 1986.

Trager, Cara. "Few Laughs for True Detectives." *New York Post,* February 3, 1987.

Wagstaff, Graham F. "Hypnosis Applied to the Collection of Evidence for Judicial Purposes." *Criminal Law Review,* March 1983.

Weglarz, Nina R. "Divorce Becomes a Big Business as Cases Grow in Size, Complexity." *Wall Street Journal,* August 28, 1985.

Yount, Johnny. *Vanish!: Disappearing through ID Acquisition.* Boulder, Colorado: Paladin Press, 1986.

Zalaud, Bill. "Winning in Court." *Security,* vol. 25, #5, May 1988.

Index